A GUIDE TO THE NEW TESTAMENT

A GUIDE TO THE
NEW TESTAMENT

by

ARTHUR W. WAINWRIGHT

LONDON
THE EPWORTH PRESS

FIRST PUBLISHED IN 1965

© THE EPWORTH PRESS 1965

Book Steward
FRANK H. CUMBERS

PRINTED AND BOUND IN ENGLAND BY
HAZELL WATSON AND VINEY LTD
AYLESBURY, BUCKS

TO

MY MOTHER

FOREWORD

THE publication of two new Biblical textbooks is an event; and particularly when they are such notable productions as this book and its sister-volume, *A Guide to the Old Testament*.

We welcome these two books with both gratitude and high expectations. Our gratitude is due to the two authors—the Rev. Arthur W. Wainwright and Mr. G. Gilbert Yates—who have devoted so much time and care to this work, and to the members of our Studies Board who collaborated with them. We are indebted also to our good friends at the Epworth Press, and their printers, who at every stage have most helpfully co-operated in the production of these two quite outstanding volumes.

We also have high expectations. These books have been prepared primarily as prescribed textbooks, to help Local Preachers 'on Trial' in their study of the Bible; and we believe that they will prove invaluable to this end. But we look for more than this; we pray that many besides those committed to this particular course of training will turn for guidance to these two books. And we dare to hope that they will find here not only new light upon God's Word, but inspiration from God Himself.

A further word is due to the student. Each of these books is *'a guide'*. They are not the only guides; nor, as they point a way forward, do they claim that theirs is the only way. As we have said before, readers will find here 'many signposts, but not a set of tram-lines'. We want to stimulate thought, not to restrict it.

Our great assurance is that beyond these and all other 'guides' there is one Guide. Travellers who desire most of all to find and follow Him will not miss their providential way. In Biblical studies as in all else He *is* the way; and His Spirit will guide us into all truth—if we are willing to receive it.

DAVID N. FRANCIS

PREFACE

THIS BOOK has been written as a textbook for Methodist Local Preachers on Trial, but it is hoped that others too will find it a useful guide to the New Testament. It attempts to provide a general introduction to the New Testament and gives comments on selected passages. The translation to which reference is made is the *New English Bible*.

I should like to express my deep gratitude to the Rev. David N. Francis, Secretary of the Local Preachers' Department, and to the members of the New Testament Panel of the Local Preachers' Studies Board (the Rev. A. John Badcock, the Rev. Dr J. Cyril T. Downes, the Rev. J. Allan Fletcher, the Rev. G. Leslie Holdsworth, Mr Philip F. Holland, the Rev. Dr Alfred H. S. Pask, and the Rev. W. Peter Stephens), all of whom have helped me in many ways. I should also like to thank my wife for helping to read the proofs.

ARTHUR W. WAINWRIGHT

NOTE TO READERS

It is important to use this book in conjunction with the *New English Bible* translation of the New Testament. When the comments on selected passages from the New Testament are being read, the actual passages in the New English Bible should be carefully studied.

LOCAL PREACHERS 'ON TRIAL'

who are using this 'Guide' in preparation for their connexional examination will find special instructions for them on p. 277.

CONTENTS

ABBREVIATIONS

NEB   *New English Bible*

RV   *Revised Version*

RSV   *Revised Standard Version*

ACKNOWLEDGEMENTS

Quotations from the Old Testament and the Apocrypha are taken from the *Revised Standard Version of the Old Testament* and the *Apocrypha*, copyrighted 1952 and 1957, by permission of Thomas Nelson and Sons, Ltd.

Quotations from the New Testament are taken from the *New English Bible, New Testament*, copyrighted 1961, by permission of the Oxford and Cambridge University Presses.

INTRODUCTION

I—THE WORLD OF THE NEW TESTAMENT

The Roman Empire

IN THE first century A D the Roman Empire included nearly all countries on the shores of the Mediterranean Sea and many lands beyond.
After years of civil strife it had found unity under the emperor Augustus,
who, by defeating his rival Antony, became its sole ruler (31 B C).
Augustus brought peace to a civilization which had grown weary of
warfare. With an efficient civil service and a comparatively small but
well-trained army he maintained order throughout his vast empire. He
died in A D 14, and although many of his successors were unworthy of
their high office, the empire continued to be ably administered.

Trade and industry flourished in this age of peace, and the growth
of prosperity was especially evident in the towns. Communications were
improved; good roads were built across the empire, and the seas were
cleared of pirates. Since there were two universal languages, Greek and
Latin, a traveller could make himself understood in most places. This
time of peace with its improved conditions for travel and its vigorous
city life provided an excellent opportunity for the Christian Church to
carry out its missionary activity.

Palestine

After a century of independence Palestine was conquered by the Roman
general Pompey in 61 B C. For many years (37–4 B C) it was ruled by
Herod the Great, who owed allegiance to the Roman authorities. He
was a cruel and ruthless tyrant, but a brilliant ruler. He enlarged the
boundaries of his kingdom, encouraged the spread of Greek culture,
and, being a devoted admirer of Augustus, was an advocate of emperor-
worship. He built the port of Caesarea on the Mediterranean coast,
founded many new cities, and restored many old ones. Himself half-
Jewish, he patronized both pagan cults and the religion of the Jews.
His most famous achievement was the rebuilding of the Temple in
Jerusalem, a work which was not completed until long after his death.

When Herod died, his kingdom was divided between his three sons,

Archelaus, Philip, and Herod Antipas. Archelaus received Judaea and Samaria, but was soon deposed for misgovernment. Thereafter his lands were administered by Roman governors, officially called procurators. Philip took over the north-eastern parts of Herod's kingdom. He was known as a just and peaceful ruler, and built the town of Caesarea Philippi. He died in AD 34. Herod Antipas ruled over Galilee and Peraea. A clever, proud, and ambitious man, he was responsible for the execution of John the Baptist, and his reign included the period of Jesus's ministry and crucifixion. He was removed from office in AD 39 for plotting against the emperor.

For a few years (AD 41–4) the Romans withdrew their governor from Judaea, and appointed Herod Agrippa I as king of the territories which had belonged to his grandfather, Herod the Great. It was Agrippa who ordered the beheading of James, the son of Zebedee. After Agrippa's death Judaea was placed under a Roman governor again.

The Romans allowed the Jews a large measure of self-government. The High Priest was the presiding officer of the Jewish supreme council, the Sanhedrin, which together with the councils of local synagogues was responsible for the administration of the law. Only when a death sentence was passed, was the Roman governor's ratification needed. The Romans recognized Judaism as a 'permitted religion', and wisely made concessions to the Jews. A special copper coinage which did not bear the emperor's image was minted for Palestine, and soldiers were forbidden to carry the standards with the emperor's effigy into Jerusalem.

Although the first century AD was generally an age of peace, the Romans had to deal from time to time with frontier wars and outbreaks of revolt. Palestine was one of the worst trouble-spots. The Jews did not easily accept the rule of a Gentile emperor, and the practice of emperor-worship appalled them. Judas of Galilee led an unsuccessful revolt in AD 6 (see notes on Acts 5³⁶⁻⁷), and there was violence and unrest during the governorship of Pilate (AD 26–36; see Mk 15⁷; Lk 13¹). In AD 40 troubles in Palestine provoked the emperor Caligula to order his statue to be erected in the Jerusalem Temple. The governor of Syria, who was instructed to carry out the order, prudently held back, knowing that the Jews would never have tolerated this insult to the Temple. Fortunately Palestine was saved from brutal warfare by the death of Caligula and the abandonment of his project.

Other insurrections followed; two of them, one led by Theudas and the other by an Egyptian, are mentioned in the New Testament (see notes on Acts 5³⁶⁻⁷; 21³⁸). The rebels were usually members of a nationalist group called Zealots. But during the governorship of Felix (AD 52–8) arose an even more fanatical group, the Sicarii, who organized political assassinations. The troubles reached a climax in the great revolt of AD 66. This was the beginning of a cruel and bloodthirsty war which dragged on until AD 70, when Jerusalem was captured and destroyed amid scenes of indiscriminate butchery.

The spirit of Jewish nationalism did not perish with the fall of Jerusalem. There were Jewish uprisings in Egypt, Cyrene, Cyprus, and Mesopotamia (AD 115–17), but all of them were crushed. The most serious revolt broke out in Palestine itself under the leadership of Bar-Cochba as a protest against the emperor Hadrian's intention of building a pagan shrine on the site of the Jerusalem Temple. When this rebellion, which lasted for three years, was suppressed (AD 135), the pagan shrine was erected, and Jerusalem, now renamed Aelia, became a Roman colony, which no Jew was allowed to enter. But although Judaism had been deprived of its Temple and sacrifices, and finally of its holy city, it had remarkable powers of survival, and was preserved through the centuries as a religion centred on the Law and the traditions.

The Christian Church and the Roman Empire

Meanwhile the Christian Church was spreading across the Roman Empire. The Acts of the Apostles and the letters of Paul show that before AD 60 there were Christian congregations in Syria, Asia Minor, Macedonia, Greece, and Rome. The early history of other Christian communities is more obscure, but by AD 150 there were churches on the north coast of Africa, including an important one at Alexandria. A few years later there is evidence of the Church's presence in Gaul (roughly the equivalent of modern France). Christianity was rapidly becoming one of the most popular religions of the empire.

At first the Romans neglected the Christians. The earliest agitations against the Church were provoked by Jews, and the Romans failed to make a clear distinction between Jews and Christians. Many Jews lived outside Palestine, mainly in the commercial centres of the empire; they were called Jews of the Dispersion, and from their number were drawn the first audiences and the first converts of the Christian missionaries. The Jews were often unpopular. In AD 38, when Herod Agrippa I was visiting Alexandria, there were savage riots in which many Jews lost their lives. In AD 49 the Jews were expelled from Rome, probably because of trouble between them and the Christians (see notes on Acts 18[2]). And when the emperor Nero was looking for scapegoats to accuse of setting fire to Rome (A D 64), he chose the Christians, knowing only that they were a despised offshoot of the despised religion of the Jews. In Nero's persecution many Christians, including probably Peter and Paul, were brutally put to death.

There is evidence in the Book of Revelation that Christians were persecuted under the emperor Domitian (about A D 90–5). In A D 112 there was a persecution in Bithynia during the reign of Trajan, and about A D 115 Ignatius, bishop of Antioch, was put to death in Rome. Forty years later Justin was martyred in Rome and Polycarp in Smyrna. Persecution took place at intervals until A D 313, when tolerance was declared by the emperor Constantine, who was himself converted to Christianity. During the first three centuries A D Christianity was regarded as an illegal religion, and its adherents were put to death for refusing to worship the emperor. The Romans were tolerant of most religions but resented Christianity's claim to be the only true faith and the Christians' refusal to worship other gods. But persecution was not the regular policy of the government. When it was inflicted, it was often carried out half-heartedly, and acted as a stimulus to the growth of the Church.

Religions of the Roman Empire

Christianity sprang from Jewish origins, and Judaism was the religion with the greatest influence on the Church's thought in the New Testament period. Before the destruction of Jerusalem there were several religious groups among the Jews. The Sadducees, who included most of the priests and formed the ruling party in Jerusalem, accepted the Law but rejected later developments like the belief in a resurrection. Another group, the Pharisees, who regarded the whole of the Old Testament and many later traditions as authoritative, had more influence than the Sadducees on the religious life of Judaism. They had a considerable popular following, and were largely responsible for the preservation of the Jewish faith after the fall of Jerusalem. A third group, the Essenes, lived in religious communities, where they shared their goods and followed a highly disciplined way of life. Some of the scrolls recently found at Qumran, near the Dead Sea, were produced by one of the Essene communities. In addition to these three groups there were the rebellious nationalists, including the Zealots and the Sicarii, who tried to hasten by force the coming of God's Kingdom.

Between 200 B C and A D 100 a number of 'apocalyptic' writings were produced, which claimed to predict the last judgement and the

Messianic kingdom. Though it is not clear how much this kind of thought was welcomed by orthodox Jewish teachers, it achieved great popularity and made its mark on the New Testament.

Another important type of Jewish thought was called Hellenistic, because it was developed by Jews who owed a debt to Greek culture and who belonged to the Greek-speaking communities of the Dispersion. Its most famous exponent was Philo of Alexandria, who used the ideas of Greek philosophy to interpret the Old Testament.

The most popular religions of the time were not Judaism or the traditional State religions of Greece and Rome. They were the mystery cults which had their origin in Egypt, Syria, Persia, and Asia Minor. These religions, which included the cults of Isis, Serapis, Mithra, and Cybele, practised secret rites. They claimed to give their initiates a new life of union with the deity, and promised them immortality. They were the great rivals of Christianity for the allegiance of the Roman world, and, unlike Christianity, they were prepared to come to terms with emperor-worship and with the traditional religions of Greece and Rome.

Another influence on religious belief was that of Greek thought, which was by no means confined to Greece itself, but was to be found in most of the cities of the Roman Empire. There was not, and never had been, one definitive system of Greek philosophy. There were different schools of thought, some of them agnostic, and others with a firm belief in a supreme and eternal being. Two of the most influential of these schools were the Stoics and the Epicureans (see notes on Acts 17[18]), and there were many others as well. But these philosophers did not touch men's hearts as much as did the mystery religions. Greek ideas, however, especially those derived from Plato, had a great influence on the thought of Jews like Philo and on the theology of the Christian Church from the second century onwards. And though the New Testament writers did not depend on Greek thought for their doctrines, there are indications in John and Hebrews, and occasionally in Paul, that deliberate use was made of language which would appeal to readers educated in the Greek tradition. Moreover, some of the false teaching which arose in the early Church bears the imprint of Greek ideas combined with astrological myths and with borrowings from the mystery religions.

The age in which the New Testament was written can be accused of cruelty, corruption, and immorality, but it cannot be condemned as godless. Although there was much scepticism and indifference in

—2

religious matters, there were many people who were deeply concerned about the ultimate purpose of life and the nature of the divine. To an impartial observer Christianity would be just one of many competing religions. Roman writers of the first century have little to say about it, and what they do say reveals an almost complete misunderstanding of its real nature. A Christian had plenty of reason for discouragement. His religion had to compete with powerful rivals in the form of Greek philosophical schools and pagan mystery cults. He knew that the Church was in a minority and that men feared or despised it. He was liable to be the object of mockery and the victim of persecution. In spite of all these reasons for doubt and disillusionment, however, the New Testament writers consistently sounded the note of joy and triumph. They were aware of the hostility and spiritual blindness of the world in which they lived, but they were convinced that God had appointed them to preach to that world the Gospel of Christ.

II—HOW THE NEW TESTAMENT CAME INTO EXISTENCE

It was by a gradual process that the New Testament came into being. The first Scriptures of the early Church were the books of the Old Testament, and it was only later that Christian writings began to gain recognition as Scriptures. Many years elapsed before there was complete agreement about the contents of the New Testament. Writings like the *Shepherd of Hermas*, the *Teaching of the Twelve Apostles*, and the *Letter of Barnabas*, were candidates for inclusion but were finally rejected. Although the Four Gospels, the Acts of the Apostles, and most of the New Testament letters were recognized by AD 200, Hebrews, James, Jude, 2 Peter, 2 and 3 John, and Revelation had to wait longer for general recognition. It was not until the Council of Carthage in AD 397 that the contents of the New Testament were finally fixed. The council's decision gave expression to a general agreement which the Church had reached gradually over a period of three hundred years.

The dates of the New Testament books cannot be determined accurately, but it is likely that all of them were written before AD 150 and most of them before AD 110. The earliest of them were the letters of Paul, written between AD 48 and 64; but the gospels and the Acts of the Apostles, although they reached their present form later, were based on oral traditions formulated in the earliest days of the Church.

The accepted list of New Testament writings is called 'the canon' of the New Testament, '*kanon*' being a Greek word meaning 'rule'. The

A GUIDE TO THE NEW TESTAMENT

into the current speech of our own time, and a rendering which should harvest the gains of recent biblical scholarship'.[1]

Throughout the following chapters the *New English Bible* translation of the New Testament will be quoted and commented on. When reference is made to the Old Testament and the Apocrypha, the *Revised Standard Version* will be used.

[1] *New English Bible, New Testament*, p. vii.

books which were finally admitted to the canon can be divided into four groups.

(i) *Gospels*, which give an account of the life and teaching of Jesus. There are four of them in the New Testament, those according to Matthew, Mark, Luke, and John. Several other gospels did not gain admission to the New Testament because they were not thought to give a realistic account of either the life or the teaching of Jesus. Among them were the gospel according to the Hebrews, the gospel of Peter, and the gospel of Thomas.

(ii) *Acts*, which describe the activities and teaching of the apostles. The only book of this nature that has been admitted to the New Testament is the Acts of the Apostles, which gives an account of the growth of the early Church, with special reference to the work of Peter and Paul. Among the books of this kind which failed to obtain a place in the New Testament were the Acts of John, the Acts of Paul, the Acts of Peter, and the Acts of Thomas.

(iii) *Letters*. There are twenty-one letters, traditionally known as epistles, in the New Testament. Thirteen of them, Romans, 1 and 2 Corinthians, Galatians, Ephesians, Philippians, Colossians, 1 and 2 Thessalonians, 1 and 2 Timothy, Titus, and Philemon, are ascribed to Paul. The letter to the Hebrews has been traditionally ascribed to Paul, but his name is not mentioned in the letter itself, or in its original titles. The New Testament also includes a letter ascribed to James, two to Peter, three to John, and one to Jude.

(iv) *Revelations* or *Apocalypses*, which claim to unfold the secrets about the final events in history, and the future era of blessedness. Many books of this nature were written between 200 B C and A D 100, but only one of them, the Revelation of John, has been given a place in the New Testament. The word 'apocalypse', which is often used to describe this kind of book, is derived from a Greek word meaning 'revelation'.

III—THE NEW COVENANT

The word 'testament' is a translation of the Greek '*diathēkē*', which also means 'covenant'. The Old Testament is in fact the Book of the Old Covenant, which was made by God with the children of Israel, when He delivered the Law to Moses. The New Testament is the Book of the New Covenant between God and men, which was established by Jesus Christ. Jeremiah records God's promise that a new covenant will be made which will enable each individual to know God. It will not be written, like the old covenant, on tables of stone, but in the hearts of men (Jer 31$^{33-4}$). The prophecy of Jeremiah was fulfilled by Jesus Christ, who established a new relationship between God and men, which was based on the Spirit rather than on the letter. It was a relationship which included a personal knowledge of God and personal communion with God. In the letter to the Hebrews Jesus is called 'the mediator of a new covenant' (12^{24}), and at the Last Supper He described the wine as 'my blood of the covenant' (Mk 14^{24}). The new covenant was sealed not with the blood of animals but with the blood of Christ, shed on the Cross. It was not made with a particular nation, but with all who trusted in Christ. The community which it established was not a people bound by ties of blood and language but the Christian Church, which is not limited by the claims of race and nation.

The traditional translations 'Old Testament' and 'New Testament' are misleading. The Scriptures are in fact the Book of the Old Covenant and the Book of the New Covenant. The Old Testament records the establishment and continuance of the Old Covenant. The New Testament records the establishment by Jesus of the New Covenant, and goes on to tell of the growth of the Church and to give evidence of the reaction of its members to the activity of the Holy Spirit.

IV—THE NEW TESTAMENT AND PREACHING

The message of Christian preachers is the Gospel, the good news about Jesus Christ and His Kingdom. The Greek word for 'gospel' is '*euangelion*', from which the word 'evangelist' is derived. It means 'good news', and the earliest Christians preached the good news that through faith in Christ men could be saved from the power of sin and death and could enter into eternal life.

Although only four books of the New Testament are actually called 'gospels', all its books contain the Gospel, because they proclaim the good news about Jesus Christ. In the letters of the New Testament we find the Gospel according to Paul, according to Peter, and according to James, because, although these letters do not include the gospel in the narrower sense of giving an account of the life and teaching of Jesus, they include the Gospel in the wider sense of giving the good news about Him. No single book of the New Testament contains the whole Gospel. There is the Gospel according to Matthew, according to Mark, according to Luke, and according to John. But the Gospel itself is greater than any of its interpreters.

The New Testament is an indispensable basis for all Christian preaching. A modern preacher ought not just to repeat what the New

Testament writers have said. His message must bear the stamp of his own experience and be directed to the needs of the situation in which he preaches. Yet he cannot give a genuine account of the Gospel unless he is faithful to the message of the earliest preachers. Although his style may be different from that of the biblical writers and he may often draw from a different stock of illustrations, and although he may consider arguments and problems which never arose in New Testament times, his essential message ought to be the same as that of the apostles. He should always measure his words by the standard of the New Testament.

V—THE NEW TESTAMENT AND DOCTRINE

There is no official creed in the New Testament, and none of its books was written as a systematic theological treatise. They are rather in the nature of tracts and popular literature, and many of them are letters written for particular situations. But although they were not intended as credal statements or theological treatises, they provide an essential basis for all accounts of Christian doctrine. The acceptance of the Bible as a standard of doctrine checks the rise of extravagant speculations, and at the same time prevents the watering-down of Christianity into a philosophy which has little to do with the essential message of the early Church.

VI—THE NEW TESTAMENT AND ETHICAL TEACHING

In recent years many people have supposed that it is possible to separate the moral teaching of Jesus from the rest of the Gospel, and to uphold Christian ethics without believing in the Lordship of Christ. No such attitude is countenanced in the New Testament. Although it contains a large amount of ethical teaching and practical instruction, the New Testament is not a detailed code of law, and does not provide an explicit answer to all the varied and complex problems which arise from day to day. Its supreme ethical teaching is that the Christian life can only be lived with Christ Himself. Nevertheless, if someone wishes to know how a Christian ought to behave in modern times, he must examine the conduct and teaching of Jesus and of the early Church. The pattern of Christian behaviour for this century cannot be discovered unless we consider the pattern of behaviour advocated in the New Testament.

VII—THE NEW TESTAMENT AND WORSHIP

The books of the New Testament were soon used for reading in public worship, and some of the ancient Church lectionaries survive today. In certain of his letters Paul gives clear instructions for his message to be read to the whole congregation. It is highly likely that the first letter of Peter was designed to be read at an Easter baptismal service. And probably one of the reasons for the writing of Matthew's gospel was the desire to provide material for the lessons at worship. Indeed the stories and sayings which were used as material for the gospels were in the early days transmitted orally, when Christians gathered together for worship and prayer.

The New Testament is a book for use in private prayer as well as in public worship. Quiet unhurried meditation on a passage from it is one of the most rewarding ways of entering into the presence of God. Moreover, much of the New Testament itself is the fruit of meditation on the stories and sayings of Jesus.

VIII—THE NEW TESTAMENT AND HISTORY

No part of the New Testament attempts to give a complete history of the times. The primary concern of its writers is to proclaim the Gospel, to convert people to Christianity, and to strengthen the faith and guide the conduct of those who are already Christians. In carrying out these fundamental tasks, however, they record the main events in the life of Jesus and the early Church. Not only the gospels and the Acts of the Apostles but also the New Testament letters and the Book of Revelation give information about the life of the early Church. Indeed there is little historical evidence about the Christianity of the first century A D except what is provided by the New Testament. One or two passing references by Jewish and Roman writers—though their understanding of Christianity is clearly limited—and some references by Christian writers of the second century, provide supplementary evidence about the early history of the Church. But the earliest and fullest information about both the life of Jesus and the history of the first-century Church is to be found in the New Testament. Although its books were not primarily intended to be historical works, they are of exceptional historical value.

IX—THE LANGUAGE OF THE NEW TESTAMENT

All the books of the New Testament were originally written in Greek, which was the international language of the countries of the Eastern

Mediterranean. It was the language of great cities like Corinth and Alexandria, where Christianity was soon established. And it was spoken both by the Jews who lived outside Palestine and by a large number of Gentile converts to Christianity.

The stories and sayings of Jesus were originally circulated in Aramaic, the language which Jesus himself spoke. But before they were incorporated into the gospels they had been translated into Greek, and it was in Greek that the books of the New Testament were written.

X—THE EARLIEST TEXTS AND VERSIONS

The earliest manuscripts of the New Testament were written on papyrus rolls—papyrus was a material made from a water-plant which grew in the Nile. A few of these rolls survive, dating back to the second and third centuries. The earliest known text of part of the New Testament is a small papyrus fragment now kept in the John Rylands Library in Manchester. It contains some words from John $18^{31-3,\ 37-8}$, and was written in the first half of the second century.

At a later date writings were copied on vellum, a material produced from animal skins, which was much more durable than papyrus. Some of the surviving vellum manuscripts date back to the fourth century, and provide the most important material for attempts to determine the original text of the New Testament.

In the early centuries of the Christian era translations of the New Testament were made into other ancient languages such as Latin, Syriac, Coptic, Gothic, and Armenian. These translations are often known as 'the versions'. For many centuries the version officially accepted throughout the Western world was Jerome's Latin translation of the Bible, which is usually called the Vulgate. And this version continues to be authoritative for the Roman Catholic Church.

When scholars attempt to determine the original text of the New Testament, they have to compare the earliest manuscripts and versions. These do not always agree with each other, because before the days of printing it was very easy for a scribe to make errors as he was writing down a fresh copy of a work. The science of textual criticism is the science of discovering the earliest form of the text, and in the last few centuries this science has been greatly developed and refined. Also in the last few centuries several early manuscripts have been discovered which have provided important additional evidence for textual critics. It has become clear that the text of the New Testament as represented by Jerome's Vulgate was not wholly accurate, and revisions have now been made, mainly in small details, but sometimes on a larger scale. These changes have little effect on the main doctrines of Christianity. But it is important that we should possess as accurate a text of the New Testament as possible.

XI—THE ENGLISH TRANSLATIONS

The first translation of the Bible into English was made by John Wyclif and others in 1382–8. In the sixteenth century a translation was made by William Tyndale and completed by Miles Coverdale. The Authorized Version, made by command of James I, was based mainly on Tyndale's version, and was finished in 1611. It has had a tremendous influence on English literature and is written in a style of incomparable majesty. But it was not based on the text found in the earliest Greek manuscripts, and in the nineteenth century the Revised Version was produced in order to make available a translation of what was believed to be the most accurate text. The New Testament of the Revised Version was published in 1881 and the Old Testament in 1885. In 1900–1 the *American Standard Version* was issued, which is in most respects the same as the Revised Version.

During the twentieth century there have been many translations of the New Testament into modern English, including those by Weymouth (1902), Moffatt (1923), who also translated the Old Testament, and J. B. Phillips (1947–57). Ronald Knox made a translation of the Latin Vulgate in 1945. And in 1946 the *Revised Standard Version* of the New Testament was issued, the Old Testament following in 1952. This is a revision of the *American Standard Version*. It takes into account the most recent discoveries in textual criticism, renders the Bible into language easily intelligible to modern men, and at the same time keeps as closely as possible to the style of the Authorized Version.

In 1961 appeared the *New English Bible* translation of the New Testament, and the translation of the Old Testament is expected to be ready in a few years' time. The *New English Bible* has been sponsored by the main religious denominations of the British Isles with the exception of the Roman Catholic Church. It is based on what modern scholars believe to be the most accurate text, and is a completely new translation, with language and style which are not dependent on any previous version. The avowed aim of the New Testament translators is to give its readers 'a faithful rendering of the best available Greek text

CHAPTER ONE

THE GOSPEL ACCORDING TO ST MARK
(INTRODUCTION AND 1^1–8^{26})

INTRODUCTION TO THE GOSPEL

The Synoptic Gospels

THE GOSPELS according to Matthew, Mark, and Luke are known as the Synoptic Gospels, because they can easily be arranged in three parallel columns, in order to make a synopsis or chart of their contents. They have a great amount of material in common, and give the same general view of Jesus's life and teaching.

The Origin of the Gospel according to St Mark

Although for many centuries Mark's gospel was regarded as an abridgement of Matthew's, the majority of non-Roman Catholic scholars are now agreed that Mark's is the earliest of the gospels. An examination of parallel passages in the three gospels shows that Matthew and Luke edited Mark's material and combined it with narratives and sayings from other sources.

A second-century writer, Papias, claims that Mark was 'the interpreter of Peter' and wrote down what he remembered of the information which Peter had given him. In addition to Peter's reminiscences Mark seems to have incorporated other material into his gospel. Many of the stories and sayings in the gospel must have been circulated orally for some years before they were written down. Some leading modern scholars, known as *form-critics*, have attempted to trace the history of the different stories and sayings in the gospels, and to show how they assumed their final form. Although their theories do not command universal assent, the form-critics have presented a strong case for the view that many of the gospel stories were first used as independent units for preaching and teaching, and only later linked together in a consecutive narrative.

It is generally thought that the gospel was written in Rome between AD 65 and 70, soon after the execution of Peter, and that since many of Jesus's first disciples were dead, Mark was satisfying the urgent need to preserve a written account of Jesus's life and teaching. Some scholars, however, are inclined to think that the gospel was written a little later, perhaps between AD 70, when Jerusalem was destroyed, and AD 75.

The Author

There are no serious reasons for challenging the traditional belief that the gospel was written by John Mark, whose mother's house in Jerusalem was a meeting-place for early Christians (Acts 12[12]). Mark was a companion of Paul on his first missionary journey, but left him before the journey was finished (Acts 13[5, 13]). Because Paul was unwilling to take him on a second journey, Mark went with Barnabas to Cyprus (Acts 15[37–9]). Later he was reconciled with Paul, who speaks well of him in his letters (Col 4[10–11], Philem 24, 2 Tim 4[11]). In Rome he was closely associated with Peter, and in the First Letter of Peter he is described as 'my son' (1 Pet 5[13]).

The Historical Accuracy of the Gospel

One of the important emphases made by the form-critics has been that the sayings and stories in the gospels were circulated orally for many years before they were first written down. They contend that, however good the memories of the early Christians may have been, the sayings and stories underwent modification during the years of oral transmission. They argue that some of the sayings were not even based on original utterances of Jesus Himself but were comments made by early Christian preachers.

It is impossible to discuss this question adequately without a detailed examination of the disputed sayings and narratives. This cannot be done within the limits of this book, but the task is attempted in several commentaries on the gospels. It is certainly obvious that Matthew and Luke have sometimes modified what they found in Mark; and Mark himself may have modified some of the traditions which he received. Nevertheless, there is a strong basis of truth in the synoptic gospels, although an element of human error may have entered into the transmission of the sayings and narratives. Some Christians, of course, accept the dogma that the scriptures cannot err. But many other Christians believe that the scriptures ought to receive the same critical scrutiny as other documents of historical importance.

The Miracle-Stories

Much of Mark's gospel is devoted to accounts of the miracles of Jesus. The word translated 'miracle' by *NEB* literally means 'work of power', and stresses the fact that God was at work in these acts of Jesus. Mark and the other evangelists regarded these works of power as a very important part of Jesus's ministry. And Jesus Himself understood them as signs of His divine mission (see notes on Luke 7[18-35]). They have caused much trouble, however, to some modern interpreters, who suspect them to be exaggerated descriptions of the original events. The healing-miracles have caused less difficulty than the others because there are modern instances of faith-healing, and some of the diseases cured by Jesus seem to have been psychological in origin. Critics are readier to accept the genuineness of a miracle-story, if there is reliable evidence of similar events in modern times. They find difficulty in stories of the raising of dead people to life, and tend to see them as exaggerated accounts of the healing of people who were in a coma but not actually dead. Their greatest difficulties arise, however, from the nature-miracles, in which Jesus is supposed to have exercised supernatural power over the forces of nature. Examples of these miracles are the Stilling of the Storm, the Feeding of the Five Thousand and the Four Thousand, the Walking on the Water, and the Cursing of the Fig-Tree.

The objection that no adequate scientific explanation can be given of these events is not in itself convincing. If Jesus Christ is the supreme and unique revelation of God, it is not surprising that events occurred, when He was present, which do not occur under normal conditions. Scientific investigation has not revealed all the secrets of nature, and may not be able to give a satisfactory explanation of what happens when the unique Son of God is active in the affairs of the world.

A weightier objection to miracles is made on theological grounds, and claims that it was not part of God's purpose to work spectacular signs through Jesus, who Himself resisted the temptation to perform such acts (see notes on Luke 4[1-13]). Jesus's redemptive work, it is argued, was achieved by sharing men's limitations rather than by a life of wonder-working.

Another important objection is the historical one, which claims that the men who passed on these stories had a tendency to exaggerate. It is argued that the stories grew in the telling, and that the original events were more normal than the gospels depict them to be. Alternative explanations of the miracles are offered. The storm stilled by Jesus is said to have been one of the typical squalls on the Sea of Galilee, which died down as soon as they arose; and the calm which followed Jesus's words is explained as a coincidence. The feeding of the five thousand is regarded as a sacramental fellowship-meal in which the numbers of the loaves and fishes were inaccurately remembered. It is claimed that Jesus never walked on the water but only by the lakeside. And the cursing of the fig-tree is said to have been told by Jesus as a parable.

These explanations cannot be regarded as more than intelligent conjectures about the original nature of the events. But unless the early Christian preachers and writers were incapable of error, it is possible that their stories were elaborated as they were handed down first orally and then in writing. On the other hand, Mark's gospel was published during the lifetime of people who had seen the events which it recorded; and the existence of eye-witnesses would restrain the tendency to exaggeration. Though some of the narratives may have been exaggerated, they have a historical basis.

It is not the purpose of this book to discuss the authenticity of every miracle, and the reader must form his own judgement about them. But certain comments must be made which apply not only to the miracles in Mark but also to those in the rest of the New Testament.

(i) Since Jesus was a unique person, who wielded unique spiritual power, an element of the miraculous is to be expected in His life.

(ii) Although the miracles are evidence of Jesus's power, He did not perform them with the express purpose of displaying that power. Any miracle which He performed was motivated by His love and compassion for men and women.

(iii) Many of the miracle-stories are not merely records of remarkable events, but convey a deeply spiritual message about Jesus's power over evil and His ability to supply men's needs.

(iv) The Christian faith does not stand or fall by the authenticity of every miracle described in the New Testament. Even if some of the accounts should prove to be exaggerated, the fundamental truths of the gospel would remain.

The Characteristics of the Gospel

It is not as easy to point out the distinctive characteristics of Mark as those of Matthew and Luke, because the distinctiveness of Matthew and Luke is revealed by comparison of them with Mark, a source which they both used. There are, however, indications that Mark was concerned to make special emphases, but to some extent these emphases have been adopted by the other synoptic evangelists.

(i) Stress is laid on *the manhood of Jesus*. He is a truly human person, who shows anger, sorrow, compassion, horror, and dismay (1^{41}, 3^5, $6^{6, 34}$, 10^{14}, 14^{33}). There is a limit too both to His power and to His knowledge (6^5, 13^{32}).

(ii) Great emphasis is laid on *the divinity of Jesus*, a belief which is implied not so much by the title 'Messiah' as by the titles 'Son of Man' and 'Son of God'. His divine authority is shown by His claim to forgive sins, His Lordship of the Sabbath, His control over the devils, His ability to heal the sick, and His power over the winds and the waves ($2^{10, 28}$, $1^{24, 34}$, etc., 4^{41}, 7^{37}, etc.). His divinity is shown too by His place at the right hand of God and the promise that He will return in power and glory (8^{38}, 13^{26-7}, 14^{62}). He is the one who fulfils and surpasses all that mattered in the Law and the prophets (9^{2-8}).

(iii) Another feature of Mark's gospel is its teaching about *the Messianic Secret*. Mark says that Jesus deliberately tried to keep His Messiahship secret ($1^{25, 34, 44}$, 3^{12}, 5^{43}) by telling people not to make known His miracles. Eventually He implicitly acknowledged His Messiahship to His disciples (8^{29-33}), and did not deny it when Bartimaeus called Him 'Son of David' (10^{48}). But it was not until His trial that He publicly admitted it (14^{61-2}). Indeed Mark seems to think that Jesus spoke in parables in order to conceal the truth about Himself from those who were not His disciples (see notes on 4^{10-12}).

(iv) An important theme of the gospel is *God's purpose of suffering for both Jesus and His disciples*. Jesus had to go the way of suffering and death, which was prophesied in the scriptures (8^{31}, 9^{12}, etc.). And His disciples had to be ready to go the same way (10^{35-40}, 13^{9-13}). True greatness lay in sacrifice and service, in denying self, and in taking up the Cross (8^{34-7}, 10^{41-5}).

(v) Another theme of the gospel is *Jesus's conflict with the powers of evil*. This is seen in the account of the Temptation, and of the driving out of devils. The theme is elaborated in 3^{22-30}. Evil is probably seen as the cause of the storm which Jesus stilled (4^{35-41}), and even Peter could be an agent of Satan (8^{33}). It is through the coming of God's Kingdom in the person of Jesus that the decisive conflict with the forces of evil has been joined. Jesus gave His life as a ransom to set men free from these forces (10^{45}). But the final conflict will occur at the end of the world, when the powers of evil will be destroyed and Jesus will return victorious (13^{14-27}).

COMMENTS ON MARK 1^1–8^{26}

Mark 1^1—*The beginning of the gospel*

John's gospel begins with a reference to the creation, Matthew's and Luke's with an account of the birth of Jesus, but Mark's gospel begins with the story of John the Baptist and of the baptism and temptation of Jesus.

Jesus Christ the Son of God. 'Jesus' is the equivalent of 'Joshua' (see notes on Mt 1^{21}).

'*Christ*' is from the Greek '*Christos*', which, like the Hebrew '*Messiah*', means 'anointed one'. In the Old Testament both kings and priests are sometimes described as anointed ones, but by the time of Jesus the word '*Messiah*' was used to describe a special deliverer and ruler, who was expected to bring a new and blessed era.

'*Son of God*' was used in the Old Testament of angels (Job 1^6), individual kings (2 S 7^{14}), and the whole people of Israel (Hos 11^1). In the pagan world the title often described a supernatural being. It is possible that it was used by the Jews of Jesus's time to refer to the *Messiah*. In Mark, as in the rest of the New Testament, it depicts Jesus as a divine being with a unique relationship to God the Father and a unique authority over mankind.

Mark 1^{2-5}—*John the Baptist*

John the Baptist, the herald of Jesus's coming, was a striking man, dressed in rough garments and reminiscent in appearance of Elijah (2 K 1^8). Baptism was already practised by the Jews, who baptized Gentile converts to their religion; and by adopting the rite John declared that he was gathering together a new nation, the distinctive feature of which was its members' repentance of their sins. Baptism was also a ceremony of cleansing, and John used it as a sign of God's forgiveness to those who repent.

Mark 1^2. This prophecy, which is from Malachi 3^1, is mistakenly ascribed by Mark to Isaiah.

Mark 1^3. This quotation is from Isaiah 40^3.

Mark 1^{6-8}—*The Coming One*

The Baptist prophesied the coming of 'one who is mightier than I', who would baptize with the Holy Spirit. Although the pupil of a Jewish rabbi used to regard it as his duty to unfasten his teacher's shoes, John did not think that he was worthy to perform even this menial task for the one who was to come.

Later John expressed uncertainty whether Jesus really was the Coming One (see notes on Luke 7^{18-35}), but the gospels make it clear that Jesus was the man in whom John's prophecy was fulfilled.

The promise of baptism with the Spirit was fulfilled after the resurrection (Jn 20^{22}), at Pentecost (Acts 2^{1-13}), and whenever men believed in Christ (Rom 8^{15}, Gal $3^{2, 14}$, 4^6).

Mark 1^{9-11}—*The Baptism of Jesus*

The precise nature of this event has been much discussed, and scholars have debated whether the opening of the heavens, the descent of the Spirit, and the divine voice were experienced by Jesus alone or by all who were present. Mark does not mention that anyone except Jesus was aware of them.

The baptism of Jesus was of great importance for several reasons :

(i) *Jesus was declared to be the Son of God*. The divine voice which said 'Thou art my Son' confirmed that Jesus had a unique relationship with His Father. This does not mean that Jesus was actually made the Son of God at His baptism, but that He became specially aware of His Sonship at that time.

The words 'Thou art my Son' are found in Psalm 2^7; and the rest of Mark 1^{11}, '. . . my Beloved; on thee my favour rests', recalls the description of the Servant of the Lord in Isaiah 42^1. This may possibly indicate that Jesus was to fulfil His Messiahship by being a Suffering Servant, but the theme is more explicitly stated elsewhere in the New Testament (e.g. 1 Pet 2^{21-4}).

(ii) *Jesus received the Holy Spirit*. The Spirit was active in Jesus before His baptism, as the birth-stories in Matthew and Luke make clear. But at His baptism the Spirit came upon Him to designate and anoint Him for His ministry (see Lk 4^{18-19}, Acts 10^{38}).

The Spirit is likened by Mark to a dove, and, since some Jewish writers described the Spirit as brooding like a dove upon the waters at the creation (see Gen 1^2), Mark may have understood the baptism of Jesus as the beginning of a new creation, the inauguration of a new world-order.

(iii) *He identified Himself with the sinful human race*. Although He was sinless, by accepting the baptism of repentance Jesus refused to exalt Himself as a different kind of being from sinful men, but identified

Himself with them. He was, like the Servant of Isaiah 53^{12}, 'numbered with the transgressors'.

Matthew (3$^{13-17}$) records that John was reluctant to baptize Jesus on the ground that He did not need the baptism of repentance. Jesus's answer, that He must 'conform with all that God requires', meant that His identification of Himself with the human race was part of God's purpose. The full meaning of Jesus's action is seen in His crucifixion, when He experienced that separation from God which is the consequence of human sin (see notes on Mk 15$^{33-41}$).

Mark 1$^{12-13}$—*The Temptation of Jesus*

That Jesus was in conflict with the powers of evil was apparent from the outset of His ministry, when He was tempted in the wilderness (or desert) by Satan, otherwise known as the devil. A fuller account of the temptation is given by Matthew and Luke (see notes on Lk 4$^{1-13}$).

Mark 1$^{14-15}$—*The Opening of Jesus's Ministry*

After John the Baptist had been arrested (see Mk 6$^{14-29}$), Jesus began to preach in Galilee. His message is summarized in this verse.

The time has come. The Messianic age, the new era of blessedness, which was prophesied in the Old Testament and other Jewish writings, has arrived with the coming of Jesus.

The Kingdom of God is upon you. A more literal translation of this would be 'The Kingdom of God has drawn near'. The Jews expected a Kingdom of God in the future, but the new feature of Jesus's teaching was that the Kingdom was present in His own ministry. 'Kingdom of God' means the kingship or reign of God, and the coming of the Kingdom means the beginning of the Messianic age which would replace 'this present evil age'. Jesus proclaimed that, although this evil age still continued, God's new age had already arrived.

Repent. In the teaching of Jesus this word means more than to be sorry for sins. It means 'to turn', and describes that act of turning to God which includes both penitence and faith.

Believe the Gospel. Gospel means 'good news', and Jesus asks men to accept the good news of the arrival of God's Kingdom.

Mark 1$^{16-20}$—*The Call of the Disciples*

Jesus called disciples to assist Him in His work and to form the nucleus of the Church. The first to be called were Simon, Andrew, James, and John, who left their work as fishermen to help Jesus to save the souls of men. They became 'fishers of men'. It was only later (Mk 3^{13-19}) that Jesus appointed twelve disciples.

Mark 1^{21-8}—*The Man with an Unclean Spirit*

Members of the congregation could be invited to expound the scriptures in a synagogue, and when Jesus went to a synagogue in Capernaum, a town on the shores of the Sea of Galilee, He was given an opportunity to speak. His teaching was distinguished by a note of authority which was contrasted with the impression created by the doctors of the Law. (For the possibility that He was a rabbi, see notes on Mark 9^5.)

While he was in the synagogue, He healed a man who was possessed by an unclean spirit. In Jesus's time certain types of wild maniacal behaviour were ascribed to the presence of devils or unclean spirits in a man. Many of Jesus's acts of healing were performed on people in this condition, and Jesus regarded this healing work as part of His fight against the powers of evil.

In verse 25 Jesus directly addresses the unclean spirit, because the voice of the man is identified with the voice of the spirit which possesses him (see also Mk 1^{34}). The spirit immediately recognizes Jesus as the Son of God, but Jesus commands it to be silent, because He does not want His Sonship to be made public at this stage of His ministry (verses 24–5; see Mk 1^{34}).

Mark 1^{29-45}—*Further Acts of Healing*

The rest of the chapter tells how Jesus healed first the mother-in-law of Simon, then a large number of sick people, and finally a leper. In Palestine lepers had to live in isolation and were outcasts. Although other men treated them as untouchable, Jesus was ready to touch them.

This section also refers to Jesus's practice of spending time alone in prayer (verse 35).

Mark 2^{1-12}—*The Paralysed Man*

This story has several important features:

(i) Jesus healed the man in response to the faith of his friends (verse 5; compare Mk 5^{21-43}, 7^{25-30}, 9^{14-29}, Lk 7^{1-10}).

(ii) He linked forgiveness with healing (verse 9). When a sense of guilt makes a man physically ill, its removal can cure the illness. Jesus knew the cause of the man's paralysis to be his sinfulness, and acted accordingly. It does not follow, however, that He regarded every illness as the consequence of sin (see notes on Jn 9^{1-41}).

(iii) He claimed the right to forgive sins, a right believed by Jews to belong to God alone (verses 5–10).

(iv) By using the title 'Son of Man' of Himself (verse 10) He implied that He was the Messiah, though He did not explicitly admit it until later (see p. 33). 'Son of Man' was a Messianic title associated with a future triumph. Jesus, however, used it to describe His earthly ministry and His suffering and death as well as His return in glory. For an examination of His use of the title, see p. 109.

The title is used of the Messiah in the *Book of Enoch*, a Jewish writing which probably took its final shape in the first century B C . Strong evidence for the title's Messianic nature is found in Jesus's own use of it to describe His return in glory.

The title could also mean 'man' (see Ps 8[4]), and some scholars argue that in Mark 2[10] and 2[28] it refers to men in general. This is certainly not Mark's understanding of the title in these or in any other sayings. It is, however, likely that, though Jesus used it primarily in a Messianic sense, He also understood it to indicate that He was the ideal man.

According to Daniel 7[13, 27], 'one like a son of man' in Daniel's vision stands for 'the people of the saints of the Most High'. It has therefore been suggested that some of the 'Son of Man' sayings refer to the community of the faithful as well as to Jesus Himself. The prophecies of His death would then imply that at the end of His early life He alone constituted the faithful community. Although some of the 'Son of Man' sayings have been influenced by the sayings in Daniel, this theory about Jesus's use of the title has not been generally accepted. It continues, however, to have supporters.

Mark 2[13-14]—*The Call of Levi*

Although the tax-gatherers were despised and feared, Jesus made one of them His disciple. Levi was also known as Matthew (Mk 3[18], Mt 9[9]).

Mark 2[15-17]—*The Friends and the Critics of Jesus*

Jesus's mission was to save sinners, and He went out of His way to befriend them and eat with them. Two types of sinful people are mentioned : *tax-gatherers*, who were servants of the Roman rulers and had a reputation for exacting more taxes than they were authorized to do ; and *sinners*, who were men and women with a name for sexual immorality and for other breaches of the Law.

Jesus's choice of friends provoked criticism from 'some doctors of the law who were Pharisees'. *The doctors of the Law*, in older translations called *scribes*, were the acknowledged exponents of the Law and the traditions. The *Pharisees* were a group of people who believed in the strict observance of the Law and the traditions. They tended to be narrow and legalistic, and were highly incensed by Jesus's attitude to the Sabbath and to certain traditional ceremonies (see Mk 7^{1-8}). In their own way they were very devout people, and it was a great tragedy that some of the leading opponents of Jesus were men who took religion seriously. The word 'Pharisees' means 'those who have been set apart'. Their chief fault was their belief in their own virtue, and Jesus's saying in verse 17 is aimed at their self-righteousness.

Jesus was not opposed by all the lawyers and Pharisees, but only by some of them.

Mark 2^{18-20}—*The Bridegroom*

Although John the Baptist's disciples observed the discipline of fasting, Jesus's disciples did not fast. Jesus explained that the time for fasting would come when He was taken away from them by death. By likening Himself to a bridegroom He foreshadowed the idea that He was the bridegroom and the Church His bride (see notes on Eph 5^{22-6^9}). This saying is the first reference in the gospel to the death of Jesus.

Mark 2^{21-2}—*New Ways*

New cloth does not fit an old coat, and new wine needs fresh skins. Similarly the new era which Jesus has brought requires a new outlook on life and new methods of action. One example of a new method was Jesus's refusal to encourage fasting among His disciples (verses 18–20). Another example was His attitude to the Sabbath (Mk $2^{23}-3^6$).

Mark 2^{23-6}—*Plucking the Ears of Corn*

One of the main quarrels between Jesus and the Pharisees was about Sabbath observance, the theme of Mark $2^{23}-3^6$. With few exceptions work was forbidden on the Sabbath, and Jesus's disciples were accused of working on the Sabbath because they plucked ears of corn as they walked through the cornfields. Jesus maintained a positive attitude to the Sabbath and was regular in His attendance at worship, but He rejected a strictly legalistic interpretation of the command that no work should be done on that day. In His reply to the Pharisees' criticism of His disciples He pointed out that, when David and his followers were hungry, they broke the Law by eating the consecrated loaves which were reserved exclusively for the priest (1 S 21^{1-6}).

Mark 2^{26}. According to 1 Samuel, the High Priest was *Ahimelech*. The mention of Abiathar in Mark must be due to an error in the transmission of the story.

Mark 2²⁷⁻⁸—*The Sabbath and the Son of Man*

Jesus stated two guiding principles in His attitude to the Sabbath. First, the Sabbath is not an end in itself, but was instituted to help men. From this principle it follows that Sabbath observance should never be allowed to stand in the way of basic needs like the need for food or for healing. Secondly, Jesus claimed to have authority over the Sabbath, and therefore assumed the right to revise the Law. For the title 'Son of Man' see notes on Mark 2¹⁻¹². An alternative interpretation is that 'Son of Man' here means not only Jesus but 'man' in general.

Mark 3¹⁻⁶—*A Man with a Withered Arm*

When Jesus healed this man in the synagogue on the Sabbath, His enemies said nothing publicly but began to plot against His life. The partisans of Herod, who joined the Pharisees in their plotting, were followers of Herod Antipas, ruler of Galilee (see notes on Mk 6¹⁴), against whom they feared that Jesus might start a revolt.

Mark 3⁷⁻¹²—*More Healings*

This brief summary is similar to Mark 1³²⁻⁹.

Mark 3¹³⁻¹⁹—*The Appointment of the Twelve Disciples*

The call of Simon, Andrew, James, John, and Levi (or Matthew), has already been described. Now Mark records the appointment of Twelve Disciples, who include these five. The number twelve stands for the twelve tribes of Israel, and the Twelve were the close associates of Jesus, who were to be leaders of the New Israel, the Christian Church. Their immediate functions were to be Jesus's companions, to preach the gospel, and to drive out devils.

Mark 3¹⁴—*as his companions*. The Greek means literally *to be with him*.

Mark 3¹⁶. *Peter* means *Rock* (see notes on Mt 16¹⁷⁻¹⁹). According to John 1⁴², Simon received the name when he was first called, and, according to Matthew 16¹⁸, he received it at Caesarea Philippi.

Mark 3¹⁸. *The Zealot party* was a violent revolutionary organization.

Mark 3²⁰⁻¹—*Jesus's Friends*

Since 'family' (*NEB*) should be literally translated 'friends', and 'For people were saying' (*NEB*) should be literally translated 'for they were saying', verse 21 could mean that Jesus's own friends said that He was out of His mind.

Mark 3²²⁻³⁰—*A Dispute about Devils*

When lawyers accused Him of driving out devils by the prince of devils, Jesus replied that if their accusation was true, Satan would be divided against himself and would therefore have no power (verses 22–6). Just as a strong man must be tied up before he can be robbed, so Satan must be overcome before men can be freed from him (verse 27). That Jesus regarded the expulsion of devils as a victory over Satan is confirmed by a saying which Luke includes in this story : 'But if it is by the finger of God that I drive out the devils, then be sure the kingdom of God has already come upon you' (Lk 11²⁰).

Jesus's statement that anyone who slanders the Holy Spirit is guilty of eternal sin (verses 28–30) implies that the lawyers were slandering the Spirit when they said that His work was Beelzebub's.

Mark 3²². *Beelzebub* was another name for Satan.

Mark 3³¹⁻⁵—*The Family of Jesus*

When His family came to look for Him, Jesus said that all who did God's will, were members of His family.

Since Joseph is not mentioned here, it is likely that he was dead by this time.

Mark 4¹⁻²—*Teaching in Parables*

This is the introduction to Mark 4¹⁻³⁴, a collection of parables which Jesus told. A parable is a story or pictorial saying, often taken from incidents in daily life, which illustrates a point of teaching. It should be distinguished from an allegory. Whereas a parable illustrates one or at most two or three points, an allegory is a story in which minute details correspond to the lesson which it conveys. When Augustine claimed that in the parable of the Good Samaritan the beaten man was Adam, the thieves were the devil and his angels, the Samaritan was Jesus, the beast was the flesh of Jesus, the inn was the Church, and the innkeeper was Paul, he was treating the parable as an allegory and reading into it lessons which were not there. The parable of the Good Samaritan teaches the nature of true neighbourliness, and is not intended to illustrate the whole plan of salvation.

Not all parables are in the form of stories. Some of them are pictorial sayings, like that about the kingdom divided against itself (Mk 3²³⁻⁶) ; and others are proverbial sayings (Mk 7¹⁵⁻¹⁷). For the most part, Jesus's parables do not just illustrate a general ethical rule but directly emphasize an aspect of His own mission. Most of them illustrate some feature of the Kingdom of God. And in their original setting many of them were intended to contrast the way of Jesus with the legalistic attitude of the lawyers and Pharisees.

Mark 4[3-9, 13-20]—*The Sower*

In this parable Jesus encourages His disciples by assuring them that in spite of much discouragement the preaching of the gospel bears much fruit through the coming of the Kingdom of God. The parable does not make it clear whether the Kingdom is already present or is expected in the future.

Mark 4[13-20]. This detailed allegorical interpretation is probably an early Christian development of Jesus's original teaching. Its outline of the different reactions of men to the preaching of the gospel is very true to life.

Mark 4[10-12]—*The Purpose of Parables*

As this saying stands, it means that the parables obscure the truth, but that Jesus by His explanations of them unfolds the secret of the Kingdom to His disciples. It is difficult to believe that Jesus took this attitude, since the obvious purpose of a parable is to illustrate a theme, not to obscure it. His words may have been misunderstood when they were translated from Aramaic, the language which He Himself spoke, into Greek, the language of the gospel. The two most attractive theories about the original form of the saying are:

(i) They do not refer to parables, since the Aramaic of verse 11 could have been translated 'to those who are outside everything comes obscurely'.

(ii) They do not describe Jesus's purpose in telling the parables, but men's actual reaction to them. The Aramaic of verse 12 could have also been translated either 'so that they look and look, but see nothing . . .' or 'to those who look and look, but see nothing . . .'.

Mark 4[12] is derived from Isaiah 6[9-10].

Mark 4[21-5]—*A Short Group of Sayings*

Jesus declares that His purpose is to reveal truth to men and not to mystify them (verses 21-3). Those who are ready to communicate their spiritual insight to others will receive fresh insight from God (verse 24). Those who possess truth will receive more truth, but those who do not possess it will become even more ignorant (verse 25).

Mark 4$^{26-9}$—*The Seed*

This parable does not refer to the gradualness of the coming of the Kingdom, but to the fact that it comes not by human effort, but on God's initiative and in God's time.

Mark 4$^{30-2}$—*The Mustard-seed*

The teaching of this parable is not that the Kingdom comes gradually but that it will be great in spite of its humble origin. As the tiny mustard-seed grows into a plant which can reach a height of ten feet, so the ministry of Jesus, short in duration and for the most part limited to a small country, will have results of supreme importance for every time and place.

Mark 4$^{33-4}$. See notes on Mark 4$^{10-12}$.

Mark 4$^{35-41}$—*The Stilling of the Storm*

This nature-miracle, which has been the subject of much critical discussion (see pp. 30–2), was clearly believed by Mark to contain important information about Jesus.

(i) It illustrates His divine power, since in the Old Testament it was God who ruled over the sea (Ps 89^9, 104$^{6-7}$, 107^{29}).

(ii) By stilling the storm He was triumphing over evil. The words 'Be still', with which He rebuked the storm, are almost the same in Greek as 'Be silent', the rebuke which He gave to the devil in Mark 1^{25}.

(iii) The story shows that, when Jesus is with men, they need not fear the dangers and uncertainties of life.

Mark 5$^{1-20}$—*The Gerasene Demoniac*

This man whom Jesus healed was called 'Legion', the Latin word for an army regiment, because of the large number of unclean spirits which possessed him. For the importance of such acts of healing, see notes on Mark 1$^{21-8}$. The man's recognition of Jesus as the Son of God (verse 7) and the identification of the man's voice with that of the evil spirits (verse 9) are typical of this kind of story.

Since Gerasa lay to the south-east of the Sea of Galilee, and was in Gentile territory, this is the first instance of Jesus's ministry to Gentiles. For the Ten Towns (verse 20), see notes on Mark 7$^{31-7}$.

The statement that Jesus allowed the evil spirits to enter a herd of pigs, which rushed into the sea and were drowned (verses 11–13), has caused difficulty. Some commentators claim that the death of the pigs was pure coincidence. Others say that the behaviour of the maniac terrified the pigs, and yet others argue that Jesus allowed the evil spirits to enter the pigs in order to prove that the man was healed. The pigs, being unclean animals, would be regarded as a suitable home for the unclean spirits.

Mark 5²¹⁻⁴³—*Jairus's Daughter and the Woman with a Haemorrhage*

Two healing-miracles are recounted in this section. The longer story tells of the healing of the daughter of Jairus, president of a synagogue. It is often thought to be an example of the restoration to life of a dead person, but, since Jesus never admits that the girl is dead (verse 39), she may have been in a coma. It is an example of a miracle which occurs in response to the faith not of the sick person, but of someone else, in this case her father (see also Mk 2¹⁻¹², 7²⁵⁻³⁰, 9¹⁴⁻²⁹).

The other miracle (verses 25–34) is the healing of a woman with a haemorrhage, who touched Jesus's cloak. It is a vivid example of healing performed by Jesus in response to the sick person's own humble faith.

Mark 5⁴¹. *Talitha cum* is Aramaic.

Mark 6¹⁻⁶—*Rejection at Nazareth*

The people of Nazareth, Jesus's home town, regarded Him merely as a member of one of their own families, and failed to acknowledge His uniqueness. Because they rejected Him, He was unable to perform many miracles there. When faith was absent, the work of Jesus was not effective.

Jesus is described as 'the carpenter', but the Greek word is wider in its meaning and refers to a man who works in stone and metal as well as wood.

In defence of the tradition of the perpetual virginity of Mary it has been claimed that the brothers of Jesus (verse 3) were His half-brothers or His cousins. But there is no good evidence to support these theories.

Another and longer account of Jesus's rejection at Nazareth is given in Luke 4¹⁶⁻³⁰.

Mark 6⁷⁻¹³—*The Mission of the Twelve*

When Jesus appointed the Twelve Disciples, He intended them not only to be His companions but also to carry out a ministry of preaching and healing (Mk 3¹⁴⁻¹⁵). In this section it is recorded that Jesus sent His disciples on a mission in Galilee without accompanying them Himself. This work would prepare them for the more extensive missionary tasks which awaited them after the resurrection of Jesus. The rules which Jesus gave about clothing and provisions were designed for missionary work in Palestine, and would obviously be unsuitable for more extended tours like those which were made by Paul.

Mark 6$^{14-29}$—*The Death of John the Baptist*

Herod's statement that Jesus was John the Baptist raised from the dead leads Mark to introduce the story of the Baptist's execution. Herod had thrown John into prison because he had criticized his unlawful marriage to Herodias, his brother's wife (see Lev 18^{16}, 20^{21}). The Jewish historian Josephus records that John was imprisoned at Machaerus, a fortress near the Dead Sea. Josephus also claims that John was put to death because Herod feared that he might start a revolt. Mark, however, says that Herod had John beheaded as a favour to Herodias's daughter, and was himself distressed at what he had been led to do. Nevertheless, Herod's fear of John was probably the underlying cause of his decision to grant her request.

Mark 6^{14}. *Herod* was Herod Antipas, son of Herod the Great. He ruled over Galilee from 4 B C to A D 39, and was under the control of the Roman government. He was officially not a king but a tetrarch. The word 'tetrarch' literally means 'ruler of a fourth part', but was often used generally of the ruler of a division of a country. Antipas ruled over a part of the territory of his father, Herod the Great.

Mark 6^{15}. *Elijah* was expected to return (Mal 4^5), and Jesus identified the Baptist with him (see notes on Mk 9$^{9-13}$).

Mark 6^{16}. The Jews thought that the age of the prophets had long ago finished and that men no longer had the prophets' direct access to God. Here it is claimed that Jesus had renewed the prophetic tradition.

Mark 6$^{30-44}$—*The Five Thousand*

This story, which is one of the nature-miracles (see pp. 30–2), *reveals the compassion of Jesus*, which was directed to both the souls and the bodies of the five thousand people who gathered round Him. He ministered to their physical needs by feeding them, but also wanted to minister to their spiritual needs by teaching them (verse 34).

The incident emphasizes that *Jesus can supply men's real needs*, and illustrates His teaching about God's providence (see Mt 6$^{25-34}$). It also shows *the fellowship of Jesus with those who follow Him*. When the disciples reflected on this meal, they may have seen it as a fulfilment of the Jewish expectation that there would be a Messianic Feast in the Kingdom of God (Isa 25[6]). And it probably foreshadowed the sacramental meal which Jesus inaugurated at the Last Supper.

The aspects of the story which have been mentioned are at least as important as its miraculous nature, and would characterize the incident, even if Mark's account was an exaggerated description of what really happened.

The story recalls the feeding of a hundred men by Elisha (2 K 4[42-4]).

Mark 6[45-56]—*Walking on the Lake*

This nature-miracle (see pp. 30–2), like that of the Stilling of the Storm (Mk 4[35-41]), shows *Jesus's divine power over nature*. In the Old Testament it was God who walked upon the waters (Job 9[8], Ps 77[19]). The story also illustrates that *men need not fear when Jesus is with them*. If the disciples had understood the incident of the loaves, which taught that Jesus would supply their real needs, they would not have been perplexed when the storm ceased at His approach (verses 51–2).

Mark 7[1-23]—*Outward and Inward Purity*

A source of controversy between Jesus and the Pharisees was the practice of ritual washing before meals. The washing of eating- and drinking-vessels and of hands has great hygienic value, but the Pharisees attached importance to these customs as ritual acts, and claimed the authority of law for what were merely traditions. When they upbraided Jesus for allowing His disciples to neglect these traditions, He denounced them for treating these outward observances as essential for true religion (verses 1–8).

The Pharisees' neglect of the real commandment of God was shown by their attitude to the fifth commandment, which deals with a man's duty to his parents. They taught that a man could evade this duty by a legal fiction. He could dedicate all his wealth to God, keep it nevertheless for himself, and, on the ground that it was devoted to God alone, refuse to assist his parents (verses 9–13).

Another saying of Jesus is added, in which He speaks of the supreme importance of a man's inward condition. It is not the food which a man eats but his inner attitude that can defile him (verses 14–15). Jesus amplifies the saying by naming some of the acts and attitudes which proceed from a man's sinful nature (verses 17–23).

Mark 7[6-7]. This quotation is from the Greek version of Isaiah 29[13], and is somewhat different from the Hebrew text on which the English versions of Isaiah are based.

Mark 7[10]. The quotations are from Exodus 20[12], and 21[17].

Mark 7[11]. *Corban* is a Hebrew word.

Mark 7[24-30]—*The Phoenician Woman.*

Jesus had already been in Gentile territory (Mk 5[1-20]), and now he left Palestine again to tour the region outside Galilee (Mk 7[24], 8[26]). His expulsion of the unclean spirit from the daughter of a Phoenician woman is an example of healing at a distance (see the Centurion's Servant, Lk 7[1-10]). It also shows how Jesus healed someone in response to another's faith (see Mk 2[1-12], 5[21-43], 9[14-27]). But it is remembered most because of Jesus's conversation with the girl's mother. At first He refused to heal the girl because she was a Gentile, and, though he relented in answer to the mother's witty reply, it is clear that His plan was to minister to Jews during His earthly life and to entrust the Gentile mission to the Church. Any work He did among Gentiles was an exception to the rule, and was a gesture pointing to the Church's future task.

Mark 7[27]. *children* refers to the Jews, and *dogs* to the Gentiles. We cannot escape the fact that Jesus spoke in language which seems to be harsh, even though the Greek word can be translated 'puppies' instead of *dogs*.

Mark 7[31-7]—*The Deaf Mute*

This healing took place in the 'territory of the Ten Towns' (or 'Decapolis'), a group of cities which lay mainly to the east of the Jordan, and had a large Gentile population.

Mark 7[34]. *Ephphatha* is Aramaic (compare Mk 5[41]).

Mark 8[1-10]—*The Four Thousand*

Mark probably intends to show that Jesus had a ministry to Gentiles as well as Jews. The Five Thousand were fed in Galilee, but the Four Thousand seem to have been fed in the area of the Ten Towns (see Mk 7[31]), which was Gentile territory.

Because of the close similarity between the stories of the Five Thousand and the Four Thousand, many scholars have come to the conclusion that they are separate accounts of the same event.

Mark 8[11-13]—*The Sign*

The Pharisees asked Jesus for a sign from heaven, which would be a spectacular demonstration of His divine power, even more dramatic than any of the miracles which He had performed. Jesus refused them a sign. If they could not accept His authority on the grounds of His previous acts and teaching, they would receive no further demonstration of it.

In similar sayings in Matthew 12$^{39-42}$ and Luke 11$^{29-32}$ Jesus affirms that the only sign He will give is His preaching of repentance and, according to Matthew, His resurrection.

Mark 8$^{14-21}$—*The Meaning of the Loaves*

When the disciples found themselves without bread, Jesus reminded them that there were lessons behind the feeding of the Five Thousand and the Four Thousand. Although He did not say what the meaning of the incidents was, they did in fact illustrate His compassion, His readiness to supply men's real needs, His fellowship with those who followed Him, and His concern to minister to both Jews and Gentiles. John's gospel goes even further and sees the Feeding of the Five Thousand as an illustration that Jesus is the bread of life (see notes on Jn 6$^{22-71}$).

Mark 8^{15}. *leaven* was often regarded as a sign of evil (see 1 Cor 5^{7}). Here it refers to the malice and hypocrisy of the Pharisees and Herod.

Mark 8^{16}. A more satisfactory translation of the Greek would omit the words *It is because*.

Mark 8$^{22-6}$—*The Blind Man at Bethsaida*

Jesus's use of outward acts in the healing of this blind man and His instruction to be silent about the event are reminiscent of the story of the Deaf Mute (Mk 7$^{31-7}$).

QUESTIONS

(1) Discuss the importance of the Baptism of Jesus.
(2) Examine Jesus's attitude to the Sabbath and to other Jewish traditions.
(3) What lessons are to be learned from the miracles of the Feeding of the Five Thousand and the Walking on the Water?
(4) Comment on : Mark 1$^{14-15}$, 2$^{19-20}$, 3^{22}, 4$^{28-9}$, 5^{30}, 7^{28}.

CHAPTER TWO

THE GOSPEL ACCORDING TO ST MARK
(8^{27}–16^8)

Mark 8^{27-33}—*Caesarea Philippi: Peter's Confession and Jesus's Prophecy of His Passion*

WHEN JESUS and His disciples were in the neighbourhood of Caesarea Philippi, an incident happened which was of crucial importance in His ministry. Peter acknowledged that Jesus was the Messiah, and Jesus prophesied His suffering, death, and resurrection. No doubt the disciples had already wondered if He might be the Messiah, and Jesus Himself had certainly hinted at His approaching death (Mk 2^{19-20}). But Caesarea Philippi was the first occasion, according to Mark's account, when a disciple openly addressed Jesus as the Messiah and when Jesus spoke explicitly about His death and resurrection.

The story is the beginning of a new section of Mark's gospel. In the earlier chapters many miracles are recorded; and Jesus's teaching is usually addressed to the crowds, and is for the most part about the coming of the Kingdom. From Caesarea Philippi onwards there are fewer accounts of miracles; and Jesus's teaching is given more often to the disciples than to the crowds, and includes sayings about His suffering, death, resurrection, Messiahship, and return in glory.

Mark's account of the incident emphasizes the contrast between Peter, who recognized that Jesus was the Messiah, and the people outside the circle of the disciples, who failed to understand who Jesus really was.

Jesus did not openly admit that Peter was right in calling Him Messiah. His reply suggests that, although He agreed with Peter, He had other important things to say about Himself. He was not just a Messiah, but a suffering Messiah who would be put to death and rise again. And He *had* to undergo death and resurrection; He does not say here why these events were necessary, but He believed them to be necessary because they were part of God's plan of redemption foretold in the scriptures (see Mk 9^{12}). He may have understood Isaiah 53 and parts of Psalm 22 as prophecies of His suffering and death, and Psalms 16^{10-11}, 49^{15}, and 73^{24-6} and Hosea 6^{1-2} as prophecies of His resurrection.

When He called Himself 'Son of Man', He was using a Messianic title (see notes on Mk 2$^{1-12}$), and no part of His teaching was more remarkable than this affirmation that the divine Son of Man had to suffer and die in order to be triumphant. The idea was so strange that Peter remonstrated with Jesus, who rebuked him and saw in his attitude the work of Satan, the tempter.

Caesarea Philippi was situated to the north of Galilee on the slopes of Mount Hermon. An ancient holy place of the local tribal religion, it later became the home of a sanctuary to the Greek nature god, Pan. Herod the Great built a temple there in honour of the Roman emperor Augustus, and Herod's son Philip founded the city of Caesarea Philippi. It was in this region, a centre of nature-worship and emperor-worship, that Peter acknowledged Jesus as Messiah.

Mark 8^{28}. For *John the Baptist, Elijah*, and *one of the prophets*, see notes on Mark 6$^{14-29}$. Perhaps the reference to *one of the prophets* is based on Deuteronomy 18$^{15, 18}$.

Mark 8^{29}. For the meaning of *Messiah* see the notes on *Christ* (Mk 1^1).

Mark 8^{31}. *elders, chief priests, and doctors of the law*. These three classes of men made up the Sanhedrin, the supreme Jewish Council, before which Jesus was put on trial.

three days afterwards. This was an idiomatic way of saying 'soon after'. A similar idiom is 'on the third day'. See Hosea 6^2.

Mark 8$^{34-8}$—*Sayings about Discipleship*

Jesus then addressed the people as well as His disciples. He told them that three things were required of a disciple: self-denial; a readiness to endure even if it meant death (such is the meaning of 'taking up the cross'); and a willingness to be with Jesus (verse 34). Real safety is obtained by self-sacrifice for the sake of Jesus and the gospel (verses 35–7). When Jesus, the Son of Man, returns at the Last Judgement, He will reject those who have been ashamed of Him (verse 38).

Mark 8^{38}. *wicked and godless* would be literally translated *adulterous and sinful*.

Mark 9^1—*The Kingdom of God in Power*

If this saying about the Kingdom speaks of the coming of Jesus at the end of the world, it is a mistaken prophecy, because, although the world has not ended, all Jesus's contemporaries have died. There is, however, a sense in which the prophecy was fulfilled by the resurrection of Jesus and the gift of the Spirit to the disciples, events in which God certainly exercised His kingship in power.

Mark 9$^{2-8}$—*The Transfiguration*

Six days after Peter's confession at Caesarea Philippi, Jesus took Peter, James, and John to a high mountain, probably Mount Hermon, which is snow-capped for almost all the year and would provide an appropriate setting for what followed. Jesus was transfigured before His disciples. His clothes appeared to be dazzling white, the colour of divine glory, and He was seen to be talking with Elijah and Moses, who symbolized the great religious traditions of Israel, Elijah representing the prophets and Moses representing the Law. They were the great men of the Old Covenant, but Jesus was greater still. He was greater than Elijah because the Word which had been spoken through the prophets was made flesh in Him (see Jn 1$^{1-14}$). He was greater than Moses, because He brought a new and deeper conception of law, which was based not on obedience to a written code but on a personal trust in Himself.

When Peter saw Jesus conversing with Elijah and Moses, he was really at a loss what to say, and suggested that three shelters should be made to honour the three men on the mountain. Then a cloud, which stood for the divine presence, appeared, and the voice of God told Peter to pay attention to Jesus. As at the Baptism of Jesus, the voice proclaimed that He was the Son of God and the Beloved (see notes on Mk 1$^{9-11}$).

The transfiguration revealed the divine glory of Jesus. It was not merely a transfiguration but a prefiguration, because it prefigured the glory of the risen Jesus.

Mark 9^4. According to Luke 9^{31}, the conversation was about the death of Jesus.

Mark 9^5. *Rabbi.* This title was given to acknowledged teachers of the Law. It is used of Jesus several times, and He may well have been a recognized teacher Himself.

Mark 9$^{9-13}$—*The Son of Man and Elijah*

Again Jesus told His disciples about His resurrection from the dead. When they asked Him about the coming of Elijah, which was prophesied in Malachi 4^5, He said that Elijah had come already, implying that John the Baptist was Elijah. He spoke also of His own future suffering.

Mark 9^{12}. See Mark 8^{31}.

Mark 9^{13}. *the scriptures.* Perhaps a lost writing is meant. Alternatively, the saying may imply that, as the first Elijah suffered at the hands of

Jezebel (1 K 19$^{1-10}$), so the second Elijah had to suffer at the hands of Herod.

have worked their will. This refers to the execution of John the Baptist.

Mark 9$^{14-29}$—*The Epileptic Boy*

The contrast of the peace and majesty of the transfiguration with the sordidness and coarseness of the world below is extremely vivid. Jesus and His disciples had to return to the sorrows and cruelties of life, as He had reminded them on their descent from the mountain (verses 9–13).

Characteristic of this kind of story is the identification of the boy's cries with the voice of the unclean spirit (verses 25–6). The story is an example of healing in response to another person's faith, in this case the father's (compare Mk 2$^{1-12}$, 5$^{21-43}$, 7$^{25-30}$). There are two distinctive features of the miracle: (i) The boy's father admitted that his faith was weak. 'I have faith,' he cried, 'help me where faith falls short' (verse 24). In spite of the man's limitation, however, Jesus was able to act, because the man's faith was an honest faith; (ii) The disciples were unable to heal the boy, but Jesus succeeded where they had failed. He explained to them (verses 28–9) that prayer was needed for effective healing.

Mark 9$^{30-2}$—*Another Prophecy of the Passion*

See notes on 8$^{27-33}$.

Mark 9$^{33-7}$—*True Greatness*

The theme that true greatness is to be the servant of all is repeated in Mark 10$^{35-45}$. The idea that to receive others is to receive Jesus is developed in the story of the Sheep and the Goats (Mt 25$^{31-46}$). The second part of verse 37 stresses Jesus's position as the representative of His Father.

Mark 9$^{38-41}$—*The Man who was not a Disciple*

Jesus's tolerance is shown by His attitude to this man who was expelling devils (verses 39–40) and by His statement about the reward which awaits those who help His disciples (verse 41).

Mark 9$^{42-50}$—*A Group of Sayings*

This is a collection of sayings which are not linked by any general theme.

(i) Those who cause the disciples of Jesus to do wrong will suffer a dreadful fate (verse 42).

(ii) It is better to make costly sacrifices than to go to hell (verses 43–8).

(iii) The disciples will be purified in the fire of suffering and persecution (verse 49).

(iv) If the disciples, whose function is to give life to the world, lose their loyalty to Jesus, who will give life to them (verse 50a)?

(v) The disciples ought to possess qualities of love and loyalty, and be at peace with each other (verse 50b).

Mark 9⁴². *lead astray.* The word literally means *cause to stumble.*
little ones means the disciples.
millstone. To hang a millstone round a man's neck was a Roman form of punishment.

Mark 9⁴³⁻⁸. *hell.* This translates the word *Gehenna,* the name of a valley used as a refuse-tip by the people of Jerusalem. In earlier days it had been the scene of child-sacrifices, and its name was adopted for the place of divine punishment. The reference to the worm and unquenchable fire, which is derived from Isaiah 66²⁴, is probably due to the fact that Gehenna was a refuse-tip. We cannot be sure how literally Jesus understood this picture of future punishment. It is certain, however, that He believed that it was a possibility to be reckoned with.

Mark 9⁴⁹⁻⁵⁰. *Salt.* The word is used to illustrate three different points: in verse 49 the purifying quality of salt; in verse 50a, the fact that under certain conditions, although it preserves the appearance of salt, it loses its saltlike qualities; and in verse 50b its seasoning qualities, which in this context stand for love and loyalty.

Mark 10¹⁻¹²—*Marriage and Divorce*

In Judaism a man had a right to divorce his wife if he found some indecency in her (Deut 24¹⁻³); but a woman had no right to divorce her husband. Jesus affirmed the equality of rights in this matter between husband and wife, by forbidding a husband to divorce his wife. When a man and woman marry, they become one flesh, joined together by God, and no man has a right to separate them. Divorce is against God's will, and anyone who remarries after divorce commits adultery.

Because Jesus did not make a practice of issuing categorical rules about conduct, many interpreters have argued that His rule about divorce was intended for His own age but not for all time. They have also claimed that obedience to the supreme law of love may sometimes require the rule about divorce and remarriage to be relaxed. Others believe that, whatever hardships Jesus's rule may bring, it is universally binding.

Mark 10^7 refers to Genesis 1^{27} and 2^{24}.

Mark 10^{11-12}. In Matthew 5^{31-2} and 19^9 Jesus is said to have allowed divorce on the ground of unchastity, but this is unlikely to have been His original teaching. The sayings in Matthew would put Jesus in agreement with the school of Rabbi Shammai, in contrast with that of Rabbi Hillel, who thought that divorce could be justified for a great variety of reasons. The rabbis disputed about the meaning of the 'indecency' mentioned in Deuteronomy 24^{1-3}, but Jesus agreed with neither of their schools.

Mark 10^{13-16}—*The Blessing of Children*

The disciples tried to keep the children away from Jesus, presumably to prevent them from troubling Him. But He insisted on receiving them, and pointed out that the Kingdom of God belonged to those who accepted it with childlike qualities, that is, with humble trust and a sense of dependence on God.

Mark 10^{17-31}—*The Rich Man, and the Peril of Wealth*

The rich man's refusal to give away all his wealth and follow Jesus was the occasion for Jesus to tell His disciples how inconceivably difficult it was for a rich man to enter the Kingdom of God, more difficult than for a camel to go through a needle's eye. But although it seemed impossible when it was regarded as something to be achieved by human effort, it was not impossible when it was understood as an act of God's mercy. 'To God everything is possible' (verses 17–27).

The incident ends with an assurance that all those who, like the disciples, had given up wealth and family ties to follow Jesus, would receive rich fellowship with others during this present age, and eternal life in the future. The order of precedence in this life would in many cases be reversed in the future (verses 28–31).

Mark 10^{17}. *eternal life* is the life of the Kingdom of God. *eternal* can mean not only 'everlasting', but also 'belonging to the Messianic age'. The Jews believed that there were two ages, *this age* and *the age to come* (see verse 30). The Messianic age was the age to come.

Mark 10^{18}. Jesus refused to be called *Good*, because He wished to emphasize that God was the source of all goodness.

Mark 10^{19}. Jesus drew special attention to those commandments which dealt with ethical duties rather than with worship and ritual.

Mark 10^{25}. There is no good reason to suppose that the *eye of a needle* was the name of a gate in Jerusalem, as some writers have conjectured.

Mark 10$^{32-4}$—*The Journey to Jerusalem*

It was part of Jesus's plan to go to Jerusalem, the very city where His enemies were strongest, and to perform His work of preaching and healing there. Although He knew that this journey would lead Him to a cruel death, He believed that it was God's will that He should go; and nothing would deter Him.

Luke's account of Jesus's last journey to Jerusalem is much longer than Mark's, and includes the record of many of Jesus's acts and sayings (Lk 9^{51}–19^{28}).

For the prophecy in verses 33–4, see notes on Mark 8$^{27-33}$.

Mark 10$^{35-45}$—*James and John: Greatness and Service*

When James and John showed a false sense of values by asking for the chief places in the Kingdom, Jesus answered that it was not His task to assign these places. He could only promise them a share in His cup of suffering and in His baptism of death (verses 35–40). He then told the Twelve that true greatness consisted in service to others (see Mk 9^{35}), and that He Himself had come to be a servant and to give His life as a ransom for many (verses 41–5).

The words of verse 45 are of great importance. They show that Jesus fulfilled His mission through service and self-sacrifice, and that by surrendering His life He gave men liberty. A ransom was a price paid to liberate a captive or slave, and, although we ought not to press the metaphor too far by asking to whom the ransom was paid, this saying emphasizes that at great cost to Himself Jesus set men free from the power of sin and death.

Mark 10$^{38-9}$. For the *cup* as a description of suffering see also Mark 14^{36}. For *baptism* as a description of Jesus's death see Luke 12^{50}. A difficulty arises because, though James died a martyr's death (Acts 12^2), John seems to have died peacefully in old age. It is possible, however, that this saying contains the seed of Paul's teaching about mystical incorporation into the death and resurrection of Christ, and does not refer to martyrdom.

Mark 10^{45}. *many* does not imply that there were some for whom Jesus did not die. The word may have been used under the influence of Isaiah 53$^{11-12}$, but it is by no means certain that this saying implies that Jesus is the Suffering Servant.

Mark 10$^{46-52}$—*Bartimaeus*

At Jericho Jesus healed the blind man, Bartimaeus, in response to his faith. When the blind man called Him by his Messianic title 'Son of

David', Jesus did not attempt to silence him, because He was soon to enter Jerusalem openly as the Messiah.

Mark 11[1-11]—*The Entry of Jesus into Jerusalem*

It seems that Jesus deliberately entered Jerusalem on an ass's colt in order to fulfil the prophecy about the coming of a king who would be 'humble and riding on an ass' (Zech 9[9]). The ass was a symbol of peaceful government by contrast with the horse which a warrior king would have chosen. But although Jesus claimed to be a peaceful king, He nevertheless claimed to be a king. And this was one of the reasons why His opponents decided that the time was ripe to arrest Him. His action had declared His claim to Messiahship.

The reference to the waving of palm branches by the crowd is found in John 12[13].

Mark 11[9-10]. *Hosanna* is a Hebrew word, meaning *Save now*, which occurs in Psalm 118[25]. *Blessings on him who comes in the name of the Lord* is from Psalm 118[26]. This psalm was used in the liturgy for the Passover.

Mark 11[12-14, 20-1]—*The Fig Tree*

This story of how Jesus cursed a fig-tree, which afterwards withered, has caused great difficulty. It is strange that the tree should have been condemned for having no fruit, when, as Mark says (verse 13), 'it was not the season for figs'. And it is even stranger that Jesus should have performed a destructive act like this. Some commentators believe that Jesus did in fact cause the tree to wither in order to convey with special vividness the lesson which He wished to teach. They argue that the incident was an acted parable. Others think that Jesus did not curse a tree, but told a parable like Luke 13[6-9], which was later misunderstood as the record of an actual event.

The fig was a symbol of the nation of Israel, and the story indicates that, because the Jews, like an unfruitful tree, had failed in their loyalty to God, they would cease to be the chosen people.

Mark 11[15-19]—*The Cleansing of the Temple*

In the outer court of the Temple, which was known as the Court of the Gentiles, wine, oil, salt, and birds were sold for use in sacrifices. It was possible in this court to exchange money for the special Temple coinage in which the Temple tax had to be paid. People also used the court as a short cut from one part of the city to another. Jesus objected to these practices, because they prevented Gentile visitors from worshipping God in the one part of the Temple which was open to them. He drove out the traders and their customers, upset the tables of the money-changers, and stopped people using the court as a thoroughfare. The Temple, He said, should be 'a house of prayer for all the nations' (Isa 56[7]), that is, for Gentiles as well as Jews. It should not be 'a robbers' cave' (Jer 7[11]).

Jesus's action was a direct challenge to the Jewish authorities, who intensified their plans to do away with Him. The incident reveals His deep concern for the religion of the Jews. He did not plan to overthrow it but to cleanse its institutions. Like some reformers in later years, He was rejected by those whose traditions He tried to reform, and His rejection led to the establishment of a separate community.

John places this story in the early part of Jesus's ministry (Jn 2[12-22]), but Mark's date is probably correct, since an incident of this nature is likely to have provoked a conspiracy against Jesus. It is improbable that Jesus cleansed the Temple twice.

Mark 11[22-5]—Faith and Prayer

Jesus taught that there was no limit to what a man can do when he has a genuine and completely sure faith. If he really believes that his prayer will be answered, then it will be answered (see notes on Mt 7[7-11]). For verse 25 see also Matthew 6[12].

Mark 11[27-33]—A Question about Jesus's Authority

During this final ministry in Jerusalem Jesus was asked some difficult questions. The first was about the source of His authority, and was asked by the chief priests, lawyers, and elders, the men who were members of the Sanhedrin. Jesus refused to answer the question directly, because they would have accused Him of blasphemy if He had claimed a unique divine authority. He replied therefore with a counter-question which not only implied that His authority came from God, but also put His opponents in a dilemma and silenced them.

Mark 12[1-12]—The Vineyard

This parable has obvious allegorical elements in it (see notes on Mk 4[1-2]). The owner of the vineyard represents God, and the tenants stand for the Jews, who were God's chosen people. The servants who were beaten and killed are the Hebrew prophets, and the son of the owner is Jesus. Perhaps also the vineyard stands for Israel. The climax of the parable is the execution of the tenants, who had murdered the owner's son, and the appointment of new tenants. Its lesson is that when the

Jews reject Jesus and put Him to death, they will forfeit their right to be God's people, and the followers of Jesus will become the new people of God. The death of Jesus will lead to the establishment of a new Israel, the Christian Church.

The quotation from Psalm 118²²⁻³ (verses 10–11) makes a similar point. Jesus, the stone rejected by the builders, has become the main corner-stone of a new Temple, which is not a building made with hands but the community of His disciples.

Mark 12²⁻⁵. These verses refer to the Jews' treatment of the prophets, evidence for which is found, for example, in 1 Kings 18¹³, 22²⁷, 2 Chronicles 24²⁰⁻², Nehemiah 9²⁶, Jeremiah 26²⁰⁻³, 37¹⁵.

Mark 12¹⁰. *The corner-stone* can be either the stone at the corner, holding the walls of a building together, or the keystone of an arch or gateway.

The quotation in verses 10–11 was often used in the early Church (see Acts 4¹¹, 1 Pet 2⁷, Eph 2²⁰), and had probably been included in a collection of proof-texts.

Mark 12¹³⁻¹⁷—A Question about Taxes

Jesus had already been questioned about the source of His authority (Mk 11²⁷⁻³³). Now the Pharisees and the men of Herod's party asked Him if they were allowed to pay taxes to the Roman emperor. It was a trick question, because, if Jesus had answered 'Yes', He would have lost the support of some of His sympathizers, and if He had answered 'No', He could have been accused of seditious talk. His answer was that taxes should be paid to Caesar (see also Mt 17²⁴⁻⁷), and that God also should be given the service and honour which was His due. It was indeed the second part of Jesus's saying, 'Pay God what is due to God', to which men needed to give chief attention.

Mark 12¹⁸⁻²⁷—A Question about the Resurrection

This question was asked by Sadducees, the members of the aristocratic and priestly party from which the High Priest was chosen. They were conservative in outlook, venerated the Law, and did not believe in a resurrection. When they asked Jesus who would be a woman's husband in heaven if she had been married to seven men on earth, He answered that men and women do not marry in heaven. Marriage is an institution designed for life on earth. He also challenged the Sadducees about the resurrection of the dead, quoting Exodus 3⁶ to show that Abraham, Isaac, and Jacob were alive at the time of Moses, long after their physical deaths.

Mark 12²⁸⁻³⁴—*The Two Great Commandments*

In answer to a lawyer's question Jesus said that the first commandment of all was the commandment to 'Love the Lord your God with all your heart, with all your soul, with all your mind, and with all your strength', and the second commandment was to 'Love your neighbour as yourself'. The first of these commandments, which is found in Deuteronomy 6⁴⁻⁵, was repeated daily by devout Jews. The second is from Leviticus 19¹⁸. It is not certain that Jesus was the first person to link these two commandments as a summary of the Law, but He showed their meaning supremely in His life, and gave a uniquely searching interpretation of them in His teaching. The love of which He speaks is not a desire for pleasure or personal gain, but a self-giving love which is full of care and concern for the person loved. It is the kind of love which Jesus Himself showed in His life and death. It is the kind of love which God has for men, and which led Him to send His Son to seek and to save the lost.

These two commandments sum up the teaching of the Ten Commandments and go beyond them. The commandment to love God sums up the first four of the Ten Commandments, which deal with a man's duty to God, and the commandment to love one's neighbour sums up the last six commandments, which deal with a man's duty to his neighbour. But whereas the Ten Commandments are mostly negative, the two commandments of Jesus instruct men to take up a positive attitude to God and their neighbours.

Mark 12³⁰. *love*. The Greek verb is *agapan*, and the corresponding noun is *agapē*, which is the usual word for *love* in the New Testament. *Agapē* emphasizes the self-giving nature of love, whereas *erōs*, the normal word for *love* in non-biblical Greek, emphasizes love as desire.

with all your mind. This phrase does not appear in the Old Testament form of the commandment. The saying means that a man should love God with his whole self, and there is no need to make distinctions between the meanings of *heart*, *soul*, and *mind*.

Mark 12³⁵⁻⁷—*The Son of David, and the Lord*

Jesus now put a question Himself. How could the Messiah be David's son, when David himself had addressed him as his Lord (Ps 110¹)? It is not clear whether Jesus implied that the Messiah was David's son or not. What the saying does make clear is that the traditional belief that the Messiah would be a descendant of David does not by itself do full justice to the nature of the Messiah. The Messiah is Lord, a title which was used in the Old Testament not only of kings but of God Himself. Jesus's use of 'Lord' in this saying suggests that He is of divine origin and authority. The title was used of Him regularly in the early Church, and has been accepted by Christians ever since.

Mark 12[36]. It is now generally thought that David did not write Psalm 110; but in Jesus's time David was thought to be the author of all the psalms, and Jesus accepted the prevailing view.

Mark 12[38-40]—*The Doctors of the Law*

Jesus warned men against the doctors of the Law, whose outward show He contrasted with their underlying rapacity.

Mark 12[39]. *the chief seats in synagogues* were on the bench in front of the ark.

Mark 12[40]. *who eat up the property of widows.* They were ready to persuade widows to make them gifts which they could ill afford.

Mark 12[41-4]—*The Poor Widow*

The outlook of this widow, who gave her two coins, worth only a farthing, to the Temple, was completely the opposite of that of the doctors of the Law. She counted for little in the eyes of the people, but was utterly dedicated and sincere. And Jesus did not measure the value of her gift by its quantity, but by its cost to her.

Mark 13[1-37]—*The Future*

This chapter, which is a collection of predictions about the future, has many of the characteristics of an apocalypse (see p. 19), with its details of the events which would precede the coming of the Son of Man. It is probable that many of these sayings were originally uttered in different situations, and were later grouped together.

The chapter opens with a prophecy of the destruction of Jerusalem (verses 1–2), which was fulfilled in A D 70, when a Roman army destroyed the city after a Jewish revolt. The rest of the chapter is an answer to the question, 'When will this happen?' (verse 4). Although the question asks for an account of the destruction of Jerusalem, Jesus's answer describes the disasters, persecutions, and supernatural portents, which will be signs of the end of the world. It should be remembered, however, that, if Mark was writing at a time when the Roman armies were either preparing to attack Jerusalem or were actually besieging it, he might have expected the end of the world to follow soon after the city's destruction.

The work of Jesus's disciples in bearing witness to Him even in the face of persecution, and the Spirit's guidance of them in the words they spoke (verses 9–13), are illustrated by many incidents in the Acts of the Apostles (e.g. Acts 4^8, 5^{32}, 7^{55-6}). For the belief that before the end the gospel must be preached to all nations, see notes on Matthew 28^{20}.

The phrase 'abomination of desolation' (verse 14 : see Dan 9^{27}, 11^{31}, 12^{11}) refers to the supremely evil power which, according to a widespread tradition, would appear on earth before the end of the world. This saying prophesies the entry of such a being into the Temple, 'a place which is not his'.

The description of the coming of Jesus as Son of Man at the Last Day (verses 26–7 ; see also Mk 8^{38}, 14^{62}) is based on Daniel 7^{13}.

Jesus's admission of ignorance about the precise time of the end (verse 32) is evidence of the reality of his human nature.

The parable of the Door-keeper (verses 33–7), with its emphasis on the sudden and unexpected nature of Jesus's coming and the need to be ready for it, may be compared with the parable of the Ten Bridesmaids (Mt 25^{1-13}).

Mark 13^{30}. This prophecy, which was not fulfilled, was probably uttered at first in a different context.

Mark 14^{1-2}—*The Plot against Jesus*

For the date of Jesus's death, see notes on Mark 14^{12-25}.

Mark 14^{3-9}—*The Anointing at Bethany*

According to John 12^3, the woman who anointed Jesus was Mary, the sister of Martha and Lazarus. There is no evidence that she was Mary of Magdala, as is sometimes supposed. John also records that it was Judas Iscariot who criticized her for wasting money (Jn 12^{4-5}).

Jesus's prediction of His death (verse 8) was correct in its assumption that His body would not be anointed after the crucifixion (see notes on Mk 16^1). The story shows that Jesus believed true discipleship not just to consist of good works, but to be based on adoration (see notes on Lk 10^{38-42}).

Mark 14^{10-11}—*Judas Iscariot*

It is hardly likely that the prospect of financial gain was the main motive for Judas's betrayal of Jesus. He was probably disillusioned with Jesus because He was not his ideal of a Messiah. Or perhaps he was trying to force Jesus into a spectacular display of Messianic power.

According to Matthew 26[15], the chief priests paid Judas thirty pieces of silver.

Mark 14[12-25]—*The Last Supper*

According to Mark, the Last Supper was the Passover meal, which was eaten on the first day of the Passover Feast, the 15th day of the month Nisan (it should be remembered that a Jewish day begins at sunset). According to John 19[14], however, Jesus was crucified on the afternoon of the 14th Nisan, and John's date is supported by Paul's description of Christ as a Passover sacrifice (1 Cor 5[7]), and perhaps by Mark 14[1-2]. John, however, may have been influenced by the theological idea that Christ was the true Passover lamb. The question of the date of these events continues to be debated. But even if the Last Supper was not actually the Passover meal, it contained characteristic features of the meal, like the breaking of the bread and the passing of the cup.

Jesus gave the meal a special relationship to His death by saying that the bread was His body and the wine was His blood (verses 22–4). Because the word 'is' did not occur in the Aramaic, we cannot be sure from His words whether the bread and wine actually were His body and blood or merely represented them. Since He was standing there in His own flesh and blood, it is likely that He intended the bread and wine to represent or symbolize His body and blood. In any case, the word 'is', which occurs in the Greek version of the saying, could in this context mean 'stands for'.

The reference to 'my blood of the covenant, shed for many' (verse 24) implies that the death of Jesus was a covenant sacrifice, in which He fulfilled the prophecy of a new covenant (Jer 31[31]) by establishing a new and personal relationship between God and men. As the covenant of the Law had been sealed by the sacrifice of animals (Ex 24[5-8]), so the new covenant was sealed by the sacrifice of Jesus on the Cross. 'Blood' stands for life which is offered to God and renewed by Him (see Lev 17[11, 14]). The life of Jesus, offered to God, was made available to men as life in God's Kingdom.

Other ideas may be present in this saying about the blood of Jesus. There is probably a suggestion that Jesus was a Passover sacrifice, marking a deliverance not from captivity to Pharaoh, but from captivity to sin. The words 'for many' possibly, but by no means certainly, imply a connection with the Suffering Servant of Isaiah 53[11-12], who gives himself as an offering to remove sin (see notes on Mk 10[45]).

Although the Last Supper itself was an anticipation of Jesus's sacrificial death, all subsequent celebrations of the meal have been regarded as a *remembrance* of it, and in Paul's account (1 Cor 11$^{24-5}$) Jesus actually says, 'Do this as a memorial of me.'

The Supper is also an act of *communion* in which the taking of bread and wine stands for a present relationship with Christ, who is with His followers and in them, whenever they participate in the meal. And as they have fellowship in Christ, so they have fellowship with each other. These points are made by Paul, when he says that those who bless the cup and break the bread share in the body and blood of Christ, and that the one loaf is a sign of the unity of Christians in Him (1 Cor 10$^{16-17}$).

The Supper also has a forward look. Jesus's prophecy that He would drink wine again with His disciples (Mk 14^{25}) seems to have been fulfilled in the events of the resurrection. But, according to Paul, Jesus said during the Supper, 'For every time you eat this bread and drink the cup, you proclaim the death of the Lord, until he comes' (1 Cor 11^{26}). The Supper is an *anticipation* of a communion with Christ at the end of the world.

It is clear that the early Christians gathered together regularly to share in the Supper, which at first was a proper meal. The practice of consuming only token quantities of bread and wine developed later. In Christian tradition the meal has been called the Lord's Supper, Holy Communion, the Breaking of Bread, and the Eucharist. It is described as the Lord's Supper in 1 Corinthians 11^{20}, and as Communion (or, in *NEB*, 'sharing') in 1 Corinthians 10$^{16-17}$. The allusions to breaking bread in Luke 24^{35} and Acts 2^{42} may possibly refer to it. And the title 'Eucharist' is derived from the Greek *eucharistein*, 'to give thanks', which occurs in Mark 14^{23}.

Mark 14^{22}. The version of these words in 1 Corinthians 11^{24} is, *This is my body, which is for you.*

Mark 14^{24}. 1 Corinthians 11^{25} reads, *This cup is the new covenant sealed by my blood.*

Mark 14$^{26-31}$—*The Journey to Gethsemane*

The hymn which the disciples sang after the meal was probably from Psalms 115–18. Psalm 118 is especially important for an understanding of the events of Jesus's Passion (see Ps 118$^{17-26}$).

The prophecy of the disciples' desertion of Jesus is taken from Zechariah 13^{7}.

Mark 14³²⁻⁴²—*Jesus in Gethsemane*

During this time of prayer in Gethsemane Jesus had to decide whether to go to His death or to turn back. Although He felt an inclination to avoid the cruel death which awaited Him, He committed the issue to God, pledging obedience to His will. Indeed Jesus's pledge of obedience (verse 36) was God's answer to His prayer.

Jesus's use of the Aramaic word *Abba* to address His Father demonstrates the closeness of their relationship, because it was an intimate form of address which was normally used only for a person's human father. In calling upon God it was customary to use the more formal *Abinu*, 'Our Father'.

The firm resolve of Jesus to do His Father's will shows that His voluntary obedience to God was an important aspect of His death. As Paul wrote, Jesus 'in obedience accepted even death—death on a cross' (Phil 2⁸).

This period in Gethsemane is often described as Jesus's agony. He did indeed say, 'My heart is ready to break with grief' (verse 34), and Luke refers graphically to His 'anguish of spirit' (Lk 22⁴⁴). The reason for this anguish was partly Jesus's own inner conflict as He faced the prospect of death, and partly His sorrow over men's tragic failure to be what God intended them to be. Christian tradition has taught that in Gethsemane Jesus was sorrowing over the sins of the whole world.

In sharp contrast with Jesus were His disciples, who even at this moment of crisis were unable to keep awake and watch with Him (verses 37–41).

Mark 14³². *Gethsemane* seems to have been an olive plantation, near the Mount of Olives.

Mark 14³⁶. *cup* refers to suffering (see Mk 10³⁸⁻⁹).

Mark 14⁴³⁻⁵²—*The Betrayal of Jesus*

Judas's co-operation enabled the priests to arrest Jesus with a minimum of disturbance. If they had taken Him by day, there might have been a riot. But in Gethsemane there was no violence apart from a short scuffle, in which the High Priest's servant was wounded. Judas may also have lodged information with the priests about some of the claims which Jesus had made for Himself in private conversation with His disciples.

The young man who escaped naked from the scene (verses 51–2) is often thought to have been Mark, who may have inserted this account as a personal reminiscence. But there is no real evidence to support the theory.

Mark 14[44]. Judas kissed Jesus because the arresting party would find it difficult to recognize Him in the darkness.

Mark 14[47]. According to John, it was Peter who struck the man, whose name was Malchus (John 18[10-11]); and, according to Luke, Jesus restored the wounded man's ear (Lk 22[51]).

Mark 14[53-65]—*Jesus and the High Priest*

The preliminary examination of Jesus was held before the High Priest at an informal meeting of the Sanhedrin, the supreme Jewish Council. False and conflicting evidence was brought against Jesus, including the charge that He had said He would destroy the Temple and build another not made with hands. This charge was a distortion of the truth, which may have had its origin in a saying of Jesus reported in John 2[19]. The examination reached its climax when the High Priest asked Jesus if He was 'the Messiah, the Son of the Blessed One'. When Jesus admitted that He was, and prophesied His return as Son of Man, He was judged guilty of blasphemy and worthy of death.

Mark 14[53]. *The High Priest* at this time was Caiaphas. The *chief priests* probably included, in addition to the High Priest, deposed high priests and members of leading priestly families.

Mark 14[61]. *the Blessed One* is a reverential phrase for God.

Mark 14[62]. *I am.* Matthew's version, *the words are yours* (Mt 26[64]), may be original. In any case Jesus was admitting His Messiahship, and His prophecy about the Son of Man shows that He claimed a unique divine status.

Mark 14[66-72]—*Peter's Denial*

Peter's denial that he had any connection with Jesus provides an important insight into his character. He was quick to deny Jesus, but quick to repent. His strength was his readiness to admit that he was wrong. Although there is ample evidence in the New Testament of Peter's faults (see Mk 8[32-3], 9[5-6], Mt 14[28-33], Gal 2[11-14]), there is also in the Acts of the Apostles plenty of evidence of his loyalty and courage.

Mark 15[1-15]—*Jesus and Pilate*

The next morning, after another session of the Council, Jesus was handed over to Pilate, the Roman governor, who had authority to sentence people to death. The accusation which had most weight with Pilate was that Jesus had claimed to be king of the Jews. During Pilate's governorship there had been several armed rebellions in Palestine, and it was his task to stamp out any possible cause of revolt. When he asked Jesus if He was king of the Jews, Jesus's answer, 'The words are yours', implied that He was in fact their king, although He was a different kind of king from the one whom they expected. Nevertheless, Pilate suggested that Jesus should be released, in accordance with a custom that a prisoner should be set free during the festival. The crowd, however, asked for the release of Barabbas, a violent revolutionary, and demanded the crucifixion of Jesus.

Although the chief priests and lawyers were the real agents of Jesus's death, Pilate was officially responsible, because without his consent the crucifixion could not have taken place. The gospels emphasize that Pilate did not believe Jesus to be guilty of any serious crime. Nevertheless he was ready to let Him be crucified, and the reasons for his attitude are not hard to find.

(i) Even though Jesus was innocent, He was a potential revolutionary leader, who would be safer out of the way.

(ii) The Jewish leaders had been roused to a high pitch of anger and excitement. There was danger of a riot, and it was worth the sacrifice of a life to keep the peace.

(iii) It is likely that Pilate had borrowed money from the High Priest in order to improve the water supply at Jerusalem. If he offended the High Priest by releasing Jesus, his financial difficulties might be reported to the Emperor.

Pilate attempted to wriggle out of his responsibility for making the final decision about the fate of Jesus. According to Luke, he tried to leave the matter to Herod (Lk 23$^{6-12}$). Mark describes his attempt to persuade the crowd to ask for Jesus's release (verses 6–15). And, according to Matthew, he publicly washed his hands to show that he was not responsible for shedding Jesus's blood (Mt 27^{24}). But the decision to crucify Jesus had to be made by him, and, in the words of the Creeds, Jesus suffered and was crucified 'under Pontius Pilate'.

Mark 15^1. *Pilate.* Pontius Pilate was Governor, or Procurator, of Judaea from A D 26 to 36. He lived at Caesarea on the Mediterranean coast, not to be confused with Caesarea Philippi, but he had come to Jerusalem to maintain order during the Passover.

Mark 15$^{16-20}$—*Mock Homage to Jesus*

This account of the mock homage paid to Jesus by the soldiers underlines the fact that Jesus suffered and died as king of the Jews. Some of the descriptions of the Suffering Servant (Isa 50[6], 53[3]) provide a fitting comment on this incident.

Mark 15[21-32]—*The Crucifixion*

On the way to the place of the crucifixion, Simon, a man from Cyrene on the north coast of Africa, was compelled to carry the Cross, probably because Jesus was fainting under its weight. The crucifixion took place on a mound called Golgotha, which was outside the walls of Jerusalem. The fact that Jesus 'suffered outside the gate' (Heb 13[12]) was later regarded as a sign of His rejection by the Jewish nation. The inscription on the Cross was 'The king of the Jews', because the main charge for which He was executed was that He claimed to be king.

Crucifixion was a Roman form of punishment—the traditional Jewish method of execution was stoning. Normally crucifixion was a lengthy process. After being scourged and stripped the condemned man was tied or nailed to a cross by his arms and feet, and was left to hang there, sometimes for several days, until finally he died from exhaustion. Jesus, however, died comparatively quickly, six hours after His crucifixion had begun.

Mark's narrative emphasizes the way in which the event was foreshadowed in the Old Testament. The dividing of Jesus's garments recalls Psalm 22[18]; the taunts of the passers-by reflect Lamentations 2[15], Psalm 22[6-8], and Psalm 69[9]; and the placing of Jesus between two bandits suggests a fulfilment of Isaiah 53[12]. Mark implies that, since everything happened according to the scriptures, it happened according to the will of God.

Mark 15[21]. *Simon* was probably a Jew who had come to Jerusalem for the feast. IIis sons, *Alexander and Rufus*, may be mentioned because they were known to Mark and to the Roman church. A Rufus is mentioned by Paul in Romans 16[13].

Mark 15[22]. *Golgotha* is Aramaic for *skull*. The Latin equivalent, *calvaria*, is the origin of the word *Calvary*.

Mark 15[25]. *nine in the morning.* The Greek means literally *the third hour*, because the Jews reckoned the hours by a different method from ours.

Mark 15[27]. *Two bandits.* Only Luke (23[39-43]) records that one of these bandits asked Jesus to remember him.

Mark 15[33-41]—*The Death of Jesus*

Jesus's cry, 'My God, my God, why has thou forsaken me?', which is a quotation from Psalm 22[1], implies that He feared that God had abandoned Him. Some commentators have tried to soften the force of the words by suggesting that Jesus intended to quote the whole of the psalm, which ends on a joyful note. It is more likely that, when Jesus uttered this cry, He meant what he said. He felt what it was like to be abandoned by God. Although He was not a sinner, He entered into the sinner's experience of separation from God.

The tearing of the curtain of the Temple after Jesus's death is seen by Mark as a sign that the barrier between God and men had been removed by the crucifixion. The curtain, which was either that which hung before the Holy of Holies or that which hung before the Holy Place, was regarded as a veil hiding God from men.

The centurion, who through no fault of his own had to supervise the crucifixion, recognized the superhuman quality of Jesus. Because he was a pagan, his affirmation that Jesus was 'a son of God' meant that he regarded Him as a divine being, though not necessarily a unique one.

Mark 15^{33}. *midday* : literally *the sixth hour*. *three in the afternoon*: literally *the ninth hour*.

Mark 15^{34}. The Aramaic words which Jesus spoke are quoted.

Mark 15$^{35-6}$. The people seem to have misunderstood Jesus's cry *Eli* as an appeal to Elijah.

Mark 15^{40}. For *Mary of Magdala* see also Luke 8^2 and John 20$^{1-18}$. *Salome* was probably the mother of the sons of Zebedee (see Mt 27^{56}).

Mark 15$^{42-7}$—*The Burial of Jesus*

In Palestine the dead had to be buried before sunset on the day of death, and this was specially important when the next day was a Sabbath. Joseph of Arimathaea, a member of the Sanhedrin, who buried the body of Jesus, was a devout man who obviously had sympathies with Jesus.

Mark 16$^{1-8}$—*The Resurrection of Jesus*

This brief story of the empty tomb is the climax of the gospel. It emphasizes that Jesus rose again, as He had predicted (Mark 8^{31}, 9^{31}, 10^{34}), and was victorious over death. It mentions, although it does not describe, the appearance of the risen Jesus to His disciples (verse 7), and therefore points to Him as the living Lord of the Church, the 'main corner-stone' (Mk 12^{10}) of the new community. The story also stresses the astonishment and terror with which the women reacted to their discovery of the empty tomb (verses 5 and 8). These emotions, which Jesus aroused on many occasions during His ministry (Mk 1^{27}, 2^{12}, 4^{41}, 5$^{20, 42}$, 6$^{50-1}$, 7^{37}, 9^6, 12^{17}, 15^5), were natural reactions to His manifestation of divine power and glory. It is not surprising that they were the emotions experienced by these women, when they saw the evidence of His resurrection, in which His divine power and glory were supremely manifested.

Mark 16^1. *intending to anoint him.* Jesus had already been anointed by the woman at Bethany (Mk 14^8), and these women at the empty tomb (see also Mk 15$^{40-1}$) did not have any opportunity to perform this customary rite.

Mark 16^2. *Sunday morning.* Literally, *the first day of the week.*

Mark 16^5. *a white robe* suggests that the youth was an angel.

Mark 16^7. *Galilee.* This verse implies that the first resurrection appearances were in Galilee, whereas Matthew, Luke, and John imply that they were in Jerusalem. Either Mark did not know of the Jerusalem appearances, or this saying was inaccurately preserved.

THE ENDING OF THE GOSPEL

Two endings of the gospel have survived, and both are given in the *New English Bible*. The shorter of them has no verse number, and the longer is found in verses 9–20. Neither of them is contained in the oldest and most reliable manuscripts, and they were both produced at a later date in order to supply what seemed to be a deficiency in the gospel, which ends abruptly and gives no description of the resurrection appearances of Jesus. Scholars have long debated whether Mark deliberately ended the gospel at 16^8, or the final paragraphs have been accidentally lost. One thing is certain: the genuine text of the gospel does not go beyond the story of the empty tomb.

QUESTIONS

(1) Discuss the importance of Jesus's conversation with His disciples at Caesarea Philippi.

(2) Why did Jesus enter Jerusalem on an ass, and why did He cleanse the Temple?

(3) Examine the meaning of Jesus's agony and prayer in Gethsemane.

(4) Comment on: Mark 9$^{3-4}$, 10^{45}, 13^{32}, 14^{24}, 15$^{38-9}$, 16^8.

CHAPTER THREE

THE GOSPEL ACCORDING TO ST MATTHEW

INTRODUCTION TO THE GOSPEL

The Author

THIS GOSPEL is traditionally ascribed to Matthew, the tax-gatherer, who was also known as Levi, and was one of the Twelve Disciples (Mk 2^{13-14}, 3^{18}, Mt 9^9). This tradition has been seriously questioned, because an apostle would not have been likely to use Mark as a source for his gospel. But even if Matthew did not prepare the final version of the gospel, there must have been some reason for his name to be associated with it, and he was probably responsible for one of its sources.

The Date and Place of Writing

The gospel seems to have been written between AD 75 and 90. Antioch has been suggested as a place where it may have originated. But no certain conclusion can be reached about either date or place.

The Sources of the Gospel

It is generally thought that the gospel used three main sources.

(i) *Mark.* The gospel reproduces ninety per cent of Mark's subject matter in language which is usually almost identical with that of Mark.

(ii) *Q.* It also includes large sections which have close parallels in Luke. These passages are thought by many scholars to have been taken from a collection of sayings, which has been called 'Q' (from the German *Quelle*, meaning 'source'). But considerable doubt has been cast on the theory that there was one large source for this type of material. The evangelists may have used several such sources.

(iii) Much of the material in the gospel is not found elsewhere, and seems to be from a third source. This material may have been provided by Matthew—although some scholars have suggested that Matthew was the author of 'Q'—but we cannot be sure. It may be a collection of independent stories and groups of sayings which had been handed down separately. On the other hand it may include items which were known to Mark or Luke but passed over by them.

THE GOSPEL ACCORDING TO ST MATTHEW

The Characteristics of the Gospel

The arrangement of the teaching into large groups suggests that the gospel was intended for the instruction of Church members and candidates for membership. It may also have been planned for use in religious services. The frequent use of Old Testament quotations and the general tone of the gospel indicate that it was written from a Jewish standpoint, but it does not follow that it was written exclusively for Jewish Christians. It gives the impression, however, that Church organization had developed, and that some of the material had been selected to give guidance for the corporate life of the Church.

Among the main emphases of the gospel are the following :

(i) The life, death, and resurrection of Jesus are seen as *the fulfilment of Old Testament prophecy*. This is a characteristic of all four gospels, but Matthew[1] shows a greater eagerness than the others to mention Old Testament passages which can be interpreted as predictions of the gospel story.

(ii) Matthew sees Jesus as the giver of *a New Law*. There are five great blocks of teaching in the gospel (Mt 5–7, 10, 13, 18, 23–5), which seem to correspond to the five books of the Jewish Law. Jesus emphasizes that He has come not to destroy the Law but to fulfil it (Mt 5^{17}) and implies that His way is superior to that of the Law (Mt 5^{21-48}).

(iii) Matthew's gospel lays emphasis on the importance of *the Church*. It is the only gospel which actually uses the word 'Church' (Mt 16^{18}, 18^{17}), and it gives instruction about behaviour within the Christian community (Mt 18^{15-22}) and about the authority of Peter and the other disciples (Mt 16^{17-19}, 18^{18}).

(iv) More than the other gospels Matthew stresses the theme of *the future judgement and kingdom*. The idea is brought out with special clarity in the parable of the Wheat and the Darnel (Mt 13^{24-30}) and in the story of the Sheep and the Goats (Mt 25^{31-46}).

(v) The gospel is also concerned to stress *the divinity of Jesus*. This is, of course, a major concern of all the gospels, but a special feature of Matthew is his tendency to modify statements in Mark which suggest that the power of Jesus was limited. Whereas Mark says of Jesus's ministry in Nazareth, 'He could work no miracle there' (Mk 6^5), Matthew says, 'He did not work many miracles there' (Mt 13^{58}). And Mark 10^{17-18}, according to which Jesus refuses to be called 'good', is completely revised by Matthew (Mt 19^{16-17}) in order to remove the suggestion

---

[1] For convenience, the author of the gospel will be called Matthew, irrespective of who he actually was.

that Jesus had no claim to be called 'good'. Moreover, Matthew's gospel begins with the supernatural birth of Jesus, and ends with His appearance in Galilee when He declares that He has complete authority over the whole universe. Both the beginning and the end of the gospel stress the unique and divine nature of Jesus.

COMMENTS ON SELECTED PASSAGES FROM MATTHEW'S GOSPEL

Matthew 1 [18-25]—*The Birth of Jesus*

The birth of Jesus is narrated only by Matthew and Luke, both of whom agree that He had no human father but was born of Mary and conceived by the Holy Spirit.

Many scholars have questioned the historical accuracy of the story, because, apart from these two narratives, the rest of the New Testament is silent about the Virgin Birth, and even in the synoptic gospels Joseph is described as the father of Jesus. They claim too that it would be more fitting for the incarnate Son of God to undergo a normal human birth than to have no human father.

Those who accept the historical accuracy of the narratives believe that Mary herself was the authority for the story, and that it was not widely publicized until after Mark and the Pauline letters had been written. They point out that, although Luke and Matthew are using independent sources for their accounts of Jesus's birth, they agree about its miraculous nature. It is also argued that a unique person ought to have a unique birth. The traditional view, which soon won acceptance, is mentioned by second-century writers, and is included in the Creeds.

It has been possible only to give a brief résumé of some of the arguments in a complex and much-discussed problem. There are, however, important aspects of the event, which do not depend for their validity on the virginity of Mary. Matthew was concerned to emphasize the activity of the Spirit in the birth of Jesus, and to stress that Jesus was Son of God, Messiah, and Saviour, and that in Him God was with men. Whether Matthew reported the event accurately or not, he correctly understood its meaning.

Matthew 1 [18-19]. Betrothal was a legal relationship under Jewish law and needed a legal act for its cancellation.

Matthew 1 [21]. The name *Jesus* is equivalent to the Hebrew *Joshua*, and means *saviour*. As Joshua saved the Israelites from slavery by bringing them to Canaan, so Jesus saves men and women from slavery to sin, and leads them into the Kingdom of God.

Matthew 1²³. This quotation is from Isaiah 7¹⁴; but the original Hebrew speaks of a young woman and not necessarily of a virgin. It is the Greek version of the Old Testament, the Septuagint, which speaks of a virgin.

The name *Emmanuel* emphasizes that God was present in Jesus.

Matthew 2¹⁻¹²—*The Astrologers from the East*

Since the astrologers were Gentiles, the story shows how Jesus was acknowledged by wise men and Gentiles. In Christian tradition the event is celebrated on 6th January, the Feast of the Epiphany. The word 'Epiphany' means 'manifestation', and refers to the manifestation of Christ to the Gentiles.

Matthew 2¹. *Herod* the Great was king of Judaea and Galilee, under Roman overlordship, from 37 B C. He was an able ruler, but had a reputation for extreme cruelty. He executed or murdered many of his own relatives. Since Herod died in 4 B C, Jesus must have been born before that date, perhaps about 6 B C. It is not surprising that an error of a few years was made in calculating the date of Jesus's birth, because it was not decided until about A D 550 to number the years from it.

astrologers. These men were Magi, members of a class of Persian astrologers. In the older translations they are called *wise men*, since at that time astrology was the study to which clever men naturally turned. The tradition that they were kings is purely conjecture, and may be derived from Isaiah 60³. There is no evidence in Matthew that there were only three of them.

Matthew 2⁶ is based on Micah 5².

Matthew 2⁹. The movement of the star suggests that it may have been a comet.

Matthew 2¹¹. For *gold* and *frankincense* see Isaiah 60⁶.

Matthew 2¹³⁻²³—*The Massacre of the Children, and the Flight to Egypt*

This story illustrates the viciousness of the sin from which Jesus had come to save men.

Matthew 2¹³. Herod feared Jesus as a possible rival for his throne.

Matthew 2¹⁵. These words from Hosea 11¹ originally referred to the Exodus.

Matthew 2¹⁸ is from Jeremiah 31¹⁵.

Matthew 2²³. There is no such saying in the Old Testament.

*   *   *

Matthew 5[1-2]—*Introduction to the Sermon on the Mount*

The Sermon on the Mount, as Matthew 5–7 is called, is the first and most famous of the five large sections of teaching in the gospel.

Matthew 5[1]. *took his seat.* It was the custom for Jewish teachers to remain seated when they were giving instruction.

Matthew 5[3-12]—*The Beatitudes*

These sayings, traditionally known as the Beatitudes, provide an ideal of character and conduct for the followers of Jesus.

(i) *How blest are those who know that they are poor* (verse 3). A literal translation of the Greek would be, 'Blessed are the poor in spirit', but *NEB* interprets it correctly. The beatitude refers not to those who are lacking in spirit but to those who recognize their own spiritual poverty and admit their need of God's help. 'How blest are you who are poor' (Lk 6[20]) may be the original version of the saying, but 'the poor in spirit' explains the meaning of 'the poor', which had become almost a technical term in Palestine for 'the devout', because during centuries of pagan rule the poor people had been the most loyal to God.

the kingdom of heaven is theirs. Matthew tends to use the phrase 'Kingdom of Heaven' where Mark uses 'Kingdom of God' (see notes on Mk 1[14-15]). Although the present tense is used, it is possible that the saying speaks of the Kingdom as a state of blessedness both in this life and in the life to come.

(ii) *How blest are the sorrowful* (verse 4). These are the people who sorrow over the sin and suffering of the world. It is not a selfish sorrow, but is like the sorrow of Jesus over the doomed city of Jerusalem (Lk 13[34-5]) and in Gethsemane (Mk 14[34]).

they shall find consolation. 'Consolation' or 'comfort' is a characteristic of the Messianic age. The anointed servant of the Lord was expected to 'comfort all who mourn' (Isa 61[2]). The use of the future tense 'they shall find . . .' does not exclude the possibility of consolation in this present life.

(iii) *How blest are those of a gentle spirit* (verse 5). This verse is based on Psalm 37[11], and the older translations read 'Blessed are the meek'. The meek or gentle man is not fearful and weak-willed. He is self-effacing and compassionate. He does not fling his weight about, and is prepared to surrender his personal rights in order to avoid unnecessary conflict with others. But he is not prepared to be false to his principles. Jesus was a man of gentle spirit, who was always ready to understand others, to forgive them, and to make sacrifices for them. But He could be severe in criticizing men, and speak to them harshly. Always, however, He spoke in love. The gentle spirit is a spirit of love.

they shall have the earth for their possession. This does not mean that they will own great properties and lands but that they are the people to whom the new heaven and the new earth belong. It means that they will enter the Kingdom of God, a blessing to be shared in the present as well as in the future.

(iv) *How blest are those who hunger and thirst to see right prevail* (verse 6). Older versions read : 'Blessed are they that hunger and thirst after righteousness.' *NEB* draws out the meaning of the Hebrew idea of righteousness, which is not just a standard of good behaviour but God's vindication of His righteous cause. The true follower of Jesus passionately desires to see God's righteous cause prevail. He wants it to prevail in his own inner life, in order that he may live after the pattern of Jesus Himself. And he wants it to prevail throughout the world, in order that men and women may enter God's Kingdom, and God's rule may be acknowledged.

they shall be satisfied. Satisfaction will come to them when right prevails everywhere. It also comes now, when right prevails in their own inner lives. The Jews looked forward to a great feast in the Messianic age, when all their hunger and thirst would be satisfied. The Christian's feast is his enjoyment of satisfaction at the triumph of God.

(v) *How blest are those who show mercy* (verse 7). Jesus Himself was ready to show mercy to all kinds of people, the sick, the sinful, and even those who put Him to death. Mercy is one of the chief ways in which love is manifested.

mercy shall be shown to them. Men cannot expect God to have mercy on them, unless they have mercy on others, an idea which is present in the Lord's Prayer and the Parable of the Unmerciful Servant (Mt 6^{12}, 18^{23-35}).

(vi) *How blest are those whose hearts are pure* (verse 8). This does not merely refer to moral chastity, but describes the single-mindedness of the man whose overriding purpose in life is to do the will of God. It is the quality of the man who sets his mind 'on God's kingdom and his justice before everything else' (Mt 6^{33}), a quality which is seen supremely in Jesus.

they shall see God. Some interpreters think this refers to a vision of God which belongs entirely to a future life. Yet it could also refer to communion with God in the present. The Jews often used the phrase 'to see God' in the sense of appearing before God at worship in the Temple. And this beatitude may refer to the inner communion with God which is attained through worship in Spirit and in truth.

(vii) *How blest are the peacemakers* (verse 9). Jesus taught the importance of being reconciled with those with whom we have quarrelled or had a misunderstanding (Mt 18[15-17]). Jesus did not choose to be a warlike Messiah, and men who follow Him must seek the way of peace.

God shall call them His sons. Although Jesus teaches that God is Father, He does not teach that all men are by nature God's sons. They can become sons through God's own act (see Mt 5[45]).

(viii) *How blest are those who have suffered persecution for the cause of right* (verse 10). Jesus, who Himself suffered, asked others to suffer persecution for His sake.

the kingdom of Heaven is theirs. See Matthew 5[3].

The theme of this final beatitude is developed in verses 11-12, which speak of the future glory of the persecuted. For the persecution of the prophets, see notes on Mark 12[1-12].

Matthew 5[13-16]—*The Christian in the World*

For the saying about salt, see notes on Mark 9[50a]. The saying, 'You are light for all the world', can be fittingly linked with the statement in John's gospel that Jesus is 'the light of the world' (Jn 8[12], 9[5]). Any light which the Christian gives to others has first been obtained from Jesus.

Matthew 5[17-20]—*Jesus and the Law*

Jesus came not to abolish the Jewish Law, but to complete or fulfil it (verse 17). He did this by proclaiming an ethical standard, which, as verse 20 claims, was far higher than that of the Pharisees and lawyers, because it dealt with a man's motives and desires as well as his actions, and was grounded in the Law of Love and the example of Jesus Himself. In the remainder of this chapter (verses 21-48) examples are given of Jesus's fulfilment of the Law.

Matthew 5[18-19] seems to enjoin complete obedience to every detail of the Law, a position which is inconsistent with Jesus's usual attitude. Perhaps the original version of verse 18 is to be found in Luke 16[17], *It is easier for heaven and earth to come to an end than for one dot or stroke of the Law to lose its force*, a saying which is an ironical criticism of the inflexibility of the lawyers and Pharisees. Many scholars think that verse 19 was added by Matthew to explain verse 18. If Jesus uttered it, He probably did so in another context, which is unknown to us.

stroke means an ornamental stroke used in Hebrew writing.

letter translates a word which refers to the smallest letter in the Hebrew alphabet.

Matthew 5²¹⁻⁴—*Murder*

Six times in this chapter Jesus contrasts His teaching with the Law of Moses (verses 21–2, 27–8, 31–2, 33–4, 38–9, 43–4), implying that His teaching is greater than that of the Law, and that He is the giver of a new Law. In this section about murder, He goes further than the commandment of Exodus 20¹³, and condemns anger, abuse, and sneering, all of which reveal hatred, the inner attitude at the root of murder.

His teaching is given practical application in the statement (verses 23–4) that a man must settle personal quarrels before he makes an offering in the Temple.

Matthew 5²². *abuse.* Literally translated, this means *say Raca*, which may be interpreted *call stupid. sneer* could be literally rendered *say Fool*.

Matthew 5²⁵⁻⁶—*Avoiding a Court Case*

This saying, in which debtors are advised to come to terms with their creditors, is probably in its right context in Luke 12⁵⁷⁻⁹, where it illustrates the need for a man to acknowledge his debt to God and to make peace with Him.

Matthew 5²⁷⁻³⁰—*Adultery*

External obedience to the commandment against adultery (Ex 20¹⁴) is not enough. Men must avoid lustful thoughts, which are inward adultery. Sayings are added (verses 29–30) about the need to discipline the body in order to avoid the punishment of hell (see notes on Mk 9⁴³⁻⁸).

Matthew 5³¹⁻²—*Divorce and Remarriage*

See notes on Mark 10¹⁻¹². The clause about unchastity is probably an addition to the original saying.

Matthew 5³³⁻⁷—*Oaths*

The Jewish Law enjoined that a man must not swear falsely by God's name, and must keep the vows which he has made to God (Ex 20⁷, Lev 19¹², Num 30², Deut 23²¹⁻³). Jesus, however, taught that truthfulness was required at all times, not just in connection with oaths. Indeed oaths are not needed at all. Plain 'Yes' or 'No' is enough.

Matthew 5³⁵ points out that oaths which refer to what God has created or controls are in fact oaths by His name.

Matthew 5³⁸⁻⁴²—*Revenge*

The Law provided that the punishment inflicted should be equivalent to the injury done (Lev 24¹⁹⁻²⁰), and originally this was a humane enactment to prevent blood-feuds. Jesus, however, taught that a man should not return violence when he is attacked. If he is sued at law, he must give more than is asked. If the authorities enforce him to do a personal service, like carrying a load for a mile, then he must do twice as much as is required.

These sayings are Jesus's injunctions to his disciples about their behaviour when they personally might be attacked. It is not clear that the injunctions also apply to a situation in which a man may feel responsibility to defend others who are attacked. Many people believe that Jesus's teaching refers also to such situations, but this is a debatable question.

Matthew 5³⁹. *Do not set yourself against the man who wrongs you* could be literally translated, *Do not resist the evil man.*

Matthew 5⁴³⁻⁸—*Love*

The Jewish Law taught men to love their neighbours (Lev 19¹⁸), and by neighbours meant fellow-Jews. It also told them to love the strangers or foreigners who lived among them (Lev 19³⁴), but this aspect of the Law was not given as much publicity as the former. The Law does not instruct men to hate their enemies, though 'hate your enemy' (verse 43) represents the attitude of a large number of Jews in Jesus's day, as indeed it represents the attitude of most people in all ages. Jesus, however, taught that men should love everyone, even their enemies, and that if men behaved in this way, they could be children of God.

'Love' in the New Testament is basically a self-giving, sacrificial love, and not a desiring love (see notes on Mk 12²⁸⁻³⁴). It is the love which God Himself shows for men, when He cares for them all, whether they are good or bad (verse 45).

Matthew 5⁴⁵. Men are not naturally *children of God*, but God can make them His children (see Mt 5⁹).

Matthew 5⁴⁸ can be literally translated, *You therefore shall be perfect, just as your heavenly Father is perfect.* The saying need not necessarily be a command, as *NEB* interprets it. And it does not imply that men will reach perfection in this life. What it clearly states is that goodness in men must be derived from the goodness of God.

Matthew 6¹⁻⁸—*Almsgiving and Prayer*

Jesus had no use for ostentation in religion, but told men to give their charity and say their prayers in secret.

Matthew 6⁷. *babbling* probably refers to the magic formulae and incantations used in heathen religions.

Matthew 6⁹⁻¹³—*The Lord's Prayer*

Jesus gave His disciples this prayer as a pattern prayer. It has two versions, the longer and more formal one in Matthew, and the shorter and more informal in Luke (Lk 11²⁻⁴). Matthew's version is the better known, and, with the addition of a doxology which is not found in the earliest manuscripts, is the basis of the form that is in regular use.

Our Father in heaven. Matthew uses the formal 'Our Father', which is suitable for public use and was a recognized Jewish mode of address to God. Luke, however, has simply 'Father', the intimate form of address used in Gethsemane (see Mk 14³⁶).

'In heaven' does not mean that God is far removed from men, but that He is great and glorious.

Because God is Father, He can be expected to answer the requests which are made in this prayer.

Thy name be hallowed. This is a petition first that God Himself should hallow (make holy) His name by acts of power among men, and secondly that men should hallow (call holy) His name by acknowledging Him and obeying Him.

Thy kingdom come. This refers both to the future Kingdom, when God's purpose will be completely fulfilled, and to the present Kingdom, which can come to individuals who put their trust in Jesus.

Thy will be done. This prayer is that God's will should be done everywhere, and also that it should be done in the life of the person who offers the prayer. It is an act of dedication and obedience, like Jesus's prayer in Gethsemane when He said, 'Yet not what I will, but what thou wilt' (Mk 14³⁶).

On earth as in heaven. God's Kingdom has already come and His will is already being done in heaven. The prayer asks that what happens in heaven should also happen on earth.

Give us today our daily bread. God is asked to supply us with all that we need for the immediate future (see Mt 6³²⁻³). The word translated 'daily' can also be used of a soldier's rations for the coming day.

Forgive us the wrong we have done,
As we have forgiven those who have wronged us.

We cannot expect God to forgive us unless we are ready to forgive others. This point is repeated in verses 14–15 and is illustrated by the parable of the Unmerciful Servant (Mt 18²³⁻³⁵).

The word translated 'wrong' literally means 'debts'. When we do wrong, we have failed in our duty to God, and are therefore in debt to Him.

And do not bring us to the test. The older translations use the word 'temptation' instead of 'test'. The Greek word can have either meaning, and in fact temptation is a kind of test or trial. This is a petition that we should not be brought to face trials we cannot endure. We are bound to be tested and tempted. But as Paul says, God 'will not allow you to be tested above your powers, but when the test comes he will at the same time provide a way out, by enabling you to sustain it' (1 Cor 10¹³).

But save us from the evil one. Trials become unbearable only when we fall into the power of evil. As long as God is there to deliver us, and as long as we trustingly ask for His protection, we shall be safe. 'The evil one' means 'Satan', the chief agent of evil.

Matthew 6¹⁴⁻¹⁵—*Forgiveness*

These verses are a comment on the clause about forgiveness in the Lord's Prayer (verse 12).

Matthew 6¹⁶⁻¹⁸—*Fasting*

Jesus did not stress the importance of fasting as much as John the Baptist did (Mk 2¹⁸), and was even accused by His enemies of being 'a glutton and a drinker' (Lk 7³⁴). Nevertheless He did not reject fasting, but practised it Himself during His temptation (Lk 4²) and gave instructions about it to His disciples in this passage, insisting that it should be done in secret, without ostentation.

Matthew 6¹⁹⁻³⁴—*Material and Spiritual Wealth*

A large number of people in Jesus's day, as in these days, thought that the most important aim in life was to amass money and property (see the parable of the Rich Fool, Lk 12¹⁶⁻²¹). But Jesus affirmed that the purpose of life was to obtain heavenly treasures (verses 19–20). A man's real allegiance is to what he values most (verse 21). He can have only one master, and if his master is to be God, it cannot be Money (verse 24). Even food and drink should not cause a man anxiety. If God provides for the birds, the flowers, and the grass, He will provide for men also. They should set their thoughts on entering God's Kingdom and accepting His justice, and should not be consumed with anxiety about their material needs (verses 25–34).

Verses 22–3 may not have originally been in this context. They mean that, just as a healthy eye gives light to the whole of a man, so, if he puts God first, his whole life will be fundamentally sound.

Matthew 6^{24}. *Money*. The original word is *Mammon*, which means property in general.

Matthew 7$^{1-5}$—*Judging Others*

Men ought not to judge others, but should deal with their own faults before pointing out what is wrong with other people. 'Judge' in this passage probably refers not only to carping criticism but also to the habit of taking private disputes to court.

Matthew 7^{16}—*A Difficult Saying*

This saying may mean that Christian teaching should not yet be given to Gentiles (for this use of the word 'dogs', see Mk 7$^{27-8}$). It could also mean that advanced instruction ought not to be given to those who were unprepared for it. Many scholars doubt if Jesus actually uttered these words, and, in any case, we do not know the original situation for which they were intended.

Matthew 7$^{7-11}$ *Further Teaching about Prayer*

Jesus teaches that earnest and sincere prayer will not remain unanswered (see the parable of the Judge and the Widow, Lk 18$^{1-8}$). But He does not say that we always receive precisely what we ask for. This saying should be considered in conjunction with those sayings which ask that God's will be done (Mt 6^{10}, Mk 14^{36}). It is only 'good things' which God gives in answer to prayer (verse 11).

Matthew 7^{12}—*The Golden Rule*

This verse is often known as 'the Golden Rule' because it provides a basic principle for conduct. Like the Law of Love (Mk 12$^{28-34}$) it has a positive note, in contrast with a saying from the Old Testament Apocrypha, 'What you hate, do not do to anyone' (Tobit 4^{15}), which is purely negative. The Golden Rule is similar in content to the command, 'Love your neighbour as yourself'. Jesus says that it is 'the Law and the prophets', meaning that it summarizes all that the Hebrew scriptures say about a man's duty to others.

G.T.N.T.—6

Matthew 7¹³⁻¹⁴—*The Narrow Gate and the Narrow Road*

It is the narrow way of a disciplined faith in Jesus which leads to salvation. The wide road of an easy, lax, uncommitted life leads to destruction.

Matthew 7¹⁵⁻²⁰—*False Prophets*

A false prophet is not so much a man who makes untrue predictions as one who falsely claims to speak for God. Jesus says that the genuineness of a prophet can be discerned by the nature of the work which he does.

Matthew 7²¹⁻⁷—*True and False Disciples*

A man who claims Jesus as his Lord, but fails to obey God, will be rejected (verses 21–3). Such a man has established his life on a weak foundation, which will crumble (verses 26–7). The man who acts upon Jesus's teaching has built his life on a secure foundation (verses 24–5).

Matthew 7²⁸⁻⁹—*Conclusion of the Sermon on the Mount*

A similar formula is used to conclude each of the other four main sections of teaching in Matthew (11¹, 13⁵³, 19¹, 26¹).

* * *

Matthew 10²⁹⁻³¹—*God's Infinite Love*

This saying is part of the second large group of sayings in Matthew (10⁵⁻⁴²) most of which is commented on in the discussion of Mark and Luke. In this particular saying Jesus stresses the way in which God cares for all His creatures.

* * *

Matthew 11²⁵⁻⁷—*The Father and the Son*

This saying claims for Jesus a unique relationship to His Father and a unique function as the revealer of God.

The knowledge of God which the Son possesses, and which men can receive through Him, is not a mere credal or theoretical knowledge. It is a personal relationship of men to God, in which they recognize His activity in their lives and acknowledge their dependence on Him. It is the knowledge which Jeremiah said would be a characteristic of the New Covenant (Jer 31³¹).

Matthew 11$^{28-30}$—*The Yoke of Jesus*

These words are similar to sayings in Ecclesiasticus 51$^{23-7}$, part of the Old Testament Apocrypha. But whereas Ecclesiasticus promises material prosperity to those who receive the yoke of divine Wisdom, Jesus promises spiritual 'relief' or 'rest' to those who take His yoke upon them. The Jews spoke of the 'yoke of the Law', because the Law was like the heavy yoke which rested upon an ox when it was ploughing. It is probably of the 'yoke of the Law' that Ecclesiasticus is thinking. Jesus is greater than the Law, and calls men not to obedience to a burdensome written code of conduct but to a joyous life in communion with Himself. Taking the yoke of Jesus means living with Him. Compared with the commands of the Law, the requirements of Jesus are light to bear.

Jesus's description of Himself as 'gentle and humble-hearted' (verse 29) sets a pattern for His disciples (see Mt 5^5, and Mk 10^{15}).

*   *   *

Matthew 12$^{38-42}$—*The Sign of Jonah*

According to Mark 8$^{11-13}$, Jesus refused to give the Pharisees any spectacular sign of His divine power. But according to this saying in Matthew, He told them that they would receive no sign except the sign of Jonah, namely, preaching which evoked repentance (Jonah 3$^{1-10}$). Matthew also sees the experience of Jonah in the whale—and here he includes an idea which is absent from the parallel passage in Luke 11$^{29-32}$—as a sign of the resurrection of Jesus. So the saying means that the only signs given by Jesus are His preaching and His resurrection (verses 38–40).

The paragraph ends (verses 41–2) by contrasting the Jews' rejection of Jesus with the Ninevites' acceptance of Jonah and the Queen of Sheba's attitude to Solomon (1 K 10$^{1-13}$).

Matthew 12$^{43-5}$—*The Unclean Spirit and the Seven Other Spirits*

It is not sufficient to drive an evil spirit from a man. If God does not rule within him, other evil spirits will take possession of him.

*   *   *

Matthew 13²⁴⁻³⁰, ³⁶⁻⁴³—*The Wheat and the Darnel*

This chapter contains the third large collection of sayings in Matthew, and its theme is the Kingdom of Heaven. Much of it is derived from Mark 4, but the sections now to be discussed are found only in Matthew.

The point of the parable of the Wheat and the Darnel is that Christians should not attempt to exclude heretics or wicked people from the Church but should exercise patience and tolerance. God will pass judgement when the time comes.

Matthew 13²⁴. *kingdom of Heaven* means the same as 'kingdom of God' (see notes on Mt 5³).

Matthew 13²⁵. *darnel* is a type of weed.

Matthew 13³⁶⁻⁴³ are probably a later development since they turn the parable into an allegory, finding detailed lessons in each aspect of the story.

Matthew 13³³—*The Yeast*

The parable of the Yeast, like that of the Mustard Seed (Mk 4³⁰⁻²), contrasts the small beginnings of the Kingdom with its great outcome.

Matthew 13⁴⁴⁻⁶—*The Buried Treasure and the Costly Pearl*

These two parables teach that man must be ready to sacrifice all his possessions in order to enter God's Kingdom, in comparison with which everything else is worthless.

Matthew 13⁴⁷⁻⁵⁰—*The Net with Good and Bad Fish*

The point of this parable is that all kinds of people enter the Kingdom of Heaven, and that the good will be separated from the bad in the Last Judgement.

Matthew 13⁵¹⁻²—*The New and the Old*

The Kingdom of Heaven includes the blessings of both the old Jewish dispensation and Christ's new dispensation.

*   *   *

Matthew 16¹⁷⁻¹⁹—*Peter and the Church*

These words, which are included in Matthew's account of Jesus's reply to Peter at Caesarea Philippi (see notes on Mk 8²⁷⁻³³), are not found in other gospels. According to Matthew, it was on this occasion that Jesus gave Simon the name of Peter. The actual Aramaic word which Jesus used was 'Cephas', meaning 'rock' or 'stone', and Peter is derived from the Greek equivalent. Although this saying designates Peter as the first leader of the Church, it mentions nothing about his link with Rome or his right to delegate powers to his successors. The *keys* which he is promised are the keys of authority in God's Kingdom in so far as it is present within the Church. And the authority is exercised by deciding what actions are allowed or forbidden, a right which is given also to other disciples (see Mt 18[18]).

Although Peter was the Church's leader in its early days (see Acts 1–12), there is no evidence in either the Acts or the New Testament letters that he exercised any unique authority in the Church. Indeed in Jerusalem it was James, the brother of Jesus, who became the Church's leader (see Acts 12[17], 15[13-21], 21[17 ff]).

Matthew 16[18]. Mark 3[16] and John 1[42] suggest that Simon was called Peter at an earlier date.

forces of death is a correct interpretation of words which mean literally *gates of Hades*.

Matthew 16[19]. *forbid* and *allow* are correct renderings of words which literally mean *bind* and *loose*. They do not, as is often supposed, refer to the refusal and granting of absolution of sins. See notes on John 20[19-23].

✳   ✳   ✳

Matthew 18[15-22]—*Church Life*

These sayings are taken from Matthew's fourth great discourse (18[1-35]), which is about the Church.

The first saying (verses 15–17) is a rule that only when three kinds of private consultation have failed, should an offender cease to be treated as a Christian brother.

The second saying (verse 18) gives Christ's followers the authority already given to Peter in Matthew 16[19]. There is no evidence that this authority was confined to the Twelve Disciples.

The third saying (verses 19–20) teaches that God answers corporate prayer, because Jesus is with men whenever they meet in His name.

The fourth saying (verse 22), that there is no limit to the number of times a Christian should forgive his fellow-Christian, assumes that the sinner repents before he receives forgiveness (see Lk 17[4]).

Matthew 18[17]. *congregation* translates the Greek *ekklēsia*, which can also be translated *church*.

Matthew 18[20]. There is a Jewish saying that, when two sit together and words of the Law are between them, the Divine Presence is with them.

Matthew 18$^{23-35}$—*The Unmerciful Servant*

The point of this parable is that a man cannot receive forgiveness from God unless he is himself ready to forgive others (see Mt 6$^{12, 14-15}$).

*   *   *

Matthew 20$^{1-16}$—*The Labourers in the Vineyard*

This parable teaches that there are no distinctions in God's Kingdom. All receive the same blessing, because God does not give to men according to their deserts but according to His own mercy and love.

Matthew 20^{16}, which does not fit the parable, is repeated from Matthew 19^{30}.

*   *   *

Matthew 21$^{28-32}$—*The Two Sons*

The lesson of this parable is that God does not want empty promises but dedicated lives.

*   *   *

Matthew 25$^{1-13}$—*The Ten Bridesmaids*

This parable exhorts men to be ready for the coming of Christ. It refers to His future rather than present coming, and reflects the idea that He is the bridegroom of the Church (see Eph 5$^{25-32}$).

Matthew 25$^{14-30}$—*The Bags of Gold*

The theme of this parable, which is similar to Luke's parable of the Pounds (Lk 19$^{12-27}$), is not that men are endowed with different abilities but that they ought to use every opportunity to serve God. If they serve Him, He will give them further opportunities for service. If they neglect to serve Him, He will reject them. When Jesus spoke of the man who hid his bag in the ground, He was thinking of the lawyers and Pharisees who failed to make proper use of their spiritual heritage.

'Bags of gold' translates a word which is translated 'talents' in older versions.

Matthew 25$^{31-46}$—*The Sheep and the Goats*

This graphic description (it is not, strictly speaking, a parable) of the return of Jesus at the Last Judgement (see Mk 8^{38}, 13$^{26-7}$, 14^{62}) has a message both to Christians and to those who have never heard of Jesus. Its message to Christians is that a faith issuing in deeds of love is genuine and a faith devoid of such results is false (see also Mt 7^{21-3}, 21^{28-32}). Its message to those who have not heard of Jesus is somewhat different. It teaches that they accept Jesus when they love others, and reject Him when they reject others.

Matthew 25^{46}. *eternal punishment* . . . *eternal life.* Since *eternal* can mean 'belonging to the Messianic age' as well as 'everlasting', this verse could refer to the quality of the punishment and the life rather than to their duration.

*   *   *

MATTHEW'S ACCOUNT OF THE PASSION AND RESURRECTION OF JESUS
(*Matthew* 26^1–28^{20})

Although Matthew keeps fairly close to Mark's account of the Passion of Jesus, he makes some additions, including the references to Judas's death (27^{3-5}), Pilate's wife (27^{19}), Pilate's washing of his hands (27^{24}), the rising of the dead in Jerusalem (27^{51-3}), and the setting of a guard over Jesus's tomb (27^{62-6}). Matthew's story of the empty tomb is based on Mark's, but he adds that there was an earthquake, and that an angel, who seems to be the same person as the young man in Mark's account, rolled the stone away from the tomb.

Matthew 28^{8-20}—*The Resurrection Appearances*

The events recorded in this section are found only in Matthew. An account of Jesus's appearance to the woman as they ran from the tomb (verses 8–10) is followed by the statement that the chief priests bribed the soldiers to say that the disciples had stolen Jesus's body (verses 11–15). The most important passage, however, describes Jesus's apostolic commission to His disciples in Galilee (verses 16–20).

Since Galilee was the part of Palestine nearest to the Gentiles, it symbolized the Gentile world (see Mt 4^{14-16}). It was therefore a fitting place for Jesus to commission His disciples to preach to all nations. Matthew, who emphasizes that Jesus's earthly ministry was, with few exceptions, for Jews only (Mt 10^6, 15^{24}), now shows that the risen Jesus has through His disciples a ministry to the whole world (verses 19–20). In words reminiscent of Daniel 7^{14}, Jesus announces that He has universal authority (verse 18). And, as the gospel begins with the message that 'God is with us' in the coming of Jesus (Mt 1²³), so it ends with the promise that the risen Jesus will always be with his disciples (verse 20).

Matthew 28¹⁹. The validity of the saying about baptism has been questioned because it commands baptism in the name of the Father and the Son and the Holy Spirit, whereas in the Acts of the Apostles baptism is always in the name of Jesus alone. There is slight evidence for the existence of a version of Matthew 28¹⁹ which mentions baptism in the name of Jesus alone. Whatever may have been the original form of this saying, baptism would not have been readily accepted by the early Church, unless Jesus had in some way commanded it.

Matthew 28²⁰. *the end of time.* According to Matthew 24¹⁴ and Mark 13¹⁰, the end will not come until the gospel has been preached to all nations.

QUESTIONS

(1) Discuss the qualities of a Christian which are described in the Beatitudes.

(2) Examine the teaching of the Sermon on the Mount about Worship and Prayer.

(3) What are the special emphases of the Gospel according to St Matthew?

(4) Comment on : Matthew 1¹⁸, 6²⁴, 13³⁰, 16¹⁸⁻¹⁹, 25¹⁴⁻¹⁵, 25⁴⁰.

CHAPTER FOUR

THE GOSPEL ACCORDING TO ST LUKE

INTRODUCTION TO THE GOSPEL

The Author

THE TRADITION that Luke is the author of the third gospel is
well supported and generally held to be true. Luke was a medical
practitioner, who was on several occasions the companion of Paul (Col
4^{14}, Philem 24, 2 Tim 4^{11}). Since the book has a good Greek style and
shows a special interest in Gentiles, it has been suggested that Luke
himself was a Gentile. But of this we cannot be certain. The gospel is
the first of two volumes written by Luke, the second being the Acts of
the Apostles, which continues the story of the early Church after the
resurrection of Jesus.

The Date and Place of Writing

No certainty can be attained about either the date or the place of the
gospel's composition, but, like Matthew's gospel, it was probably written
between AD 75 and 90.

The Sources of the Gospel

Luke's gospel includes a great amount of material which has been derived from Mark, although it does not reproduce as much of Mark as
Matthew does. It also includes a large number of sayings and a few
incidents which are found in Matthew but not in Mark. These passages
are often described as the 'Q' source, although it is not certain that there
was only one written source from which this material was drawn (see p.
70). Finally, there is a large amount of material in Luke which is not
found in any other gospel.

Matthew used Mark as the framework of his gospel, and many
scholars believe that Luke followed a similar procedure. But some influential scholars have suggested that Luke's gospel reached its present
form in a different way. They argue that Luke used 'Q' and other
material to make the first draft of a gospel, which they describe as 'Proto-
Luke'. He then incorporated material from Mark to form the present

gospel. The arguments for and against this hypothesis are very technical, and cannot be discussed here.

It is also possible that the gospel first began at 3^1, which seems to be a natural opening, and that the first two chapters, which are more Jewish in style than the rest of the book, were added later by Luke.

The Synoptic Problem

It is now possible to sum up what has been said about the sources of the synoptic gospels. Mark's was the earliest gospel, and was used by the other two synoptic evangelists. There is a large body of material, called 'Q' by scholars, which is found in both Matthew and Luke, but not in Mark. There is also material which is found only in Matthew, and other material which is found only in Luke.

The theory that the main sources were four different documents is challenged by many scholars, and the most that we can say for certain is that, in addition to the gospel according to St Mark, three other groups of material were used in the writing of the synoptic gospels.

The Characteristics of the Gospel

The aim of Luke's gospel (Lk 1^{1-4}) was to give an account of the life and teaching of Jesus, and it had a special concern to show to Theophilus, the high-ranking person to whom it was dedicated, that Jesus was unjustly condemned and had committed no offence against the Roman authorities. It has several noteworthy characteristics.

(i) It stresses *the universality of Jesus's work of salvation*. The deliverance has been made ready 'in full view of all the nations', and Jesus is 'a light that will be a revelation to the heathen' (2^{31-2}, compare 3^6). Repentance is to be proclaimed to all nations (24^{47}), and the ancestry of Jesus is traced to Adam, the father of all men (3^{23-38}), whereas Matthew traces it to Abraham, the father of the Jewish nation (Mt 1^{1-17}).

(ii) Luke's gospel shows special interest in the *outcasts of society*, including the poor, the tax-gatherers, and notorious sinners. This interest is revealed in incidents like the Sinful Woman, the Samaritan Leper, and the Dying Thief, and in the parables of the Good Samaritan, the Pharisee and the Tax-Gatherer, the Great Feast, the Prodigal Son, and the Rich Man and Lazarus.

(iii) Luke also understands *the importance of women* for the gospel story. With his references to Elizabeth, Mary the mother of Jesus, Anna, Martha and Mary of Bethany, and the Sinful Woman, he records much more about the part played by women than do the other synoptic gospels.

(iv) Another great theme of Luke's, *the mercy of God to repentant sinners*, is found in the parables of the Lost Sheep, the Lost Piece of Silver, the Prodigal Son, and the Pharisee and the Tax-Gatherer. It is also taught by the stories of the Sinful Woman, Zacchaeus, and the Dying Thief. And on the Cross Jesus forgives even those who crucify Him. The Son of Man had come 'to seek and save what is lost' (19^{10}), and was born to be 'a deliverer' (2^{11}).

(v) More than the other synoptic gospels, Luke stresses *the work of the Holy Spirit*. Not only was the Spirit active in Jesus at His birth and baptism, during His temptation, in His prayers, and throughout His ministry (1^{35}, 3^{21-2}, $4^{1-2, 14, 18}$, 10^{21}), but also in others, including John the Baptist, Elizabeth, Zechariah, Mary, and Simeon ($1^{15, 35, 41, 67}$, 2^{25}). And the concluding paragraph of the gospel points to the gift of the Spirit at Pentecost.

(vi) The titles given to Jesus by the other synoptic gospels are also given to Him by Luke. But in Luke there is a special emphasis on Jesus as *the Servant of God*, with several quotations from Isaiah 40–66. And in narrative passages Luke often introduces the title *the Lord* for Jesus.

(vii) There is great emphasis in Luke on *prayer, praise, and thanksgiving*. His gospel contains some of the earliest Christian hymns, the *Magnificat*, the *Benedictus*, and the *Nunc Dimittis*, and includes many accounts of the way in which Jesus and others praised God and prayed to Him. This theme is present at the beginning of the gospel, when Zechariah is ministering in the Temple, and at the end, when the disciples are 'in the temple praising God'.

COMMENTS ON SELECTED PASSAGES FROM LUKE'S GOSPEL

Luke 1^{1-4}—*Introduction*

The gospel, like the Acts of the Apostles, is dedicated to Theophilus, a man of high rank in the Roman Empire. It is not said whether he was a Christian or not.

Luke 1^{5-25}—*Zechariah and Elizabeth*

Since John the Baptist was the forerunner of Jesus, it is fitting that the gospel should begin with the promise of John's birth.

Luke 1²⁶⁻⁵⁶—*The Annunciation of the Birth of Jesus*

The angel Gabriel's message to Mary (verses 30–6) emphasizes that Jesus will be the Son of God and the Messianic king, that He will have no human father (see notes on Mt 1¹⁸⁻²⁵), and that the Spirit will be active in His birth.

Mary's great song of praise and thanksgiving (verses 46–55), traditionally known as the *Magnificat* (from the first word of the Latin translation), is reminiscent of Hannah's song in 1 Samuel 2¹⁻¹⁰. It sees in the coming of Jesus the beginning of a new order in which those who fear God and show humility will receive mercy.

Luke 1⁵⁷⁻⁸⁰—*The Birth of John the Baptist*

Zechariah's hymn of thanksgiving for John's birth (verses 68–79), which is known as the *Benedictus* (another title taken from the first word of the Latin version), praises God for raising up the Messiah and for sending John as His forerunner.

Luke 2¹⁻⁷—*The Birth of Jesus*

Luke emphasizes that Jesus was a member of the family of David, from whom the Messiah was expected to arise, and also mentions that no suitable place was provided for Jesus's birth, a fact which was symbolic of Jesus's rejection by the Jewish people. Luke may have also believed that by ordering a general registration the Roman emperor unknowingly helped to bring about the birth of the Messiah in Bethlehem.

Luke 2². *Quirinius* is known to have held a registration or census in AD 6–7. But since Jesus was born before Herod's death in 4 BC, Luke must be referring to another census. Jesus was probably born about 6 BC.

Luke 2⁵. The connection of David's family with Bethlehem is mentioned in 1 Samuel 16¹.

Luke 2⁸⁻²⁰—*The Shepherds*

According to Luke, the first men to visit the child Jesus were shepherds, men of low station, who lived a hard, unpretentious life, and were liable to criticism because their work made it difficult for them to maintain a strict observance of religious festivals.

The peace which the heavenly host promises (verse 14) is an inner peace, and the men who receive God's favour are those who acknowledge Jesus as deliverer and Lord.

Luke 2¹⁴. The Authorized Version, *On earth peace, goodwill toward men,* is not based on the most reliable manuscripts.

Luke 2²¹⁻⁴—*Observance of the Jewish Law*

Paul described Jesus as 'born under the law' (Gal 4⁴), and this section of the gospel shows how Mary and Joseph kept the Law's requirements. Jesus was circumcised on the eighth day (Lev 12¹⁻³); Mary submitted to the rite of purification prescribed for mothers (Lev 12⁶⁻⁸); and an offering was made for the redemption of Jesus as the firstborn son (Ex 13¹²).

Luke 2²⁴. *Turtle-doves* or *pigeons* were the offering for the purification (Lev 12⁸), not, as Luke mistakenly claims, for the redemption of the first-born.

Luke 2²⁵⁻³⁸—*Simeon and Anna*

Simeon is chiefly remembered for his song, the *Nunc Dimittis* (another title taken from the first words of the Latin version), which speaks of the deliverance and revelation which Jesus brings to all nations (verses 29–32). He also predicted the rejection of Jesus and the agony which it would bring to Mary (verse 34). The coming of Jesus, he said (verse 35), would pass judgement on men, because it would show them as they really were.

Anna (verses 36–8), like Simeon, was a person of deep spiritual quality, who recognized Jesus and thanked God for His coming.

Luke 2²⁵. *restoration* translates a Greek word which literally means *consolation* and was used to describe the condition of the Messianic age (see Mt 5⁴).

Luke 2³⁹⁻⁵²—*The Boyhood of Jesus*

The only recorded incident of Jesus's life between His infancy and His baptism is His visit to Jerusalem when He was twelve years old. At this age a Jewish boy was accepted as 'a son of the commandment', a person who was capable of carrying out the Law. Mary's words reveal her failure to understand Jesus fully. His reply shows His awareness of a special mission in life and a special relationship to God the Father (verses 48–9).

*   *   *

Luke 3⁷⁻²⁰—*The Preaching of John the Baptist*

Part of the Baptist's teaching has already been discussed (see notes on Mark 1²⁻⁸). A considerable amount of further teaching is recorded by Luke, and some of this material is found also in Matthew. The main themes of the Baptist's teaching are as follows:

(i) *Repentance and the New Nation.* Baptism was a sign both of

cleansing and of entry into a new nation (see notes on Mark 1^{2-8}).
When John told his audience that they should not rest in the assurance
that Abraham was their father (verse 8), he meant that their Jewish
ancestry was not of supreme importance. What really mattered was
that they should repent, and prove their repentance by dedicated lives.
If they accepted John's message, they would become the new people of
God, the true children of Abraham.

(ii) *Ethical Teaching*. John insisted that true repentance issued in
good works (verse 8), and told his disciples to make sacrifices for the
needy (verse 11). He attacked two of the major scandals of Palestine,
the extortionate practices of the tax-gatherers and the bullying and
blackmailing behaviour of the soldiers (verses 12–14). In his fearless
denunciation of evil he was ready even to incur the wrath of Herod
by condemning his illegal marriage (verse 19; see notes on Mk 6^{14-29}).
With his passion for social justice and individual righteousness John
was in the true succession of the great Hebrew prophets.

(iii) *The Coming One and Judgement*. According to Luke, the 'one
to come' (see notes on Mk 1^{7-8}) will baptize with fire as well as with the
Holy Spirit. Those who are baptized with the Spirit are gathered into
God's kingdom like wheat into a granary, and those who are baptized
with fire—fire means judgement—are condemned like chaff that is
burnt (verses 16–17). Indeed the judgement has already begun with the
ministry of John (verse 9).

Luke 3^8. In the original Aramaic the words *children* and *stones* would
be very similar.

Luke 3^{16}. Many scholars claim that the original prophecy was about
baptism with fire, and that the reference to the Spirit was added because
of the Church's experience of the gifts of the Spirit.

*   *   *

Luke 4^{1-13}—*The Temptations of Jesus*

Luke and Matthew give a much fuller account of this incident than
Mark does (Mk 1^{12-13}), and their information presumably came from
Jesus Himself. Matthew records the temptations in a different order
from Luke (Mt 4^{1-11}), but otherwise the two accounts are almost identical.

The devil is described as a person, an idea which many people find
difficult to accept. It is true that the gospels use the language and ideas
of their own day, but whether we choose to call the devil a person or
not, it is an essential part of the gospel message that the forces of evil

are more powerful than any merely human person, that they take control of individuals and corrupt them, and that they can only be decisively overthrown by God's intervention in Christ.

In this story Jesus is tempted to use unworthy methods to assert that He is Son of God. It was God's will that His divine Sonship should be revealed through His suffering, death, and resurrection. But the devil tried to persuade Him to demonstrate His Sonship first by turning a stone into bread, secondly by winning political power over the whole world, and thirdly by performing a sensational act of magic. They were all temptations to use spectacular miracles to achieve His aim, and, if He had yielded, He would have surrendered Himself to the devil.

Jesus resisted these temptations. He knew that such methods did not win a way into men's hearts. He knew too that, in order to accomplish His mission. He had to overcome the powers of evil. He was led in this crisis by the Spirit (verses 1, 2, 14), and was helped by meditation on familiar words of the scriptures which he quoted in answer to the temptations (Deut 8^3, 6^{13}, 6^{16}).

These three temptations were not the only ones which Jesus had to face. Temptation came through Peter, who tried to dissuade Him from going to the Cross (see notes on Mk 8^{27-33}). He was tempted also in Gethsemane, when He wondered if He could escape a violent death (Mk 14^{35-6}). His resistance to temptation was part of His fight against evil, and He was indeed 'tested every way, only without sin' (Heb 4^{15}).

Luke 4^3. The temptation to turn stone into bread would be specially great, because Jesus had gone a long time without food, and also because such a miracle could be interpreted as a sign of His desire to provide for men's material needs.

Luke 4^{10-11} quotes Psalm 91^{11-12}.

Luke 4^{14-30}—*The Rejection at Nazareth*

This seems to be a more detailed account of the incident mentioned in Mark 6^{1-6}. Luke places it earlier in the ministry than Mark does, and mentions that the people tried to kill Jesus. He also says that in the synagogue Jesus read from Isaiah 61^{1-2}, a passage which well described the nature of His mission.

Luke $4^{14\ and\ 18}$ stress the activity of the Spirit in the ministry of Jesus.

Luke 4^{17}. For the practice of inviting people to read in the synagogue, and the possibility that Jesus was a rabbi, see notes on Mark 1^{21-8} and 9^5.

Luke 4^{18}. *anointed* is an important word because 'Messiah' means 'Anointed'.

Luke 4²⁶. *Elijah*. See 1 Kings 17⁸⁻²⁴.
Luke 4²⁷. *Elisha*. See 2 Kings 5¹⁻¹⁴.

*   *   *

Luke 7¹⁻¹⁰—*The Centurion's Servant*

This miracle, which is also recorded in Matthew 8⁵⁻¹⁰, is performed at a distance (see also Mark 5²¹⁻⁴³), and in response to another's faith. It illustrates Jesus's readiness to help Gentiles—the centurion, probably an officer in the army of Herod Antipas, was not a Jew (verse 5)—and it contrasts the Gentile's faith with the Jews' unbelief (verse 9).

Luke 7¹¹⁻¹⁷—*The Widow's Son at Nain*

Many scholars argue that the young man whom Jesus raised was not actually dead, but in a coma. Luke himself, however, clearly understands this to be a miracle of raising the dead. Nothing is said about the widow's faith, but the whole emphasis is on Jesus's compassion for her. The miracle is similar to those performed by Elijah and Elisha (1 K 17⁸⁻²⁴, 2 K 4⁸⁻³⁷).

Luke 7¹⁸⁻³⁵—*John the Baptist and Jesus*

Probably because he did not understand what kind of Messiah Jesus was, John the Baptist sent two of his disciples to ask if Jesus really was 'the one who is to come' (verses 18–20). Jesus's answer (verses 22–3) meant that His works of healing and preaching proved Him to be the Coming One. He went on to say that, although John, as the herald of the Messiah (see Mal 3¹), was the greatest man of the old order, he was less than anyone in the new order (verses 24–8). And He denounced the Pharisees and lawyers for being equally critical of John who led a highly ascetic and abstinent life, and of Himself who ate with tax-gatherers and sinners (verses 31–4). God's wisdom, He claimed, is shown to be right by all who, like John and Jesus, truly serve him (verse 35).

Luke 7²². Jesus's work is described in language taken from Isaiah 29¹⁸, 35⁵⁻⁶, 61¹.

Luke 7²⁸. This saying does not imply that John will always be excluded from the Kingdom of God. Indeed, according to Luke 13²⁸⁻⁹, the great men of Israel share in it.

Luke 7³². Jesus is probably alluding to the refusal of some children to play with their friends at games of either weddings or funerals. Nothing pleases them.

Luke 7[36-49]—*The Sinful Woman*

Jesus defended this woman's action by telling the parable of the Two Debtors. Since the parable teaches that those who have been forgiven most will love most (verses 41–3), the woman must have already repented and received forgiveness. Jesus's words in verse 48 are therefore an assurance that her sins have already been forgiven rather than an actual pronouncement of forgiveness. Presumably it was Jesus Himself who in the first place forgave her, and in doing so He was exercising a function which the Jews regarded as divine (see also Mk 2[5]). Like a similar story in Mark 14[3-9], this event shows the importance of adoration in the Christian life.

*   *   *

Luke 9[51-6]—*Rejection by the Samaritans*

This is the beginning of a long section (Lk 9[51]–19[28]), which describes the journey of Jesus to Jerusalem, and consists mainly of material that is not found in Mark. In this introductory paragraph Luke understands Jesus's crucifixion, resurrection, and ascension as part of one event, which he describes as being 'taken up to heaven'; and he stresses Jesus's determination to go the way which God had appointed for Him.

The Samaritans rejected Jesus because of their hostility to the practice of making pilgrimages to Jerusalem. They regarded Mount Gerizim and not Jerusalem as the holy place (see also John 4[20]). The disciples' request (verse 54) proves how much they trusted in Jesus's power, and His reaction (verse 55) is evidence of His new way of dealing with enemies (see Mt 5[44]).

Luke 9[57-62]—*Three Would-be Disciples*

These sayings do not mean that every Christian should be homeless, refuse to attend his father's funeral, and fail to say good-bye to his relatives. But they do mean that a man should be prepared to make these sacrifices, if Jesus calls him to do so. The Kingdom of God has the first claim on a Christian's loyalty.

We are not told whether or not the three men to whom Jesus spoke finally followed Him.

Luke 9[58] is an important saying about the humiliation of the Son of Man.

Luke 9[61]. Jesus requires more of His disciples than Elijah did of Elisha (1 K 19[19-21]).

Luke 10[1-20]—*The Mission of the Seventy-two*

This missionary charge, which in many ways resembles those of Matthew 10[5ff] and Mark 6[7-13] (on which see notes), emphasizes that the Kingdom of God has drawn near (verses 9, 11) and that the disciples' success in driving out devils is a sign of the defeat of Satan and of the beginning of a new age (verses 17–20).

The number seventy-two (verse 1), which is a multiple of 12, may be connected with the twelve tribes of Israel, and may indicate that this mission was directed to the Jews. Some manuscripts read seventy instead of seventy-two, and, since there were thought to be seventy nations of Gentiles, this would imply that the mission was to Gentiles. In either case the incident shows that there were more than twelve disciples to whom Jesus gave authority to preach and heal.

Luke 10[12-14]. *Sodom, Tyre,* and *Sidon* had been in former times notorious for their immorality. For their fate see Genesis 19[24-8], Isaiah 23[1-18], Ezekiel 26[1]–28[4], Amos 1[9-10].

Chorazin, Bethsaida, and *Capernaum,* cities of Galilee, are condemned for their rejection of Jesus and His disciples.

Luke 10[18]. Jesus describes a vision which He has experienced.

Luke 10[20]. The real motive for a Christian's joy is not his successful exercise of spiritual power but his knowledge that God has chosen him for eternal life.

Luke 10[21-2]—*Father and Son*

See notes on the parallel passage, Matthew 11[25-7].

Luke 10[23-4]—*The Time of Fulfilment*

This is further evidence that the new age had already come with the ministry of Jesus.

Luke 10[25-37]—*The Good Samaritan*

This parable does not give a direct answer to the lawyer's question, 'Who is my neighbour?' Its lesson is that a man ought to behave like a neighbour to anyone who is in need. From this lesson, however, it is easy to deduce an answer to the lawyer's question, namely, that anyone who needs a man's help is his neighbour.

The parable contains an implied criticism of orthodox Jews, represented by the priest and the Levite, who kept the letter of the Law but failed to show a genuine compassion for the needy. It shows also that someone who was not an orthodox Jew could give real obedience to

God, and that love is not merely shown by obedience to rules but by creative conduct in new and challenging situations.

Luke 10$^{25-8}$. See notes on Mark 12$^{28-34}$.

Luke 10^{32}. *a Levite* was an assistant of the priests.

Luke 10^{33}. *a Samaritan*. The Samaritans, who accepted only the five books of the Law as scripture and regarded Mount Gerizim, not Jerusalem, as their holy place, were despised by the Jews. See also Luke 9$^{52-6}$, 17$^{11-19}$, John 4$^{8-26}$.

Luke 10$^{38-42}$—*Martha and Mary*

Jesus's words to Martha and Mary show that in a life of true discipleship the most important thing is not to do good works, but to be with Jesus and to hear His message. The zealous activity of Martha was not wrong in itself, but Mary's reaction to Jesus was better.

Luke 10^{38}. *a village*. This was Bethany (see Jn 11^1).

Luke 10^{39}. *Mary* ought not to be identified with Mary of Magdala.

Luke 11$^{1-4}$—*The Lord's Prayer*

Luke's version is shorter and more informal than Matthew's (see notes on Mt 6$^{9-13}$).

Luke 11$^{5-8}$—*The Friend at Midnight*

This parable teaches that sincere and single-minded prayer is answered by God (see also the parable of the Judge and the Widow, Lk 18$^{1-8}$). Verses 9–13 have parallels in Matthew 7$^{7-11}$.

*   *   *

Luke 12$^{13-21}$—*The Rich Fool*

In answer to a man who wanted Him to settle a family dispute about property, Jesus refused to settle it, and in this parable warned the man to avoid greed, because material wealth is of no ultimate value (compare Mt 6$^{19-34}$).

*   *   *

Luke 13$^{31-3}$—*Jesus and Herod*

This saying emphasizes that there was a divine necessity about Jesus's death (see notes on Mk 8$^{27-33}$).

Luke 13^{32}. *that fox*. A fox typified both a low cunning and insignificance of character.

I reach my goal could also be translated *I am perfected*. In either case it means that Jesus's work reached fulfilment in the crucifixion and resurrection.

Luke 13³⁴⁻⁵—*Jesus's Lament over Jerusalem*

Jesus expresses His great love for the people of Jerusalem, even though He knows that they will reject Him.

Luke 13³⁴. Uriah (Jer 26²⁰ᶠᶠ) is an example of a prophet who was murdered (see also I K 18⁴, ¹³, 19¹⁰). There is a Jewish legend that Isaiah was put to death.

Luke 13³⁵. *forsaken by God*. This prophecy was fulfilled when the city was destroyed in A D 70.

until the time comes. It is not certain whether this refers to Jesus's entry into Jerusalem before His death or to His return at the end of the world.

Blessings on him . . . is a quotation from Psalm 118²⁶.

Luke 14¹⁻⁶—*Healing on the Sabbath*

In curing a man's dropsy on the Sabbath Jesus asked His critics two awkward questions which left them silent. If in answer to the first (verse 3) they had said that cures were allowed, they would have been accused of laxity; if they had said that cures were forbidden, they would have been accused of harshness. If in answer to the second (verse 5) they had agreed that animals should be rescued on the Sabbath, they would again have been accused of laxity; if they had said that rescue was forbidden, they would have incurred the wrath of animal-owners. For Jesus and the Sabbath, see also notes on Mark 2²³⁻3⁶.

Luke 14⁷⁻¹⁴—*The Chief Place at the Feast*

Jesus's words in verses 8–11 are not just an instruction about etiquette at meals but about behaviour in general. A Christian should not push himself, but should leave it for God to honour him. Compare Proverbs 25⁶⁻⁷.

Another saying is added (verse 12–14) about hospitality to the poor and crippled.

Luke 14¹⁵⁻²⁴—*The Great Feast*

An element of allegory is present in this parable, the main point of which is that outcasts and Gentiles will become God's people instead of the Jews who have forfeited this privilege. The people who refused the invitation (verses 17–20) represent the Jews who rejected Jesus.

The poor, crippled, blind, and lame (verses 21–2) represent the outcasts of society. The people in highways and hedgerows (verses 23–4) are Gentiles.

Matthew's version of this parable (Mt 22[1-14]) has an extra paragraph about the punishment of a guest who appeared without correct wedding-dress. This guest stands for the lawyers and Pharisees who were not ready to receive Jesus.

Luke 14[20]. Jesus demands more of men than the Law does (see Deut 24[5]).

*   *   *

Luke 15[1-10]—*The Lost Sheep and the Lost Piece of Silver*

These two parables were Jesus's answer to the criticism that He fraternized with sinners. They both teach that God is ready to make great sacrifices to find those who are lost, and that, when He finds them, there is joy in heaven. They imply that it is God who takes the initiative in bringing back the sinner.

The reference to 'ninety-nine righteous people who do not need to repent' (verse 7) is an ironical comment on the complacency of the lawyers and Pharisees (see also Mark 2[17]).

Luke 15[11-32]—*The Prodigal Son and His Elder Brother*

This parable, which, like the previous two, is an answer to the criticism that Jesus was the friend of sinners, is not only about the prodigal son, but also about his elder brother. The first part (verses 11–24) tells of God's merciful love for those sinners who indulge in reckless and immoral living. The second part (verses 25–32) teaches that God loves the self-righteous man as much as the profligate, the lawyers and Pharisees as much as the tax-gatherers and sinners. At the end of the parable the elder brother is still outside the house, and we are not told whether he accepted or rejected his father's invitation to return. Thus the climax of the parable challenges the lawyers and Pharisees to return to God, from whom their self-righteousness has estranged them, and to show friendship to those whom they have treated as outcasts.

The behaviour of the father, who goes out of the house to speak both to the prodigal and to the elder son (verses 20 and 28), illustrates the way in which God takes the initiative in seeking sinners. The father's readiness to accept the prodigal as a son, when he asked only to be a servant, is characteristic of God's desire to give men greater blessings than they expect or deserve.

Luke 15[12]. The younger son is given the right to use his share of the inheritance immediately, even while his father is alive.

Luke 15[15]. *pigs*. There was no more degrading occupation for a Jew than to look after pigs, which he regarded as unclean animals.

Luke 15[22]. The *ring* is a symbol of sonship, and the *shoes* are a token of liberty.

Luke 16[1-8]—*The Dishonest Bailiff*

It is not the bailiff's dishonesty which is commended for imitation, but his promptness and astuteness in dealing with a crisis. The parable teaches men to show a similar promptness and understanding of the situation in their dealings with God. They must make their peace with Him while they have opportunity.

Luke 16[9-12]—*Sayings about Wealth*

Probably these sayings were not originally connected with the parable of the Dishonest Bailiff.

Luke 16[9]. *to win friends* in this verse means to win the friendship of God. The saying urges a right use of material wealth.

*   *   *

Luke 16[19-31]—*The Rich Man and Lazarus*

This parable is aimed at the Sadducees, the ruling class of Jews, who did not believe in the resurrection of the dead. The rich man is clearly supposed to be a Sadducee, and the parable teaches that, if a man is not persuaded by the scriptures of the need to care for others and of the reality of the judgement which awaits him, then he will not be persuaded by spectacular apparitions.

Luke 16[22]. *with Abraham*. This phrase, which is literally translated *in Abraham's bosom*, shows that man can have life immediately after death, even before the final resurrection (see also Lk 23[43]).

Luke 16[24, 26]. The description of the rich man's torment uses conventional Jewish language, and there is no need to suppose that Jesus meant it all literally. The essential meaning of this description of hell is that it is a state of complete separation from God.

*   *   *

Luke 17[7-10]—*Servants and their Duty*

These sayings teach that, however much a man does for God, he earns no special merit but is as dependent as ever on God's love and mercy.

Luke 17[11-19]—*The Ten Lepers*

The story about the Samaritan leper's gratitude to Jesus is evidence both that Jesus's ministry was not confined to Jews and that non-Jews were capable of the appropriate response to Him. For the importance of Samaritans in this gospel, see notes on Luke 10[25-37].

Luke 17[19]. *cured*. The word literally means *saved*. Jesus not only healed the leper physically but made possible his complete spiritual renewal.

Luke 17[20 37]—*The Day of the Son of Man*

The saying in verses 20–1 affirms that the Kingdom of God is already present through the ministry of Jesus (see notes on Mk 1[14-15]). Although the most natural translation of the Greek would be 'the Kingdom of God is within you', it is unlikely that Jesus would have said this to Pharisees. The Aramaic words which He probably used could also be translated 'the Kingdom of God is among you', and in this context 'among' is to be preferred to 'within'.

The rest of this section (verses 22–37) describes the suddenness of the future coming of the Son of Man in judgement (see also Mk 8[38], 13[26-7], 14[62]).

Luke 17[26-33]. For *Noah* and *Lot* see Genesis 6[ff], 19[23-8].

Luke 17[31], which seems to prophesy an event such as the fall of Jerusalem, may have originally been uttered in a separate context.

Luke 17[37] means that in the end, wherever men are, judgement will come to them as certainly as vultures gather round a corpse.

Luke 18[1-8]—*The Judge and the Widow*

The point of this parable is that God will answer the persistent prayer of His servants by acting on their behalf (see also Mt 7[7-11], Lk 11[5-13]).

Luke 18[7]. *his chosen* are those who have been called to serve God faithfully, even, if need arises, through suffering and persecution.

Luke 18[8] probably refers to the future rather than present coming of the Son of Man.

Luke 18[9-14]—*The Pharisee and the Tax-Gatherer*

This parable condemns the self-righteousness which was typified by Pharisees, and urges the need for repentance and humility. The tax-gatherer is forgiven, because he admits his own worthlessness and his dependence on the mercy of God.

＊   ＊   ＊

Luke 19$^{1-10}$—*Zacchaeus*

By his acceptance of Jesus, his sacrifice of half his possessions, and his readiness to repay the money he had extorted, Zacchaeus showed himself to be a genuine son of Abraham, a true heir of God's promises (see Lk 3^8).

Verse 10 is an important statement of the nature of Jesus's ministry. It was a distinctive feature of Jesus that He took the initiative in going out to seek and save the sinners.

Luke 19^2. *superintendent of taxes.* For Jesus's friendship with the despised class of tax-gatherers, see notes on Mark 2$^{15-17}$.

*   *   *

THE PASSION NARRATIVE IN LUKE
(*Luke* 19^{28}–23^{56})

In his passion narrative Luke does not keep as close to Mark as Matthew does. He includes several incidents and sayings which are not found in Mark, as, for example, Jesus's lament over Jerusalem (19$^{41-4}$), a separate account of the Last Supper, in which the cup is given before the bread (22$^{14-23}$), an extremely graphic description of Jesus's anguish in Gethsemane (22$^{43-4}$), and a reference to the healing of the High Priest's servant (22$^{49-51}$). Some striking features of Luke's narrative, however, are found in the passages which are now to be discussed.

Luke 22$^{24-38}$—*The Discourse at the Last Supper*

The sayings about service (verses 24–7) are not unlike Mark 10$^{42-5}$ (on which see notes).

In verses 28–30 Jesus appoints His disciples to a position of authority in the Christian Church, which He describes as 'the twelve tribes of Israel' because it is the new people of God. The word translated 'vest' by *NEB* is connected with the Greek word for 'covenant'. Its use in this context reminds us that in the events of Jesus's passion and death a new covenant was being established (see notes on Mk 14$^{12-25}$).

The scattering of the disciples and Peter's denial of Jesus (verses 31–4; see also Mk 14$^{27-31}$) are seen as the work of Satan, the great accuser and tempter, who asks for the disciples as he formerly asked for Job (Job 1$^{6-27}$).

In the final paragraph of this discourse (verses 35–8) Jesus tells His disciples that they can rely no longer on the goodwill and hospitality of others, as they did during a former mission (Lk 10$^{1-12}$). His reference to a sword is not intended to be taken literally, but means that the disciples must be ready for trouble.

Luke 22^{37} is a reference to Isaiah 53^{12}.

Luke 23$^{6-12}$—*Jesus before Herod*

This incident, which is recorded only by Luke, shows that Herod Antipas, like Pilate, found no real case against Jesus. According to Acts 4$^{25-8}$, the part played by Pilate and Herod in the death of Jesus was a fulfilment of Psalm 2^2. For Herod, see notes on Mark 6$^{14-29}$.

Luke 23$^{32-48}$—*The Crucifixion*

Luke omits all reference to the cry, 'My God, my God, why hast thou forsaken me?' (see Mk 15^{34}), but includes two sayings which are not found in the other gospels. The first of them (verse 34) is a prayer of Jesus for the forgiveness of His murderers, and the second (verse 46) is derived from Psalm 31^5 and emphasizes Jesus's trust in His Father even at the approach of death.

The story of the thief who admitted his own guilt and recognized the innocence of Jesus (verses 39–43) is found only in Luke. The thief asked for forgiveness when Jesus returned in judgement at some unknown date in the future, but Jesus promised him life immediately after his death (see notes on Lk 16^{22}).

Luke 23^{43}. *Paradise*, which is derived from a Persian word meaning 'garden', refers to the home of the blessed after death.

Luke 23^{47}. Where Mark 15^{39} reads 'a son of God', Luke reads *innocent*.

*   *   *

THE RESURRECTION
(*Luke* 24$^{1-53}$)

Like Mark and Matthew, Luke gives an account of the discovery of the empty tomb by the women. Instead of one young man by the tomb, there were, according to Luke, 'two men in dazzling garments', and Luke's version of the saying about Galilee omits any suggestion that Jesus was actually going there (Lk 24$^{6-7}$, see Mk 16^7). In contrast with Mark 16^8, Luke says that the women reported what they had seen to the other disciples. He then gives some narratives of resurrection appearances that are not mentioned in the other gospels.

Luke 24$^{13-32}$—*The Journey to Emmaus*

This famous and moving story of the appearance of Jesus to Cleopas and another disciple has several noteworthy features. The first is that the disciples did not recognize Jesus until He had expounded the scriptures to them and broken bread with them. The second is that, when Jesus expounded the scriptures to them, they felt their hearts on fire, but were not able to understand the cause of their experience until afterwards. A third feature of the story is that, when the disciples had seen the risen Jesus, they were eager to tell others about Him (see verse 33).

We cannot be certain what passages of scripture were expounded by Jesus. They would probably include those parts of the Old Testament which refer to the Messiah, the Son of God, the Son of Man, and the Suffering Servant. Hosea 6$^{1-2}$, Daniel 12$^{2-3}$, Psalms 16$^{10-11}$, 49^{15}, and 73$^{24-6}$, are passages which may have been interpreted as prophecies of the resurrection of Jesus.

The manifestation of Jesus to the disciples in the breaking of bread may have been regarded as the first celebration of the Lord's Supper after the resurrection.

Luke 24$^{33-5}$—*The Appearance of Jesus to Simon*

This is probably the appearance to Peter which is mentioned by Paul in 1 Corinthians 15^5.

Luke 24$^{36-53}$—*The Appearance of Jesus to His Disciples*

The reference to the flesh and bones of Jesus and His ability to eat food (verses 39–43) was probably included by Luke in order to refute the argument that the risen Jesus was no more than a ghost, and also in order to answer the heresy of Docetism, which denied the genuine humanity of Jesus and argued that He did not really die (see p. 132 and Jn 1^{14}).

The preaching of repentance to all nations (verse 47) may have been understood as a fulfilment of passages like Genesis 12^3, Psalm 22^{27}, and Isaiah 49^6. For prophecies of Jesus's death and resurrection (verse 46), see notes on Luke 24$^{13-32}$.

As in Matthew and John (Mt 28$^{19-20}$, Jn 20$^{21-3}$), the risen Jesus commissions His disciples for their apostolic work (verses 48–9). Luke's account also includes a promise of the gift of the Spirit (see Acts 2$^{1-4}$).

The final paragraph tells of Jesus's departure from His disciples at Bethany and their return to Jerusalem (verses 50–3). The gospel which began in the Temple (Lk 1^{5-25}) ends there, and, as its early chapters are full of joy and praise, so it concludes with the disciples rejoicing and praising God.

Luke 24^{48}. Jesus is said by Luke and John to have commissioned His disciples in Jerusalem, whereas Matthew claims that this happened in Galilee. Disagreements like this show that there is no concerted attempt to harmonize the different traditions of the resurrection. The very discrepancies of the accounts are evidence of their genuineness. Early Christians would find it difficult to remember with complete accuracy the events of those momentous days. They would be so overwhelmed with joy that they might easily have been confused about the time, place, and order of events. But although there is disagreement about the place where Jesus appeared, Matthew, Luke, and John agree that the risen Jesus commissioned His disciples for their work.

Luke 24^{51}. Some manuscripts add here a reference to the ascension of Jesus, but this is an attempt to bring Luke into harmony with Acts 1^9. The best manuscripts of Luke do not record the ascension.

QUESTIONS

(1) Discuss the temptations of Jesus.

(2) Give an account of the teaching about repentance and forgiveness in Luke's parables.

(3) What do the synoptic gospels record about the life and teaching of John the Baptist?

(4) Comment on : Luke 2^{49}, 9^{51}, 10^{41-2}, 17^{21}, 23^{42-3}, 24^{32}.

CHAPTER FIVE

THE TEACHING OF JESUS ACCORDING TO THE SYNOPTIC GOSPELS

AN ATTEMPT will now be made to gather together the teaching of Jesus as it is recorded in the Synoptic Gospels. In the last four chapters the teaching has been examined in the order in which it occurs in the gospels. Now the main themes of the teaching will be considered, and illustrated from all three gospels.

I—THE FATHERHOOD OF GOD

Although God is sometimes called Father in the Old Testament, and the title was often used of Him by Jews in Jesus's time, it was Jesus who really set the Fatherhood of God at the centre of religious teaching. He taught that God was creator, ruler, and judge of the universe. He taught about the Lordship, power, and glory of God. But above all He taught that God was Father.

According to His teaching God is *the Father who cares for His creatures.* He gives good things to those who ask Him (Mt 7^{11}). He feeds the birds, clothes the grass in the fields (Mt 6^{25-30}), and marks the fall of the sparrow to the ground. But He cares even more for men and women (Mt 10^{29-31}).

The Fatherhood of God is shown in *His mercy and forgiveness.* The parables of the Lost Sheep, the Lost Piece of Silver, and the Prodigal Son (Lk 15^{1-32}), tell of His unbounded mercy to the repentant sinner and His joy at the sinner's return. His love is a seeking love, which was active in the ministry of Jesus, who came 'to seek and save what is lost' (Lk 19^{10}).

God's Fatherhood is shown in His readiness to enter into *a new relationship with men.* Jesus taught men to love God (Mk 12^{28-34}) and call Him Father. He Himself addressed God by the informal title *Abba* (see notes on Mark 14^{32-42}), a specially intimate form of the word 'Father'. And in Luke's version of the Lord's Prayer He tells His disciples to address God simply as 'Father' (Lk 11^2).

Although God is the Father of all men, they are not automatically His children. Sonship is a privilege which He can give or withhold.

Peacemakers, and men who love their enemies and pray for their perse-cutors, will be children of God (Mt $5^{9, 44-5}$).

The Fatherhood of God is revealed in *His relationship to Jesus,* who had a unique knowledge of Him and gave a unique revelation of Him (Mt 11^{27}). At Jesus's baptism and transfiguration God addressed Him as 'Son' (Mk 1^{11}, 9^{7}). Nowhere is the closeness of the relationship more obvious than in Jesus's prayer to the Father in Gethsemane (Mk 14^{36}) and in His words to the Father during His crucifixion (Lk $23^{34, 46}$).

II—THE PERSON AND WORK OF JESUS

(a) *The Titles which He accepted*

Son of Man. By claiming this title for Himself, Jesus implied that He was the Messiah (see notes on Mk 2^{1-12}). Although the title had already been used in connection with the Messiah's final victory, Jesus gave it wider associations. He used it to describe *the nature of His earthly ministry.* As Son of Man He had the right to forgive sins, was sovereign over the Sabbath, and came to seek and save what was lost (Mk $2^{10, 28}$, Lk 19^{10}). He associated the title with *His humiliation, suffering, death, and resurrection.* As Son of Man He had 'nowhere to lay his head' (Lk 9^{58}), performed a ministry of service to others (Mk 10^{45}), and would suffer, die, and rise again (Mk 8^{31}, $9^{12, 31}$, $10^{33-4, 45}$). He also preserved the title's link with the future by using it of *His return as judge and ruler at the last day.* He would be 'seated on the right hand of God and coming with the clouds of heaven' (Mk 14^{62}). He would be ashamed of those who were ashamed of Him (Mk 8^{38}), but would gather His chosen from all corners of the earth (Mk 13^{26-7}). He would separate the righteous from the unrighteous, as a shepherd separates the sheep from the goats (Mt 25^{31-46}).

Son of God. This title, which may have been used by Jews in Jesus's time describes the Messiah, expresses the uniqueness of His relationship to God (see note on Mk 1^{1} and Mt 11^{25-7}). At His baptism and trans-figuration He was called God's Son (Mk 1^{11}, 9^{7}), and was recognized as such by devils (Mk 5^{7}). In the parable of the Vineyard the son of the owner represents Jesus, the Son of God (Mk 12^{1-12}). Even though He did not go out of His way to advertise it, Jesus was inwardly certain that He was Son of God, and that He stood in a unique relationship to His Father. Indeed His continual emphasis on the Fatherhood of God was the result of this awareness of His Sonship. Although He was reluctant to admit publicly that He was the Son of God, when at last He was openly challenged by the High Priest He did not deny it (Mk 14[61-2]).

Christ, or *Messiah*. The Greek *Christos* and the Hebrew *Messiah* both mean *Anointed* (see notes on Mk 1[1]). In Jesus's time the title was used to describe the king who was expected to bring a new era of liberty and blessedness. Jesus did not admit that He was Messiah until His ministry was well advanced. Even in His reply to Peter at Caesarea Philippi (Mk 8[29-33]) He did not admit it directly but only by implication. Later, however, when Bartimaeus called Him Son of David, a Messianic title (Mk 10[48]), He did not command him to be silent. And the manner of His entry into Jerusalem implies that He regarded Himself as Messiah (Mk 11[1-10]). Finally, at His trial He admitted to the High Priest that He was both Messiah and Son of God (Mk 14[61-2]). He was reluctant to make this admission because He was not the kind of deliverer whom the Jews expected. Instead of being a conquering king He was a Suffering Servant and a Prince of Peace.

Other titles such as Rabbi, Rabboni, Teacher, and Master, were accepted by Jesus, and in one passage He implies that He is Lord (Mk 12[35-7]). Although He never actually calls Himself Suffering Servant, some of His teaching may have been influenced by the Servant Songs of Isaiah 40–66 (see Mk 10[45], Lk 22[27]).

(b) The Work which He claimed to do

Even more important than the titles which Jesus claimed for Himself were the functions which He assumed, functions which set Him apart from the rest of men.

He forgave sins. Forgiveness was regarded by the Jews as a gift which could be granted only by God. That Jesus claimed the right to forgive sins is shown by the stories of the man who was paralysed (Mk 2[1-12]) and the sinful woman (Lk 7[36-49], see notes).

He saved men and women. Salvation meant more than forgiveness. It meant that a man was not only rescued from the power of sin but also brought into the life of God's Kingdom. Jesus came 'to seek and save what is lost' (Lk 19[10]), not to 'invite virtuous people, but sinners'

(Mk 2^{17}), a message which is affirmed in the parables of the Lost Sheep, the Lost Piece of Silver, and the Prodigal Son (Luke 15^{1-32}).

He brought the Kingdom of God to men and women. One of the distinctive features of Jesus's teaching was that the Kingdom of God was present in His work of preaching and healing. He said that the Kingdom had drawn near in His ministry (Mk 1^{15}) and that when He cast out devils, the Kingdom had come upon men (Lk 11^{20}).

He was the new Lawgiver. Jesus claimed to complete the Law of Moses, and He completed it by going beyond it (Mt 5^{17}). He contrasted His words with those of Moses (Mt 5^{21-44}), implying that He was the new legislator for the new covenant.

He would be judge. He predicted that He would come as Son of Man to exercise divine judgement on mankind and to separate those whom God had chosen from those whom he had rejected (Mk 8^{38}, 13^{26-7}, Mt 25^{31-46}).

(c) His Death and Resurrection

Jesus knew that He would die a violent death. Early in His ministry He told His disciples that He would be taken away from them (Mk 2^{19-20}); and on several later occasions, beginning at Caesarea Philippi, He prophesied His death and resurrection (Mk 8^{31}, $9^{12, 31}$, $10^{33-4, 45}$).

He believed that there was a divine *necessity* about His death, and taught that the Son of Man *had* to suffer, die, and rise again (Mk 8^{31}). He regarded these events as necessary because they were part of God's plan of redemption, foretold in the scriptures (Mk 9^{12}, 14^{21}).

Jesus spoke of His mission in terms of *service* (Mk 10^{45}, Lk 22^{27}); and His life of service culminated in His death, when He gave Himself as 'a ransom for many' (Mk 10^{45}). It is possible but not certain that this aspect of His teaching was influenced by the idea of the Suffering Servant in the Old Testament. It is clear, however, that when He said that He gave Himself 'a ransom for many', He meant that His death would set men free from sin and death, and bring them to God's Kingdom and to eternal life.

He also described His death in terms of a *covenant-sacrifice*. He established a new covenant, which was sealed not by the sacrifice of a dumb animal but by His own voluntary self-offering (Mk 14^{24}). Through this new covenant was formed the people of God, the Christian

Church, which succeeded the Jewish nation as God's chosen race (Mk 12$^{1-12}$).

Jesus compared His suffering and death to a *baptism* (Mk 10$^{35-40}$, Lk 12^{50}). His death and resurrection were indeed like a descent into the waters and a rising up again; but they were also a baptism because they were a new beginning, the inauguration of a new age and a new people.

The crucifixion and resurrection were the climax of Jesus's ministry, and the work which He came to do was not complete until this climax was reached. His sayings themselves do not give a full explanation of the events. But although His death and resurrection remain a divine mystery, His sayings help us to understand their wonder and power.

III—THE KINGDOM OF GOD

(a) The Kingdom of God in the Ministry, Death, and Resurrection of Jesus

The new and unexpected feature of Jesus's teaching about the Kingdom of God was His affirmation that it had come in His own ministry. The Kingdom or Reign of God, which was expected as a future climax to God's purpose in history, had, according to Jesus's teaching, already broken into the course of history through His own coming. 'The time has come,' He said, 'the kingdom of God is upon you' (Mk 1^{15}). In His own work of casting out devils, He claimed, 'the kingdom of God has already come upon you' (Lk 11^{20}). His acts of healing and preaching were signs that He was the bringer of the new age (see notes on Luke 7$^{22-3}$). This was the time of fulfilment which prophets and kings had longed for (Lk 10$^{23-4}$). The Kingdom of God was among men (Lk 17^{21}), and it was possible for men to enter it (Lk 16^{16}).

Some of Jesus's words imply that the Kingdom was not actually present but would come in the lifetime of His disciples. This is the implication of Mark 9^1 and probably of Mark 14^{25}, prophecies which seem to have been fulfilled by the resurrection of Jesus, when the Kingdom really came 'in power'. There is no fundamental conflict between these sayings and those which imply that the Kingdom was present during the ministry of Jesus. Although the Kingdom was present in His ministry, the inauguration of the Kingdom was not complete until His ministry had reached its climax in His death and resurrection.

(b) The Kingdom of God and the Future

Jesus also spoke of the Kingdom of God which would come at the end of history. This aspect of His teaching is in agreement with traditional

Judaism, and cannot be ignored. The future state is 'the feast in the kingdom of God' (Lk 13^{29}), and will begin when Jesus returns in glory as Son of Man (Mk 13^{26-7}, 14^{62}; see also Mt 25^{31-46}). No one knows when it will come, not even Jesus Himself (Mk 13^{32}). It will be sudden and unexpected, catching many people unawares (Lk 17^{22-37}).

(c) The Kingdom of God and Life after Death

The teaching about the Kingdom of God which has been so far outlined does not reveal what happens to a man between the day of his death and the return of the Son of Man. Jesus is not silent about this matter. He teaches that there is life for the faithful immediately after death. Abraham, Isaac, and Jacob, are eternally alive (Mk 12^{26-7}). Lazarus was with Abraham after his death (Lk 16^{19-31}), and the dying thief was promised that he would the same day be with Jesus in Paradise (Lk 23^{43}).

(d) The Nature of the Kingdom of God

The life of the Kingdom is 'eternal life' (Mk 10^{30}), and 'eternal' means not only 'everlasting' but 'belonging to the Messianic age'. Although this life is essentially too wonderful to describe in detail. Jesus gave some indication of its nature. Its incomparable value is the theme of the parables of the Buried Treasure and the Pearl of Great Price (Mt 13^{44-6}), which teach that a man ought to be ready to surrender all his possessions in order to enter it. Its blessedness is described in the Beatitudes (Mt 5^{1-10}). It is a state of divine consolation in which right prevails, and men receive mercy, have a spiritual vision of God, and are called His sons. These blessings belong both to the present and the future. At present they are enjoyed amid tensions and conflict, but in the future they will be enjoyed without limit or restraint.

Above all, the Kingdom is God's. It comes through God's power, not through human activity (see the parable of the Seed, Mk 4^{26-9}). It is a sudden and wonderful manifestation (see the parables of the Mustard Seed and the Leaven, Mk 4^{30-2}, Mt 13^{33}). No setbacks or hindrances can prevent its coming, and, even though the preaching of the Kingdom often meets with an unfavourable response, the message nevertheless bears fruit, because there is at least some soil in which the seed takes root (Mark 4^{3-9}).

The Kingdom is not a reward which men earn, but the gift of God's love. It is not a question of what men deserve but of what God chooses to give (see the parable of the Labourers in the Vineyard, Mt 20^{1-16}; and also Lk 17^{10}). The life of the Kingdom is life with Jesus Himself

(Lk 22^{30}), who invites men to come to Him, take His yoke upon them, and find relief (Mt 11$^{28-30}$). His yoke is the yoke of God's Kingdom, and the relief which He offers is the peace and joy of eternal life.

(e) Entry into the Kingdom of God

Although the Kingdom is an undeserved gift from God, there are certain conditions for entry into it.

(i) *Acknowledgement of dependence on God.* Men must accept the Kingdom like little children (Mk 10^{15}) by admitting their absolute need of God.

(ii) *Repentance and humility.* They must recognize their own spiritual poverty (Mt 5^3), and, like the tax-gatherer in the parable, be ready to admit their own sinfulness (Lk 18$^{9-14}$).

(iii) *Loyalty to God.* A man must not look back longingly for the life which he has abandoned (Lk 9^{62}), but must have a loyalty to God which nerves him for endurance in the face of persecution (Mt 5^{10}). It is the man 'who holds out to the end' who will be saved (Mk 13^{13}).

(iv) *Acceptance of Jesus.* To receive Jesus is to receive His Father (Mk 9^{37}). The man who follows Jesus, and loses himself for His sake, will win eternal life (Mk 8^{35}, 10^{21}).

(v) *Self-sacrifice.* A man must be prepared to give up everything for Jesus. He may be required to sell all his possessions and to leave his family and friends (Mk 10$^{17-22, 28-31}$). He must certainly be ready to exclude anything from his life which distracts him from following Jesus (Mk 9^{45}). He must leave self behind, take up his cross, and follow Jesus (Mk 8$^{34-5}$).

(vi) *Obedience to God's Will.* It is not enough to pay lip-service to Jesus. 'Not everyone who calls me "Lord, Lord"', He said, 'will enter the kingdom of God, but only those who do the will of my heavenly Father' (Mt 7^{21}). Those who care for the needy have cared for Jesus Himself, and will receive eternal life (Mt 25$^{31-46}$). A higher righteousness is required of Jesus's disciples than the righteousness of lawyers and Pharisees (Mt 5^{20}). It is the righteousness which is based on the Law of Love and shown by the qualities enumerated in the Beatitudes.

(vii) *Watchfulness.* Men must be alert and ready for the coming of the Kingdom (see the parables of the Doorkeeper and the Ten Bridesmaids: Mk 13$^{33-7}$, Mt 25$^{1-13}$). And an alert man is one who makes use of those opportunities of service which God gives him (see the parable of the Bags of Gold: Mt 25$^{14-30}$).

Jesus's teaching about entry into the Kingdom of God does not always make it clear whether He is thinking of the present or the future. Often, indeed, He may be referring to both at once. The conditions of entry into the future Kingdom are also the conditions of entry into the present Kingdom. And they are not meritorious works which earn salvation, but the response by which a man accepts Jesus as his Lord.

IV — THE LAW OF LOVE, THE GOLDEN RULE, AND THE BEATITUDES

There is no better summary of Jesus's teaching about conduct than the two commandments about love of God and love of neighbour (Mk 12²⁹⁻³¹), and the Golden Rule, 'Always treat others as you would like them to treat you' (Mt 7¹²). And there is no better guide to Jesus's teaching about the Christian character than the Beatitudes (Mt 5³⁻¹²). All these passages have already been discussed, and reference should be made to what has been said about them, because they are fundamental to Jesus's teaching about the Christian life.

V — JESUS AND THE JEWISH LAW

Jesus did not come to destroy the Law, but to complete it (Mt 5¹⁷); and He completed it by asking men to penetrate to its inner spirit. A man must refrain from anger, abuse, and sneering, as well as from murder. He must avoid lust as well as adultery (Mt 5²¹⁻², ²⁷⁻⁸). Higher standards are required from the followers of Jesus than from the Pharisees and the doctors of the Law (Mt 5²⁰). Jesus's teaching is in some respects more rigorous than the Law. He forbids divorce to men as well as to women (Mk 10¹⁻¹²). He insists that people should always tell the truth, whether they take oaths or not (Mt 5³³⁻⁷). They ought not to seek retribution for wrongs, but to give way to those who injure them. They should love their enemies as well as their neighbours (Mt 5³⁸⁻⁴⁸).

Jesus stressed the moral rather than the ritual aspect of the Law. He refused to interpret overscrupulously the commandment about observance of the Sabbath (Mk 2²³⁻3⁶), and taught that outward observances like ritual washing were not essential to religion (Mk 7¹⁻⁸). The commandments to which He gave an extremely rigorous interpretation were moral commandments about murder, adultery, perjury, revenge, and love. In these matters He went further than the Jewish Law, because He established a new conception of Law based on the commandment of love, and, above all, on loyalty to Himself.

His ethical teaching was primarily concerned with a man's inner attitude. He attacked evil thoughts like anger and lust (Mt 5²², ²⁸), and showed that the evil of a man is in his heart (Mk 7$^{14-23}$). He detested the hypocrisy which was content with outward show and failed to penetrate to the truth of things. Worship and prayer were chiefly matters of inner intention, and conduct should spring from a heart full of love. Purity of motive could be adequately sustained only by personal loyalty to Jesus. The Jews spoke of the yoke of the Law, but He invited men to bend their necks to His own yoke (Mt 11$^{28-30}$). It was not enough to obey a code of commandments. Men must follow Jesus Himself.

VI—WORSHIP, PRAYER, AND THE SACRAMENTS

Worship and prayer are means by which a man can obey the commandment to love God. Though Jesus set an example by regular attendance at synagogue and, when He was in Jerusalem, at the Temple, He had no use for ostentation in worship, and criticized the status symbols and excessive formalities of the doctors of the Law and the Pharisees, denouncing them for making a show of their almsgiving, prayer, and fasting (Mt 6$^{1-8, 16-18}$).

He spent many hours in prayer (see Mk 1^{35}), and some of the great moments of His life, as, for example, His baptism, His transfiguration, Gethsemane, and the crucifixion (Lk 3^{21}, Mk 9$^{2-8}$, 14^{32ff}, Lk 23$^{34, 46}$), included acts of prayer. In addition to the Lord's Prayer, which has already been discussed in the notes on Matthew 6$^{9-13}$, there is plenty of evidence of His attitude to prayer. He showed the importance of thanksgiving by His practice of it during His ministry, at the Last Supper, and on the way to Gethsemane (Mt 11^{25}, Mk 14$^{23, 26}$). He set an example too by His practice of intercession for others. He prayed for children (Mk 10^{16}), for Peter (Lk 22$^{31-2}$), and for the men who put Him to death (Lk 23^{34}). Petition for His own needs had an important place in His prayers, as, for example, in His prayer in Gethsemane that the cup of suffering and death should be taken from Him (Mk 14^{36}). God did not answer this prayer by granting His request, but by guiding Him to accept His death in humble obedience. It is with this incident in mind that we should understand Jesus's statement that God will vindicate those who are persistent in prayer (Lk 18$^{1-8}$), and that, when men ask from God, they will receive. He did not promise that God would always give exactly what they requested. He would give 'good things to those who ask Him' (Mt 7$^{7-11}$). The supreme petition is 'Thy will be done' (Mt 6^{10}).

Prayer is for Jesus an act of communion with God, in which a man commits himself to God and receives His guidance. Although the prayer

'Thy kingdom come' (Mt 6^{10}) refers partly to the future, it also refers to the present. When a man prays according to the pattern of Jesus, the Kingdom of God comes into his life.

In the synoptic gospels there is a limited amount of evidence about the sacraments of Baptism and the Lord's Supper. The only saying in which Jesus actually instructs His disciples to baptize converts (Mt 28^{19}) has been the subject of much controversy. It is unlikely, however, that baptism would have been universally accepted from the first days of the Church's history, if Jesus had not in some way commanded it. Moreover, since He regarded His own death as a kind of baptism (Mk 10^{38}, Lk 12^{50}), there is a sense in which Christian baptism was inaugurated by His death. Baptism is certainly regarded as a sacrament of initiation in Matthew 28^{19}, but the synoptic record of its connection with repentance and with the gift of the Spirit is found in the teaching of John the Baptist and not in that of Jesus.

The sacrament which symbolizes and seals the corporate life of the Church is the Lord's Supper, which was instituted by Jesus on the eve of His death, and became the Church's central act of worship. For its meaning in the synoptic teaching, see the notes on Mark 14^{12-25}.

VII—POSSESSIONS

Jesus warned men of the unprofitable nature of material possessions. A man should store up treasure for himself in heaven. If he values spiritual riches, his heart will be with God (Mt 6^{19-20}). He cannot serve two masters, and must choose between God and Money (Mt 6^{24}).

This does not mean that a man ought never to own material wealth. Jesus varied His demands according to the person. He told one man that he must sell everything and give to the poor (Mk 10^{21}). Zacchaeus gave half his possessions to charity (Lk 19^{1-10}). But Jesus did not ask this type of sacrifice from everybody. He insisted, however, on the importance of using material possessions in the service of God (Lk 16^{9}), and He denounced preoccupation with wealth, as shown by the parable of the Rich Fool (Lk 12^{15-21}). Men ought not to be anxious about food, drink, and clothes. If they seek God's Kingdom and justice, these other things will be provided (Mt 6^{25-34}).

Material wealth, Jesus taught, is a great obstacle to a man's entry into the Kingdom of God. It is easier for a camel to pass through a needle's eye than for a rich man to enter the Kingdom. Nevertheless, with God everything is possible (Mk 10^{23-7}). The mercy of God can overcome even the barrier which wealth erects between a man and the Kingdom.

VIII—MARRIAGE AND THE FAMILY

Jesus taught that, when a man and woman married, they became one flesh, joined together by God, and that no man had a right to separate them (Mk 10^{5-9}). It followed that divorce was against God's will. Although, according to Jewish Law, a man had a right in certain circumstances to divorce his wife, a woman had no right to divorce her husband. Jesus, however, forbade either husband or wife to obtain a divorce (see notes on Mark 10^{1-12} for a fuller discussion).

He assumed that marriage ought to be monogamous. It was a union between one man and one woman, in which the two become one flesh (Mk 10^7). He also taught that sexual intercourse should be confined to marriage. Adultery is a sin, and so is fornication (Mark 7^{21-2}). Moreover, the loyalty of married people to each other should extend to their thoughts as well as their deeds, because lustful thoughts are adultery in the heart (Mt 6^{27-8}).

Sacred as marriage is, it is an institution for this life only, and there are no marriages in heaven (Mk 12^{25}). This does not exclude a spiritual relationship between husbands and wives in heaven, but means that in the new order of things marriage itself will have no place.

Jesus accepted the institution of the family, and Himself shared in family life from infancy to manhood. He showed great kindness and affection to children (Mk 9^{36-7}), and several of those whom He healed were children or young people (Mk $5^{21-4, \ 35-43}$, 7^{25-30}, 9^{14-29}, Lk 7^{1-17}). Indeed His reverence for marriage is evidence of His reverence for the family. But He did not believe that human families were made for eternity. God alone was the Father in heaven, and eternal relationships would be different from earthly ones.

Jesus also believed the claims of God to be more important than the claims of family. His disciples had to be prepared to leave their homes and their relatives, and even to renounce marriage, in order to follow Him (Mk 10^{28-31}, Lk 9^{59-62}, Mt 19^{12}). They must be ready to see their homes divided, and to forsake some of their most important family duties, if service to Him demanded it (Lk 9^{59-62}, 12^{51-3}).

IX—THE STATE, AND THE USE OF VIOLENCE

Jesus kept the laws of the land and never tried to provoke the Roman authorities. At a time when many people wished to organize violent uprisings against their Roman overlords, Jesus chose the way of peace. His famous utterance, 'Pay Caesar what is due to Caesar, and pay God what is due to God' (Mk 12^{17}), admits that the Romans had a right to impose taxes. And even though He thought that the Jews had no right to impose a temple-tax, to prevent needless trouble He paid it (Mt 17$^{24-7}$). He proclaimed the principle of non-resistance (Mt 5$^{38-42}$), instructing His followers to turn the other cheek and to go the second mile. The examples which He gives apply to a situation in which His disciples themselves are attacked or placed under pressure. It is not certain that His teaching applies to situations in which a man believes that he has a duty to defend others. He taught men to love their enemies and pray for their persecutors (Mt 5^{44}), but it is a matter of controversy whether His way of love would always lead to non-resistance.

X—THE CHURCH

Jesus deliberately left behind Him a community of people under the leadership of the apostles. He Himself was the corner-stone of the community, which succeeded the Jewish nation as the chosen people of God (Mk 12$^{1-12}$). The very fact that He chose twelve leading disciples reminds us of the twelve tribes of Israel, and is a sign that He was establishing a new people of God.

He did not provide detailed plans for the community which He founded, and it is called 'church' in only two of His sayings (Mt 16^{18}, 18^{17}: in the latter instance *NEB* translates 'congregation'). He appointed Peter to be the Church's first leader, and gave him and the other disciples authority to decide what actions were forbidden and allowed (Mt 16$^{18-19}$, 18^{18}). Although a few brief instructions survive about the mode of settling disputes (Mt 18$^{15-17}$), the synoptic gospels do not contain a detailed system of Church government.

The Church was conscious from the beginning of its missionary task. When Jesus first appointed the twelve disciples, their functions were not only to be His companions but also to preach and to heal (Mk 3$^{14-15}$). Both Matthew and Luke record in their different ways that the risen Jesus sent out His disciples to preach the gospel to all nations (Mt 28$^{18-20}$, Lk 24$^{46-9}$). In their task of preaching, according to Mark 13$^{9-13}$, the disciples would be guided by the Spirit. The Church has a ministry of preaching and service to the whole earth. The disciples of Jesus must be like salt to the world, giving a quality and flavour to its life. They are a light for the world, and their task is to tell men about God and to testify to His goodness by the quality of their lives (Mt 5^{16}).

QUESTIONS

(1) Examine the synoptic teaching of Jesus about His death and resurrection.

(2) What is the synoptic teaching of Jesus about the Kingdom of God?

(3) In the light of Jesus's sayings in the synoptic gospels, what should be our attitude to marriage and the family?

(4) Comment on : Mark 7^{14-15}, 10^{24-5}, Matthew 5^{17}, 20^{14-15}, Luke 10^{29} 18^{2-3}.

CHAPTER SIX

THE GOSPEL ACCORDING TO ST JOHN
(INTRODUCTION AND CHAPTERS 1 TO 12)

INTRODUCTION TO THE GOSPEL

Differences between John's Gospel and the Synoptic Gospels

JOHN'S GOSPEL is in a class by itself. While the synoptic gospels have a great deal in common, John's is vastly different from the other three.

(i) *The style of writing.* The difference of style is obvious, even in English translations. John's vocabulary is considerably smaller than that of the synoptics. He is inclined to more repetition and to longer sentences and paragraphs than the other evangelists.

(ii) *The form of the teaching.* The synoptic gospels present much of Jesus's teaching in short sayings, but, although John's gospel does contain sayings of this nature, a great amount of its teaching is presented in the form of long connected discourses. Moreover, John does not include the kind of parable which is found in the synoptic gospels; he has a preference for symbolic sayings and discourses.

(iii) *The content of the teaching.* Whereas the synoptic gospels suggest that Jesus was reluctant to admit that He was Messiah and Son of God, John records that He accepted these titles for Himself at the beginning of His ministry and regularly claimed for Himself a unique divine status. There are also marked differences of emphasis in the teaching. While the synoptics prefer to speak of the Kingdom of God, John prefers to speak of eternal life, and, although John stresses the primacy of the Law of Love, he does not include the detailed ethical teaching which is found in the synoptics.

(iv) *The account of the life of Jesus.* Important events which are not recorded by John include the birth of Jesus in Bethlehem, His baptism, His temptations, His expulsion of devils, His ministry to tax-gatherers, His visit to Caesarea Philippi, His transfiguration, His institution of the Lord's Supper, and His agony in Gethsemane. Events which are described by John, but not mentioned in the synoptic gospels include the call of Nathanael, the miracle at Cana, Jesus's conversations with Nicodemus and with the Samaritan woman, His healing of the man born blind, His raising of Lazarus, His washing of His disciples' feet, and His extended discourse at the Last Supper. John's passion narrative differs considerably from that of the synoptics, and his resurrection narrative is almost wholly different from theirs. There are other differences too. The synoptic gospels give the impression that the ministry of Jesus may not have lasted much longer than a year, but John's gospel implies that it lasted perhaps three or four years. Whereas the synoptic gospels devote much space to Jesus's ministry in Galilee, John lays more emphasis on His work in Jerusalem and its neighbourhood. And John differs from the synoptics in his dating of both the cleansing of the Temple and the crucifixion.

Similarities between John's Gospel and the Synoptic Gospels

It must not be imagined that John's gospel is wholly different from the others. Its account of the Feeding of the Five Thousand has close verbal similarities with the synoptic gospels, and some of its sayings are similar to synoptic sayings. Moreover, all four gospels agree that Jesus believed He was Messiah and Son of God, that He ministered in Galilee, entered Jerusalem on an ass, partook of the Last Supper, was betrayed by Judas, and was arrested, put on trial and crucified. They all agree too that He rose from the dead.

If John's gospel had been intended as a supplement to the synoptic gospels, there would not have been as much overlapping of content as there is. Indeed John may not have read the other gospels, since the verbal similarities could be explained by the fact that stories and sayings were circulated independently in the early Church. But before we attempt to explain why John's gospel was written, we must enquire into the problems of its historical reliability and its authorship.

The Historical Reliability of the Gospel

None of the gospels is free from an element of interpretation, and a comparison of the synoptic gospels with each other shows clearly that some of the stories and sayings have been modified to suit the different theological standpoints of the evangelists. This process of interpretation is most marked in John's gospel, especially in the lengthy discourses which he attributes to Jesus. The same style of writing is used whether the evangelist is making his own comments or recording the words of Jesus or John the Baptist. Moreover, there is no adequate way of reconciling this gospel's assumption that Jesus openly claimed a divine status with the synoptic gospels' account of His reluctance to admit that He was the Son of God and the Messiah. One or the other must be wrong, and it seems likely that the synoptic gospels are nearer the truth. But although the synoptic gospels generally give the more reliable account of the life and teaching of Jesus, it does not follow that John's gospel is without historical value. It must be used, however, with special caution, because of the large element of interpretation which it contains.

The Background of the Gospel

Some of the leading ideas of the gospel have obvious similarities with both Hebrew and Greek thought. The contrast between light and darkness, truth and falsehood, occurs in the Old Testament and in later Jewish writings—the recently discovered Dead Sea Scrolls provide evidence of the use of these ideas in Jewish religious communities about the beginning of the Christian era. These ideas are also prominent in the writings of Greek thinkers. Another idea found in Greek thought as well as in the Hebrew tradition is that of the Word, which is expounded in the prologue to the gospel.

The most reasonable explanation of these and other similarities is that, whereas the tradition behind the gospel was formulated in Palestine, the gospel received its present shape in Asia Minor, an area where Greek culture predominated. John used ideas which appealed to both Jews and Gentiles. But although he clearly knew the Old Testament, it is not certain that he was directly acquainted with any later Jewish writings or with any works of Greek philosophy.

The Author of the Gospel

According to the earliest tradition, which goes back to the second century, the gospel was written in Ephesus by the apostle John, the son of Zebedee. In recent years this tradition has been challenged because the gospel is so different from the synoptics that it is doubtful if it could have been written by one of the original disciples of Jesus. It has been suggested that it was written by John the Elder, who lived in Asia Minor and is mentioned by the second-century writer, Papias. Some support is claimed for this theory from the fact that the second and third letters of John are ascribed to the elder (2 Jn 1, 3 Jn 1). The theory is at best a conjecture, but, whether we think that John the Elder or some unknown person was responsible for the present form of the gospel, it is reasonable to suppose that the author was a disciple of John the Apostle, and used his master's reminiscences as a basis for his work. It is unlikely that the tradition about John's link with the gospel is a complete fiction, and the prominence of 'the beloved disciple', who is almost certainly John, in the gospel's narrative confirms the view that it is based on material derived from him.

The Beloved Disciple

The gospel refers several times to 'the disciple whom Jesus loved' (13^{23}, 19^{26}, 20^2, $21^{7,\ 20-3}$). It is almost certain that this disciple was John, the son of Zebedee, because, although John was a leading disciple, he is never mentioned by name in the gospel. It is unlikely that John would have singled himself out as the disciple whom Jesus loved, as it would have been obvious self-advertisement. But it would be a natural description for one of John's disciples to use, when he was editing the apostle's reminiscences. Probably John is the eyewitness mentioned in 19^{35}.

The Unity of the Gospel

Numerous theories have been suggested about possible displacements of the text of the gospel, and it has been claimed that the original order of the narrative has been somewhat confused. These theories, which are only conjectures, are discussed in the commentaries, and in the following pages the gospel will be examined in the order in which it has been preserved.

One incident, however, the story of the woman taken in adultery (7^{53}–8^{11}), is absent from some manuscripts and appears in varying places in others. It is probably a genuine tradition about the life of Jesus, which was not an original part of John's gospel. For this reason *NEB* places it at the end of the gospel.

The last chapter of the gospel, Chapter 21, presents a special problem. The final words of Chapter 20 provide a fitting conclusion to the gospel, and the last chapter seems to be a kind of appendix, probably added by a different person from the author of the rest of the gospel. It may well incorporate traditions which were derived from John himself, and 21^{24} suggests that the author believed John to have written the rest of the gospel, and was claiming John's authority for the appendix.

The Date and Place of the Gospel

The tradition that the gospel was written in Ephesus is probably correct, but the date of the gospel is by no means certain. The earliest papyrus fragment of the gospel was written about AD 120, and, because the amount of interpretation in the gospel suggests a fairly late date, we may assume that it was written between A D 90 and 110.

The Purpose of the Gospel

The gospel itself claims to be written 'in order that you may hold the faith that Jesus is the Christ, the Son of God, and that through this faith you may possess eternal life by his name' (Jn 20^{31}). It was designed to refute heretical teaching which denied the reality of the incarnation and claimed that Jesus did not really die and rise again (see notes on 1^{14}, 19$^{28, 34}$, 20^{27}). And it was written for a generation of Christians who no longer expected Jesus to return in their own lifetime. Hence there is emphasis on the fact that men have eternal life already, and the doctrine of a future resurrection, although it is present, is not prominent.

The gospel is the result of sustained reflection on the meaning of Christ's life, death, and resurrection. It is the fruit of its author's rich understanding and experience of Christ, of whom it gives a portrait which is unsurpassed for spiritual power and beauty.

The Symbolism of the Gospel

A characteristic feature of the gospel is its frequent use of symbols to express spiritual truths. For example, Jesus is the bread of life, the light of the world, the good shepherd and the real vine. There is a more frequent use of allegory than in the synoptic gospels. Not only is Jesus the good shepherd, but the sheep are the members of the Church (10$^{1-18}$). And not only is He the real vine, but His Father is the gardener and His disciples are the branches (15$^{1-6}$).

Many of the statements in the gospel contain hidden spiritual meanings, which can easily be overlooked. The references to 'night' in 3^2, 9^4, and 13^{30} imply that there is spiritual as well as physical darkness. And 'blood and water' (19^{34}) alludes to the sacraments.

Most of the miracles in the gospel have a clear symbolical meaning. In the synoptic gospels the miracles convey spiritual truths, but John[1] makes these truths more explicit than do the synoptic writers. Whereas the characteristic word for a miracle in the synoptic gospels is the Greek *dunamis*, 'a work of power', the characteristic word in John is *sēmeion*, 'sign' (see 2^{11}, 4^{54}, 6$^{2, 14}$, 9^{16}, 11^{47}, 12^{18}, 20^{30}). The miraculous acts both manifest the glory of Christ (2^{11}) and illustrate spiritual truth. They are not merely proofs of His divine power but means by which teaching is

---

[1] The name 'John' will be used henceforth for the author of the gospel, whether he was actually called John or not.

conveyed. For example, the wine in the miracle at Cana stands for the new dispensation which Jesus has brought, the feeding of the five thousand points to Jesus as the bread of life, the healing of the blind man demonstrates that Jesus is the light of the world, and the raising of Lazarus shows that Jesus is resurrection and life.

Other incidents too have symbolic meaning. The cleansing of the Temple reveals Jesus as the New Temple, and the washing of the disciples' feet shows Jesus as a servant and as one who purifies the souls of men. In the conversation with the woman of Samaria the water from Jacob's well leads Jesus to talk of the living water of the Spirit. This symbolism is based on the belief that the world is a place in which God manifests Himself, and in which the Word is made flesh. The physical world reveals spiritual reality, and the temporal points to the eternal.

The Teaching of the Gospel

There is a more deliberate attempt in this gospel than in the synoptics to present a developed theology. Indeed John and Paul rank together as the profoundest thinkers in the New Testament. Much of the gospel's teaching will be examined in the comments on selected passages, but, since there is a carefully planned exposition of ideas in the gospel, it will be helpful to consider its main themes.

(i) Father and Son

The title 'Father' is used of God more often in John's gospel than in any other writing of the New Testament. God is also described in other ways. He is the one who loves the world, raises the dead, gives life (3^{16}, 5^{21}), and is Himself 'spirit' (4^{24}). Above all, He is the Father who reveals Himself in His Son, Jesus Christ, through whom alone He can be known and understood (1^{18}, 14^6).

Jesus Christ is the Father's 'only Son'; a distinction is made between Jesus, who is 'the Son', and His disciples who are 'children of God' (1^{12-14}). Stress is laid on the fact that Jesus is the Messiah and the Son of Man, titles which have already been examined in the notes on Mark 1^1 and 8^{27-33}. But the distinguishing feature of the gospel's teaching about Jesus is its clear emphasis on His divinity. He is the Word, who was with God at the creation of the world, and was 'what God was' (1^{1-3}). He is the Lord, whom Isaiah saw in his vision (12^{37-41}). Honour granted to Him is honour granted to His Father, and He acts on His Father's behalf, passing judgement on men and giving life to them (5^{19-23}). He and the Father are one, dwelling in eternal unity (10^{30}, 17^{20-3}). He is the light, life, and truth, and is described as 'I am' ($6^{35, 41, 48, 51}$, $8^{12, 58}$, $10^{7, 9,}$ $^{11, 14}$, 11^{25}, 14^6, $15^{1, 5}$), a phrase which is used of God in the Old Testament. These indications of His divine status, which begin with the opening verse of the gospel, reach their climax in the resurrection narratives, when His divinity is openly acknowledged in Thomas's confession, 'My Lord and my God!' (20^{28}).

At the same time the gospel stresses that Jesus was a real man. The Word became flesh (1^{14}). Blood and water flowed from His side when He was crucified (19^{34}). He could grow weary and thirsty (4^{6-7}, 19^{28}), sigh and be deeply moved ($11^{33, 38}$), and His soul could be in turmoil (12^{27}). It was indeed one of the main purposes of the gospel to refute the false teachers who denied the reality of the incarnation.

(ii) Salvation and Judgement

Jesus Christ came into the world not to judge it but to save it (3^{16-17}). He came to save men from sin and death, and to give them eternal life (1^{29}, 3^{16-17}, 10^{10}). This work of salvation, which continued throughout His ministry, culminated in His death.

John uses a variety of ideas to expound the meaning of Jesus's death, and one of them is that of *victory over the devil*. Men were in the power of the devil, the Prince of this world, and at His death Jesus threw out the devil and gave men the possibility of freedom from evil ($8^{36, 44}$, 12^{31}, 14^{30-1}).

Jesus's death is also interpreted as a *sacrifice*. As the Passover Lamb (1^{29}, $19^{14, 31}$) He initiated a new Exodus, setting men free not from captivity to Pharaoh but from captivity to sin, and delivering them not from physical death but from spiritual and eternal death. And when John says that Jesus 'takes away the sin of the world', he is thinking of Jesus not only as a Passover Lamb but also as a sin-offering and perhaps as the Suffering Servant (see 1^{29}).

The idea of the *Servant* is probably behind the story of the Feet Washing, which shows that Jesus underwent humiliation in the service of others (13^{1-17}). And it was as Servant that He was glorified and lifted up in His death and resurrection (see notes on 12^{20-36}). In this moment of being lifted up He drew men of all nations to Himself (12^{32}).

The death of Jesus was the supreme manifestation of God's *love*. It was because God loved the world that He sent Jesus to save men (3^{16}). In the events of the passion Jesus showed 'the full extent of His love' (13^1), because the greatest love is 'that a man should lay down his life for his friends' (15^{13}). He was the shepherd who gave His life for the sheep (10^{1-18}). His love for men is a pattern for the love which the disciples should show to each other, and by dwelling in His love they will themselves be able to love (15^{9-12}).

John's gospel also contains teaching about judgement. Although the purpose of Christ's coming was not to judge men but to save them, they are in fact judged by their reaction to Him. While the man who trusts in Christ does not come under judgement, 'the unbeliever has already been judged in that he has not given his allegiance to God's only Son' (3^{18}). And this present judgement will be confirmed by the future judgement, when men will rise to hear their doom (5^{29}).

(iii) *Eternal Life and Resurrection*

The life for which Jesus sets men free is eternal life, which is not only everlasting life but also the life of the Messianic age (see notes on Mk 10^{17}). It is the gift of God, who has sent His son to make it possible (3^{16-17}). Indeed Jesus Himself is described as 'life' (11^{25}, 14^{6}). In order to receive this gift of life, men must believe in Christ and obey His teaching (3^{14-16}, 8^{51}). Eternal life can be a present possession, which a man may enjoy even while mortal life continues (3^{36}). It is described as 'to know thee who alone art truly God, and Jesus Christ whom thou hast sent' (17^{3}). This knowledge is fundamentally a personal relationship based on faith. Christians dwell in Christ, and Christ dwells in them (15^{4}, 17^{23}). They are children of God, born of the Spirit (1^{12}, 3^{1-8}), and the Spirit dwells with them and in them (14^{17}). Their relationship to Christ is that of branches to a vine (15^{1-8}), and Christ is the spiritual food and drink which nourishes them (6^{22-58}). Through Christ they have access to the Father (1^{18}, 14^{6}), and dwell in the Father and the Son, as the Father and the Son dwell in each other (17^{21}).

The emphasis on eternal life as a present possession does not exclude a belief in a future resurrection (5^{29}) and the return of Jesus at the end of the world (21^{22}). These two ideas, of the present blessing of eternal life and the future blessing of the resurrection, are combined in 6^{54}: 'Whoever eats my flesh and drinks my blood possesses eternal life, and I will raise him up at the last day' (see also 6^{40}).

(iv) *The Spirit and the Trinity*

The gospel has a clearly formed theology of the Spirit. At the beginning of His ministry the Spirit came upon Jesus (1^{32-3}), but in order that the Spirit may come to others, Jesus must be crucified and rise again (7^{39}, 16^{7}). After His resurrection Jesus gave the Spirit to His disciples sending them out on their missionary task, and inaugurating a new creation (20^{22}). Individuals enter the new life by being born of the Spirit (3^{1-8}). The nature of God Himself is spirit (4^{24}), and the Spirit is the new life, the living water, within the believer (7^{37-9}).

The Spirit is described as *paraklētos* (see notes on 14^{15-26}) a word which is translated Advocate or Comforter. Neither of these translations is adequate to express the meaning of this term. The Spirit is not only an Advocate who defends the cause of Christ and His disciples, but also a prosecuting counsellor who convicts the world (16^{8-11}). The comfort which the Spirit brings is no mere palliative for suffering but the strength and encouragement which are marks of life in the new age. The word *paraklētos* also suggests that the Spirit has a function of exhortation (see notes on 14^{15-26}). The Spirit is a witness to Christ, and guides men into all truth, teaching them things which they have not heard during Christ's earthly ministry (14^{26}, 15^{26}, 16^{13}).

John's gospel comes nearer than any other part of the New Testament to formulating a doctrine of the Trinity. Christ is portrayed as the Son of God who is eternally related to His Father. The idea of His divinity is more consistently expressed in this gospel than elsewhere in the New Testament, and the term 'Word' effectively conveys the paradox that Christ is 'with God' and is also 'what God is' (1^1). The Spirit is described in terms which imply that He is personal, especially through the use of the word *paraklētos*; and the gospel is clearly aware of the problem of distinguishing the activities of Father, Son, and Spirit. In his attempt to answer this problem the evangelist develops the teaching that the Son must go away in order that He may give the Spirit to men.

(v) *The Church and Sacraments*

That the Church is the successor to the Jews as the chosen people of God is made clear by the contrast between Jesus and Moses (1^{16-17}) and between the old and new orders (2^{1-11}). Jesus is the King of the Jews ($18^{33}-19^{22}$), but His own people have rejected Him, showing that their father is not God but the devil (8^{41-7}). It is not the orthodox Jew but the disciple of Jesus who is the true Israelite (1^{47}). The Church is a union of Jews and Gentiles, for both of whom Jesus laid down His life (10^{1-18}).

The apostles are the Church's leaders, and have authority to declare or withhold the forgiveness of sins (20^{23}). Peter is related to the Church as a shepherd to his flock (21^{15-17}). Emphasis is laid on the Church's unity, which is based on the relationship of Christians to Christ. He is the vine and they are the branches (15^{1-10}). He is the shepherd and they are the sheep (10^{1-18}). The unity of the Father and the Son is the pattern for the unity of all Christians (17^{20-3}).

The Church was inaugurated when the risen Jesus gave the Spirit to His disciples (20^{21-3}). Its worship is not tied to a particular shrine but is offered in spirit and in truth (4^{19-24}). Jesus Himself, crucified and risen, is its Temple (2^{12-22}).

The gospel's sacramental teaching is for the most part allusive. Baptism is regarded as the outward aspect of spiritual rebirth (3^{1-8}). The Lord's Supper is the sacrament of spiritual communion with Christ ($6^{30-58,\ 63}$), and is alluded to in the description of Him as the bread of life and the real vine (6^{35}, 15^1). The sacraments are connected with the death of Christ (19^{34}) but have their origin in His whole ministry (see notes on 6^{52-8}).

(vi) Ethical Teaching

The gospel does not contain a large and detailed body of ethical teaching like that of the synoptics. There is no instruction about marriage, money, and the use of force. The emphasis is on the fundamental principle of Christian conduct. The religion of Jesus is founded not upon law but upon grace and truth (1^{17}), and the basic commandment is one of love (13^{34}, 15^{12-14}). The disciples ought to love one another, and the greatest love is to lay down one's life for one's friends, a love which Jesus showed supremely on the Cross. It is the proper state of Jesus's disciples that they should live in unity and harmony (17^{22-3}). Self-sacrifice and readiness to serve Jesus is the root of good conduct (12^{25-6}), and the disciples must follow their master's example of humble service (13^{15}). Because they dwell in Jesus, they will bear the fruit of dedicated lives (15^5).

Although the ethical teaching of the gospel is mainly about basic principles, there are certain practical applications of them. Jesus denounced the money-changers in the Temple for their abuse of God's house (2^{12-22}), and defended His duty to heal the sick on the Sabbath (5^{1-18}). But above all, the emphasis is on the supremacy of the Law of Love. The Christian lives under the dispensation of grace and truth. He is a child of God (1^{12-13}), who enjoys freedom because he has received the truth (8^{31-6}).

COMMENTS ON SELECTED PASSAGES FROM
JOHN I TO 12

John 1^{1-18}—The Prologue

The gospel begins, not with the story of John the Baptist or an account of the birth of Jesus, but with the assertion that the eternal Word of

God, who was incarnate in Jesus Christ, was active in the creation of the world. With its reference to light, life, and the creation, the prologue of the gospel is reminiscent of the first chapter of Genesis. The evangelist is teaching that the gospel story begins at the creation of the world, because the creation was the beginning of the Word's activity in the world.

The idea of *the Word* is very important in Jewish thought. Creation occurred by God's word (Gen $1^{3, 6}$, etc., Ps 33^6), and it was the word of God which came to the prophets (Isa 2^1, Jer 1^2, Hos 1^1, etc.). The Word stood for God's revelation of Himself to men; and the opening message of John's gospel is that in Jesus Christ the revelation was not just in words but in the man Himself. 'The Word became flesh' (verse 14).

While the basic associations of this idea were Hebrew, its use would appeal to readers who had been reared in Greek thought; 'Word' is a translation of the Greek *logos*, which was used by Stoic philosophers to describe the universal reason, the fundamental principle of the universe.

The idea is especially suitable to express the mystery of Christ's relationship to God, because in some Jewish writings the Word of God is described in terms which suggest that it is a personal being, or, as some scholars explain, 'an extension of the divine personality'. Thus the gospel can say (1^1) that the Word not only was with God, but also was 'what God was' (The Revised Version actually translates: 'the Word was God'). The first chapter begins with a statement of Christ's divinity, and the twentieth chapter, which is probably the conclusion of the original version of the gospel, reaches its climax in Thomas's confession of Jesus as 'My Lord and my God!' (Jn 20^{28}).

The idea that Christ was active in the creation of the world (verse 3) is also found in Colossians 1^{16} and Hebrews 1^2. As an agent in creation, the Word is the source of *life* (verses 3–4), not only of physical life but of eternal life (see p. 128). Indeed Jesus describes Himself as life (Jn 11^{25}, 14^6), and 'life' is one of the main themes of the gospel.

The Word is also the giver of *light* (verses 4–9). In the Old Testament God is light (Ps 27^1) giving physical light to the world (Gen 1^3) and inner light to men (Ps 43^3). Here in John's gospel the emphasis is on Jesus as the giver of the inner, spiritual light which enlightens men, bringing them knowledge of God, and showing them how to live. Jesus Himself is the light, and this light is described as the 'real light' (verse 9) by contrast with the false and deceptive light of other religions and philosophies. It is a light which the darkness of sin cannot put out (verse 5), and is intended for every man (verse 9), because Jesus Himself is the 'light of the world' (John 8^{12}, 9^5).

The rejection of Christ, which culminated in His crucifixion, is contrasted with His acceptance by those who believe in Him (verses 10–13). A distinction is made between Jesus Himself, who is *the Father's only Son* (verse 14), and His followers, who are *children of God* (verse 12). Separate Greek words are used for 'Son' and 'child', in order to show that, while Jesus Christ is eternally the Son of God, His followers are not naturally children of God but only enter this state when they believe in Christ and are born anew (see notes on Jn 3$^{1-12}$).

The climax of the prologue is the statement that *the Word became flesh* (verse 14), an assertion by which the gospel answers the misleading notion that Jesus Christ was not fully human. A heresy, known as Docetism, according to which Jesus was not truly man, was beginning to develop. There were varying forms of this heresy, one of which claimed that from the beginning to the end of His earthly life, Jesus was human only in appearance, because it would have been degrading for God to take human flesh upon Himself. Another form of the heresy said that the heavenly Christ was united with the man Jesus during His ministry, but departed from Him before His crucifixion because it would have been inconceivable for God to be put to death. For other evidence of attacks on this heresy, see John 19$^{28, 34}$, 20^{27}; Luke 24$^{36-43}$, 1 John 1^1 and p. 125.

The incarnation of the Word ('incarnation' means 'being made flesh') is said by John to be a manifestation of the glory of Christ (verse 14). *Glory* is one of the key words of this gospel, and is used especially of God's manifestation of Himself to men. Jesus shared God's glory eternally (17^5), and this glory was shown in His miracles (Jn 2^{11}, 11$^{4, 40}$). The death of Jesus is His glorification (Jn 7^{39}, 12$^{16, 23}$, 13^{31}), and His glory is given to the disciples in order that they may be united through His dwelling in them (Jn 17$^{22-3}$). For the idea of glory, see also the notes on the transfiguration (Mk 9$^{2-8}$).

Jesus is described as the giver of Grace and Truth. *Grace* is the free, undeserved love of God, through which He offers eternal life to men (see notes on Gal 2$^{15-21}$), *Truth* is a word which has a more complex meaning in John than in modern usage. It means (*a*) the truth about God, which is revealed in Jesus Christ, who Himself is the truth (Jn 14^6), and (*b*) God's faithfulness and trustworthiness. The covenant of grace and truth, established by Christ, is contrasted with the covenant of the Law, given through Moses (for a similar contrast, see 2 Cor 3^6, Gal 3^{23}–4^7).

The prologue to the gospel ends with the affirmation that Jesus

Christ is the only Son of the Father, of whom He is the unique revelation (verse 18). For the titles *Father* and *Son*, see p. 126.

The prologue's reference to the testimony of John the Baptist (verses 6–9 and 15), with its emphasis on Jesus's superiority to the Baptist (see also John 1^{30}, 3^{28-30}), may well be specially intended for those disciples of the Baptist who did not accept Jesus as the Messiah.

John 1^{19-34}—*The Testimony of John the Baptist*

According to John's gospel, the Baptist said that he was not Elijah (verse 21). But, according to the synoptic gospels, Jesus claimed that the Baptist was Elijah (see notes on Mk 9^{9-13}). It is quite possible that the Baptist thought that the Messiah himself was the Elijah prophesied in Malachi 4^5, and that Jesus corrected him.

Whereas much of John's account of the Baptist's work is paralleled in the synoptic gospels (see notes on Mk 1^{2-11}), John makes no mention of the baptism of Jesus, though he records the descent of the Spirit and the divine voice (verses 32–4).

The Baptist's saying that Jesus is the *Lamb of God* who takes away the sin of the world (verse 29; see also verse 36) combines two Jewish sacrificial ideas. According to John's gospel, Jesus was put to death at the very time when the Passover lambs were being slaughtered (Jn 19^{14}). These lambs were offered in commemoration of the deliverance of the children of Israel from Egypt. According to Exodus 12^{1-20} the lambs were sacrificed at the Exodus in order to prevent the angel of death from visiting the homes of the people. Therefore, when Jesus is likened to the Passover Lamb, He is said to be the one who brings a new Exodus, this time a release from slavery to sin and a deliverance from spiritual death.

The Passover Lamb was not thought to take away sin, but in order to express the meaning of Christ's death John had to introduce the idea of taking away sin. He probably did this under the influence of Isaiah 53^{4-12}, in which the Suffering Servant who takes away sin is compared to a lamb. It is unlikely that the gospel had in mind the daily sacrifices of lambs in the Temple (Ex 29^{38-42}), since these were not offered for sins. Though sin-offerings and guilt-offerings were not usually lambs (except for Lev 5^6), the gospel may well be linking the idea of the sin-offering with that of the Passover Lamb. For a discussion of the sin-offering, see notes on Hebrews 9^{11-15}.

Attempts have been made to link the idea of the Lamb of God with that of the triumphant lamb in the Book of Revelation (see notes on Rev

21[22]). A different Greek word for lamb, however, is used by Revelation, and, in any case, the saying in John's gospel emphasizes sacrifice rather than triumph.

John 1[35-51]—*The Call of the Disciples*

This story of the call of the disciples has several distinctive features. It states that the first of the disciples, one of whom was Andrew, were followers of John the Baptist (verses 35–9). It also says that the first act of Andrew and Philip as disciples of Jesus was to bring someone else to Him, Andrew bringing Simon, and Philip bringing Nathanael (verses 40–5). And when it places the naming of Simon as Cephas right at the beginning of Jesus's ministry (verse 42), it differs clearly from Mark 3[16] and Mt 16[18].

The story of Nathanael's call is of special interest. When Jesus described him as a true Israelite, free from deceitfulness (verse 47), He was contrasting him with Jacob, the first Israelite, who was renowned for his deceitfulness. Nathanael, as a disciple of Jesus, was a member of God's new Israel and recognized that Jesus was the king of Israel (verse 49).

In the final words of this chapter, which refer to the story of Jacob's ladder (Gen 28[12]), Jesus describes Himself as the ladder between men and God, the means by which men can have access to God (verse 51).

This section about the call of the disciples is by no means in complete agreement with the synoptic accounts, and the most marked difference is that in John's gospel Jesus is openly acknowledged from the beginning of His ministry not only as Lamb of God but also as Messiah (verse 41) and Son of God (verse 49).

John 1[46]. Nathanael's scorn for Nazareth may have been local jealousy, because he himself came from Cana (Jn 21[2]). He is not mentioned in the synoptic gospels, and the suggestion that he was the same person as Bartholomew is pure conjecture.

John 2[1-11]—*The Water and the Wine*

This story of how Jesus turned water into wine is not merely an account of a miraculous event, but also teaches a spiritual lesson. It is described as a sign (verse 11), a word which is a typical designation of a miracle in this gospel (see p. 125). As a sign, it both reveals the glory of Jesus (see verse 11 and compare Jn 1[14]) and teaches that the gospel supersedes the Jewish religion. The water in the purificatory jars symbolizes the Jewish religion, and the wine stands for the gospel. The message is that Jesus has transformed Judaism into something greater (see also Mk 2^{22} for a comparison of the gospel message to wine).

Many commentators think that this story is an exaggerated account of what really happened, and some have suggested that Jesus originally told it as a parable.

John 2^4. *My hour* refers to the crucifixion. Jesus is telling Mary that, while she is mainly concerned about the shortage of wine, His chief concern is the work of redemption, which will be achieved at the hour of His death.

John 2$^{12-22}$—*The Cleansing of the Temple*

This story is placed much earlier by John than by the synoptic gospels (see notes on Mk 11$^{15-19}$). Probably the synoptic date is correct, and John places it here because, having shown in the previous section that Jesus has transformed the Jewish religion, he wishes next to depict Him as the New Temple.

John's account also differs from the synoptic accounts in ascribing to Jesus the saying 'Destroy this temple, and in three days I will raise it again' (verse 19), a saying which may well have given rise to the charge brought against Him at His trial, that He had said He would throw down the temple and build another not made with human hands (Mk 14^{58}). If the charge is based on this saying, it is a distortion of what He actually said. He does not say that He Himself will destroy the Temple, and does not refer to the Temple in Jerusalem but to the temple of His own body. He is in fact prophesying His own death and resurrection, and claiming that He is the true temple, the centre of the true, spiritual worship.

*   *   , *

John 3$^{1-12}$—*The New Birth*

The word translated 'over again' (verses 3 and 7) can also mean 'from above', and in these sayings has both meanings. A man must be born over again, and the birth is effected from above.

This new birth is 'from water and spirit'. 'Water' refers to baptism, which was the outward sign of a spiritual birth, and in New Testament times was often the actual occasion for the gift of the Spirit (Acts 2^{38}, 19$^{5-6}$). The emphasis in this story, however, is on the Spirit rather than on baptism. The Jews had a tendency to leave everything to the coming of a future Kingdom, but Jesus is saying that inward renewal is necessary for entry into the Kingdom, and, indeed, since there is a sense in which the Kingdom is already present, a man who is inwardly renewed can enter it immediately.

The New English Bible uses the word 'spirit' with a small 's', indicating that the gospel is referring to spiritual birth by contrast with physical birth. Since there were no small letters but only capitals in the original manuscripts, the meaning ought not to be so limited. Birth 'from Spirit' is not merely birth of a spiritual nature but also birth which is initiated by the Holy Spirit. This birth is beyond understanding. Like the wind, the Spirit's activity cannot be understood by men (verse 8). But Jesus is the one who testifies to the truth of the new birth (verse 11), and, if Nicodemus cannot understand Him when He talks about earthly things (i.e. uses illustrations about birth and the wind which are taken from earthly life), he will not be able to understand heavenly things (i.e. teaching which is not put forward in pictorial form) (verse 12).

John 3². *by night*. Nicodemus came by night either because he did not want his visit to be made public or because he found it easier to converse in the evening than during the day. The words *by night* may also symbolize the spiritual darkness in which Nicodemus lived (Jn 9⁴, 13³⁰).

John 3⁸. The same Greek word *pneuma* means both *wind* and *Spirit*.

John 3¹³⁻²¹—*Faith and Eternal Life*

The theme of this section is that God because of His love for the world sent Jesus, in order that through faith in Him men should receive eternal life. Although Christ's supreme purpose was to save men and not to judge them, they are in fact judged by their rejection of Him.

Eternal life, which is both everlasting life and the life of new quality in the Messianic age (see p. 128 for a fuller discussion) is received by those who have *faith* in Christ. Having faith in Christ is not merely accepting doctrinal statements about Him but trusting in Him and yielding allegiance to Him. The noun 'faith' (Greek *pistis*) never occurs in this gospel, but the verb 'believe' (Greek *pisteuein*, which *NEB* often translates 'have faith' or 'give allegiance') occurs many times.

The emphasis on God's love for the world (verse 16) shows both that God took the initiative in saving men and that His love extended to all the human race. *Love* is a sacrificial love, not a desiring love (see notes on Mk 12²⁸⁻³⁴), and in 1 John 4⁸ the statement is made that 'God is love'.

Both eternal life and judgement can be received immediately. If men have faith in Christ, they receive eternal life, and if they reject Him, they receive judgement (verse 18; see also Jn 3³⁶).

Jesus's work of salvation is illustrated from the story of the brazen serpent which Moses lifted up when the children of Israel had been bitten by fiery serpents because of their failure to trust in God (Num 21^{4-9}). Those who looked at the brazen serpent were healed of their wounds and lived; and Jesus must be lifted up on the Cross in order that men may receive eternal life (verses 14–15).

*   *   *

John 4^{1-42}—*The Woman of Samaria, the Living Water, and the Real Worship*

Luke tells of Jesus's sympathy for the despised Samaritans (Lk 9^{52-6}, 10^{29-37}, 17^{11-19}), and here John records an incident which illustrates Jesus's friendship for them. The story has two great themes:

(i) *Living Water* (verses 10–15). In the Old Testament 'living water' stands for God's activity in giving men new life. He is the 'fountain of living waters' (Jer 2^{13}), and at the last day 'living waters shall flow out from Jerusalem' (Zech 14^8). In John's gospel 'living water' stands for the Spirit (see Jn 7^{37-9}), who supplies all a man's spiritual needs and gives him eternal life.

(ii) *Real Worship* (verses 19–26). The Samaritans believed that the special place for the worship of God was Mount Gerizim in Samaria, while the Jews believed that it was the Temple in Jerusalem. Jesus says, however, that the mark of real worship will not be its association with a particular shrine but its offering in spirit and in truth. It is worship in spirit, because God is spirit (verse 24), and because worship of Him must be a spiritual act; it is also worship in spirit because it is guided by the Holy Spirit. It is worship in truth, because it is sincere, and because it is offered by those who dwell in Christ, who is Himself truth (Jn 14^6; for 'truth' see also notes on Jn 1^{14}). This real worship is possible only when the time has arrived (verse 23). 'The time' refers to the coming of the Messiah, as the woman perceives (verse 25), but in John's gospel it refers especially to the crucifixion (12^{23}, 13^1, where the same word is translated 'hour'). Hence the time has now arrived in so far as Jesus's ministry has already begun, but it is only approaching in so far as He is not yet crucified (verse 23).

The final part of this story includes some words spoken by Jesus to His disciples. First, he says that the very work which He does for God provides Him with spiritual nourishment (verses 31–4). Then He tells His disciples that there is a harvest of people ready to receive eternal life, and it is their task as apostles to gather this harvest, which others, presumably Jesus together with the Baptist and the Old Testament writers, have sown (verses 35–8; compare Lk 10^2).

*   *   *

John 6^{22-51}—*The Bread of Life*

This section follows the account of two miracles, the Feeding of the Five Thousand and the Walking on the Water, both of which are recorded by the synoptic gospels (Mk 6^{34-52}). John's gospel contrasts the people's readiness to receive the loaves with their reluctance to accept the spiritual message about the bread of life.

When Jesus says, 'I am the bread of life' (verses 35, 41, 48, 51), the words 'I am' imply that He is divine, since in Exodus 3^{14} the name of God is 'I am'. In similar sayings in this gospel Jesus says that He is the light of the world (8^{12}), the door of the sheepfold ($10^{7, 9}$), the good shepherd ($10^{11, 14}$), the resurrection and life (11^{25}), the way, the truth, and life (14^6), and the real vine ($15^{1, 5}$). Most striking of all is 8^{58}, 'Before Abraham was born, I am', a saying which implies that Christ exists eternally.

The manna or bread which God gave the children of Israel in the desert (Ex 16^{1-36}) is contrasted with Jesus who is 'the real bread from heaven'. The manna did not prevent the Israelites from ultimately dying a physical death; but the real bread will enable men to have eternal life (verses 30–4, 47–51). This real bread can be received by coming to Jesus and believing in Him (verse 35). Those who do this, will have eternal life now, and be raised up in the final resurrection (verses 39–40).

The description of Jesus as the bread of life may also mean that He is the spiritual food symbolized by the bread in the Lord's Supper (see notes on Jn 6^{52-8}, 15^{1-17}).

John 6^{52-8}—*The Flesh and the Blood*

In verse 51 there was a transition from the idea of bread to that of the flesh; and in this section Jesus speaks of His own flesh and blood as food and drink which give men eternal life and assure them of resurrection at the last day. Behind these ideas are three main lines of thought.

(i) *The crucifixion.* The flesh and the blood refer to the flesh which was torn and the blood which was shed on the Cross.

(ii) *The Lord's Supper.* This gospel has no record of the institution of the Lord's Supper, and the presence of teaching which appears to be sacramental at this stage of the gospel is evidence that John wished to relate the sacrament to the whole of Christ's incarnate life and not merely to His death. The description of Jesus's body and blood as food and drink has a clear sacramental ring about it (see notes on Mk 14$^{12-25}$).

(iii) *The disciples' share in the life of Christ*. Those who eat His flesh and drink His blood (verses 53–6) are the disciples, who outwardly participate in the sacrament and inwardly live their whole lives in the power of Christ. They dwell in Him, and He dwells in them.

John 6$^{59-71}$—*The Reaction of the Disciples*

The chapter ends with a description of the reaction of Jesus's disciples to His teaching. The Feeding of the Five Thousand had won Him great support, but, when He taught that it was the Spirit and not material food which gives life (verse 63), some of His disciples were so unprepared for the challenge of His message that they left Him. The story reaches its climax in the words of Peter (verse 68), who acknowledges that he has nowhere to turn but to Jesus and His message of eternal life.

*   *   *

John 9$^{1-41}$—*The Blind Man and the Light of the World*

This account of the healing of a blind man, of the incredulous reaction of his neighbours, and of the censorious attitude of the Pharisees, is rich in ideas.

(i) *The meaning of suffering*. The Jews believed that disease and deformity were the result of sin, but Jesus said that the man's blindness was not caused by his own or his parents' sin; its purpose was to show God's power to cure him (verse 3). Jesus's words seem to imply that God deliberately made the man blind in order to show His power, but they can also be translated, 'he was born blind, with the result that God's power might be displayed in curing him', a translation which would eliminate the idea that God had predestined the man to be blind. In the synoptic account of the healing of a paralysed man (Mk 2$^{1-12}$) Jesus links disease with sin; this is consistent with John 9^3, which does not rule out the possibility that disease and sin are sometimes connected with each other.

(ii) *Day and Night*. When Jesus is active as the light of the world, it is spiritual day. But when He is arrested and crucified, it will be spiritual night (verses 4–5). For the theological use of the word 'night', see also John 3^2, 13^{30}.

(iii) *The Light of the World*. The healing of the man's physical blindness is symbolical of Jesus's power to heal the spiritual blindness of sinners. Jesus is the light of the world (see notes on Jn 1⁴), but not everyone accepts that light. He has in fact come 'to give sight to the sightless and to make blind those who see' (verse 39); in other words He gives the light of eternal life to those who admit their spiritual blindness, but reveals the inner darkness of those who, like the Pharisees, think they have enough spiritual insight already.

(iv) *The effectiveness of Jesus.* The story makes a contrast between Jesus, who heals the blind man on the Sabbath day, and the Pharisees, who criticize His action but are themselves unable to perform works of healing. In the midst of their censorious questioning the blind man testifies to the effectiveness of Jesus: 'All I know is this: once I was blind, now I can see' (verse 25).

John 9⁵. *I am the light of the world* is not one of the 'I am' sayings (see notes on Jn 6²²⁻⁵¹), because the Greek does not have the emphatic 'I', A similar saying in John 8¹², however, is an 'I am' saying.

*   *   *

John 10¹⁻¹⁸—*The Door and the Good Shepherd*

In this discourse the work of Jesus is illustrated from the life of a shepherd and his sheep. The interpretation of the story is divided into two parts, in the first of which Jesus is described as the door of the sheepfold, and in the second of which He is described as the shepherd.

(i) *The Door of the Sheepfold* (verses 7–9). This 'I am' saying (verses 7 and 9; see notes on Jn 6²²⁻⁵¹) means that Jesus is the one through whom men have access to eternal life (compare Jn 14⁶).

(ii) *The Good Shepherd* (verses 10–18). The shepherd was a familiar sight in Palestine, and sometimes the leaders of the nation were called shepherds. The title was used for the Messiah (Ezk 34²³) and even for God Himself (Ps 23¹). In the synoptic gospels Jesus tells a parable about a shepherd who went to find a lost sheep (Lk 15³⁻⁷). It is not surprising, therefore, that He should be explicitly called a shepherd in John 10, and that the title should be used of Him also in Hebrews 13²⁰ and 1 Peter 2²⁵. The idea that the followers of Christ are His sheep is found in Luke 12³² and Mark 14²⁷.

The theme of this section is stated in an 'I am' saying (see notes on Jn 6²²⁻⁵¹), in which Jesus calls Himself the good shepherd who lays down His life for the sheep (verse 11: see also verse 14). Ideas which emerge in the allegory are:

The Shepherd's care for the sheep. Jesus knows each of His followers by name (verses 3–4, 14), and is even ready to die for them (verses 11, 15, 17–18). His purpose is to give them life 'in all its fullness' (verse 10).

The sheep's knowledge of the Shepherd. The followers of Jesus know Him (verse 14) not just with the knowledge of passing acquaintance but with the intimate knowledge shared by those who love each other, like the knowledge shared by the Father and the Son (verse 15).

The unity of the sheep. Jesus's disciples will not be limited to the Jewish nation ('this fold', verse 16). There are others, from outside Judaism, who will join the Church and be united under one shepherd.

The meaning of the Shepherd's death. Jesus gives His life of His own free will and in obedience to the Father (verse 18); and He gives it in the assurance that He will overcome death (verses 17–18). The purpose of His coming, and therefore also of His death, is to give men eternal life (verse 10), and to unite them in one Church (verses 14–16).

John 10⁶. *parable*. The Greek word is different from that which is translated *parable* in the synoptic gospels. The story of the door and the sheep is greatly different from the synoptic parables but is not a pure allegory, though it has a great deal of allegory in it.

* * *

John 11¹⁻⁴⁴—*The Raising of Lazarus: Resurrection and Life*

It is no coincidence that the two chapters which immediately precede the story of Jesus's last visit to Jerusalem foreshadow the final events of His earthly life. Chapter 10 points forward to His death, and Chapter 11 to His resurrection.

Like other miracles in this gospel, the story of the raising of Lazarus has a theological lesson, which is contained in Jesus's saying, 'I am the resurrection and I am life' (verse 25). In its immediate context this 'I am' saying (see notes on Jn 6²²⁻⁵¹) means that Jesus can at once restore Lazarus's life without waiting for the resurrection at the last day. Its deeper meaning is that Jesus, who Himself is to be raised from the dead, is the source of resurrection and life. All those who have faith in Him participate here and now in eternal life without having to wait for the last day.

The story also makes the point that the purpose of Lazarus's sickness is to reveal the glory of God (verse 4), an idea similar to that found in John 9³. For 'glory', see notes on John 1¹⁴.

This miracle is described in more precise detail than any similar synoptic stories, and many scholars believe that the narrative must have been considerably elaborated by the evangelist. It has been suggested that the story has its origin in a parable such as that of the Rich Man and Lazarus (Lk 16[19–31]), but it is quite likely that a real incident is behind it, though it has obviously been subjected to editing and interpretation. For another story of the raising of the dead, see Luke 7[11–17].

*   *   *

John 12[20–36]—The Greeks

This incident, which is taken from the account of Jesus's last visit to Jerusalem, shows that Jesus is not to be revealed to Gentiles until after His resurrection. The Greeks who asked Philip if they could see Jesus, had sufficient sympathy for the Jewish religion to have come to Jerusalem for the Passover, even though they were allowed to share in the feast only to a limited extent. Jesus's reply to Philip and Andrew implies that the Greeks would not yet be able to see Him; and there is no record that they did. The grain of wheat had to die in order to bear its rich harvest (verse 24), and Jesus had to be lifted up on the Cross before He could draw all men to Him (verse 32). But although the Greeks were denied their immediate request, it was of men like them that the risen Jesus said : 'Happy are they who never saw me and yet have found faith' (Jn 20[29]).

Much of the material in this section is similar to synoptic sayings. The reference to the grain of wheat (verse 24) recalls the parables about seed and sowing (Mk 4[3–9, 26–32]), and the sayings about self-sacrifice and service (verses 25–6) are almost the same as those in Mark 8[34–7]. The account of Jesus's inner turmoil (verse 27) is like that of His agony and prayer in Gethsemane (Mk 14[32 ff]), though John places Jesus's prayer in a different setting from Gethsemane.

The description of Jesus's death as *glorification* (verses 23, 27–8) and *lifting up* (verse 32) uses ideas found in the song of the Suffering Servant, who is to be 'exalted and lifted up' (Isa 52[13]). These terms are used by John to describe the crucifixion, but they also suggest the resurrection, both these events being regarded by John as a unity (see also Jn 3[14–15]). The moment of His death and resurrection is called *the hour* (verses 23, 27, 31 ; see also Jn 2[4], 4[21, 23], 13[1],17[1]), because it is the crucial moment in history and also the fulfilment of prophecy. His death is a victory over the devil, 'the Prince of this world' (verse 31 ; see also Jn 14[30], 16[11]), and gives men the possibility of freedom from the power of sin. It is also a time of judgement for the world (verse 31), and Jews are exhorted to seize the opportunity to trust in Jesus, before it is too late (verses 35–6). After His death the message will go to the Gentiles. It is not just for Jews but for all men that He will die (verse 32).

John 12^{24}. See also 1 Corinthians 15$^{36-8}$.

John 12^{27}. *Now my soul is in turmoil.* This is very close to the Greek version of Psalm 55^4.

John 12$^{35-6}$. The idea that a Christian is a man of light is found also in Matthew 5^{14}, 1 Thessalonians 5^5, Ephesians 5^8.

QUESTIONS

(1) Expound the prologue to John's gospel.

(2) What does John's gospel teach about eternal life?

(3) Explain the teaching about the Door of the Sheepfold and the Good Shepherd in John 10$^{1-18}$.

(4) Comment on : John 1^{29}, 2$^{9-11}$, 4^{24}, 6^{54}, 9^5, 12$^{31-2}$.

CHAPTER SEVEN

THE GOSPEL ACCORDING TO ST JOHN
(CHAPTERS 13 TO 21)
AND THE LETTERS OF ST JOHN

COMMENTS ON SELECTED PASSAGES FROM
JOHN 13 TO 21

John 13$^{1-20}$—*The Washing of the Disciples' Feet*

THE GOSPEL'S story of the Last Supper differs considerably from the synoptic accounts. Although it does not mention the institution of the sacrament of the Lord's Supper, it contains much more of the teaching at the Supper than do the synoptics. And it is the only gospel which records the washing of the disciples' feet, a story which has several important themes.

(i) *The humility of Jesus and His readiness to serve others.* Although the menial task of washing feet was undertaken by children for their parents and by disciples for a rabbi, Jesus insisted on reversing the normal order of things by washing the feet of His disciples. The story is a vivid illustration of Jesus's work as a Servant (see notes on Mk 10^{45} and compare Lk 22^{27}).

(ii) *The cleansing power of Jesus.* The washing of feet was a sign that Jesus could make men inwardly clean. This is the underlying meaning of verse 10, 'A man who has bathed needs no further washing; he is altogether clean', a saying which may allude also to the meaning of baptism.

(iii) *The fellowship between Jesus and His disciples.* Jesus's action shows His close relationship with His disciples (see verse 8), which is established by His sacrificial service and by His power to cleanse men's souls.

(iv) *The example of Jesus.* Jesus was setting an example to His disciples to serve each other (verses 12–17), and, in so far as they followed it, they were His faithful messengers (verses 16 and 20).

(v) *Not everyone accepts the benefits which Jesus offers.* Throughout this story we are reminded of the presence of the traitor, Judas Iscariot (verses 2, 10, 18). The cleansing power of Jesus is of no avail to the misguided man who sets his heart against Him.

John 13^1. *his hour.* See notes on John 12$^{20-36}$.
John 13^{18} quotes from Psalm 41^9.

* * *

John 13$^{31-8}$—*Introduction to the Farewell Discourses*

This introductory paragraph to the great discourses of 13^{31}–17^{26} speaks of the glorification of the Son of Man (see notes on Jn 12$^{20-36}$), the commandment to love one another (which is parallel to the commandment to love one's neighbour; see notes on Mk 12$^{28-34}$), and the prophecy of Peter's denial (see also Mk 14$^{29-31}$).

John 14$^{1-14}$—*The Way, the Truth, and Life*

Jesus tells His disciples that eternal dwelling-places await them, and that He must die in order to prepare the way for them. He is indeed Himself the Way to God (compare Jn 1^{51}, 10$^{7-9}$). He is also the Truth, because He reveals the truth about God and is the unique manifestation of God's faithfulness to men (see Jn 1^{17} and p. 132). And He is Life (see Jn 1$^{3-5}$, 11^{25} and p. 128), because He is the giver of eternal life (verses 1–6).

The rest of the section (verses 7–14) develops the theme of Jesus as the revelation of the Father, and ends with a promise that prayer in Jesus's name will be answered (see also notes on Mt 7$^{7-11}$).

John 14^2. *many dwelling-places.* Some scholars claim that this refers to temporary resting-places on a journey, and implies that there is progress in heaven. But the saying is unlikely to mean this.

John 14^6 is one of the 'I am' sayings (see notes on Jn 6$^{22-51}$).

John 14$^{15-26}$—*The Spirit*

One of the main themes of the farewell discourses is that Jesus must go away in order to send the Holy Spirit, who is described in Greek as *paraklētos* (verses 15 and 26; see also Jn 15^{26}, 16^7), which can be translated 'Advocate' or 'Comforter', and probably has both meanings in this discourse. 'Advocate' is the normal translation of the Greek, but the word is used here in a general sense to describe the function of the Spirit, not only as a defending counsel but also, according to John 16$^{7-11}$, as a prosecuting counsel. The idea that the Spirit is the counsel who pleads for men and women before God, is not clearly present in John's gospel. The advocacy which the Spirit exercises is His witness to Christ in defending the cause of Christ and enabling the disciples to make their testimony (Jn 15$^{26-7}$). The Spirit's work as a prosecuting counsel is to convict the world of its sin in rejecting Christ (Jn 16$^{7-11}$).

The Spirit is the Comforter in so far as He brings men both consolation and encouragement; to comfort is to strengthen as well as to console. And because the Messianic age was supposed to be a time of consolation, the word 'Comforter' implies that the Spirit is bringing the blessings of that time.

The use of the word *paraklētos* also suggests that the Spirit is the Spirit of exhortation, by whom the truth about Christ is communicated to the disciples and by whom they themselves are enabled to proclaim God's truth to others. Indeed the Spirit is called the Spirit of truth (14^{27}, 15^{26}, 16^{13}), whose function is to bear witness to Christ (15^{26}), to remind men of the teaching of Jesus (14^{26}), and to give them further instruction (16$^{12-15}$) (for the meaning of 'truth' see p. 132 and also Jn 1^{17}, 14^{6}).

The Spirit will come to the followers of Jesus and will dwell with them and in them (verses 15–20). This does not mean that the Spirit is the same as the risen Christ. The description of the Spirit as 'another' is evidence that there is a distinction between them, and that Jesus Himself is also a *paraklētos*, as indeed He is described in 1 John 2^{1}. Jesus goes away in order that the Spirit may come, but it is Jesus who returns at His resurrection to give men the Spirit (verse 18), an event which is recorded in John 20^{22}.

The description of the Spirit as *paraklētos* implies that the Spirit is a person, as do also the references to the Spirit as one who guides, witnesses, and convicts (15^{26}, 16$^{7-15}$).

John 14$^{27-31}$—*Peace and Victory*

'Peace be with you' was the usual Jewish form of greeting and farewell, but the peace which Jesus gives His disciples is more than a formal act of farewell (verse 27). It is the underlying peace which comes to those who trust in God and have received forgiveness. It is the peace which Christ Himself wins for men by His self-offering (see also Jn 20^{19} and Gal 1^{3}).

The gospel regards the crucifixion as the occasion of Christ's decisive victory over the Prince of this world, the devil (verses 30–1; see also Jn 12^{31}, 16^{11}). Because Jesus has lived a sinless life, the devil has no rights over Him and cannot overcome Him.

John 15$^{1-17}$—*The Real Vine*

This allegorical picture of Jesus as the vine, His Father as the gardener, and His followers as the branches, is full of teaching about the inner life of Christians and the corporate life of the Church.

(i) *The Real Vine and the Church.* The vine was regarded as a symbol of the nation Israel. In Jeremiah God says to the nation, 'Yet I planted you a choice vine (literally, 'a vine of truth')' (Jer 2^{21}). But, as Jeremiah points out, the vine had turned degenerate. The Christian Church is the new Israel, and draws its life from Christ, who is called the real or true vine.

The saying 'I am the real vine' is one of the 'I am' sayings discussed in the notes on John 6$^{22-51}$.

(ii) *The Real Vine and the Lord's Supper.* These words about the vine have their setting at the Last Supper, and there is an obvious allusion to the wine which was used at the meal. Just as Jesus is the bread of life (Jn 6^{35}, etc.), so He is the real vine. He is Himself the spiritual bread and wine which give men eternal life.

(iii) *The Barren and Fruitful Branches.* The barren branches which are cut off (verse 6) refer both to the Jewish nation, which failed to fulfil its function as God's people, and also to any followers of Jesus who break away from Him. The fruitful branches (verses 2 and 5) are the faithful Christians. Just as fruitful branches have already been pruned, so these men have already been inwardly cleansed by Christ. They are united with Him, dwell with Him, and draw their life from Him. The fruit which they bear is a life based on the commandment of love, a life dedicated to the service of others and used to bring others into communion with Christ.

(iv) *The Greatest Love.* The greatest love is to lay down one's life for one's friends (verse 13). In this way Jesus Himself has shown His love for men. It is the supreme fulfilment of the command to love one another (verse 12; see Mk 12$^{28-34}$, Jn 13^{34}). The self-offering of Christ makes it possible for men to dwell in Christ's love; they have a fellowship of love with Christ and are empowered to exercise a Christ-like love to each other. Jesus showed His love by choosing the disciples to be His friends and to perform their apostolic mission. The relationship was initiated not by the disciples but by Jesus Himself, who chose them (verses 14–16).

John 15^{18}–16^{15}—*The Spirit and Persecution*

Jesus warns the disciples that they will be persecuted, and assures them that the Spirit will be present with them. For the description of the Spirit as *parakletos* and Spirit of truth, see notes on John 14$^{15-26}$. In this section the Spirit's function as a witness is emphasized. The Spirit performs His witness by testifying inwardly to the disciples, and through the disciples to others (15$^{26-7}$). Although the link between the Spirit's witness and the disciples' witness is not made explicit, it is in fact through the guidance of the Spirit that the disciples are able to bear witness to Christ (see 16^{13}).

Another feature of this section is its account of the Spirit as a prosecuting counsel who confutes and convicts the world because of its rejection of Jesus, and who by doing so convinces men that Jesus is right and that the devil is condemned (16$^{7-11}$).

An important paragraph (16$^{12-15}$) predicts that under the guidance of the Spirit the followers of Jesus will be led to understand more about the truth than they did before. God does not guide men only through the teaching of Jesus and the written words of the scriptures but through the preaching and teaching of the Church and through the religious experience of individuals.

The theme that Jesus must go away and return in order to send the Spirit is found in 15^{26} and 16^{7}.

The statement that men have no longer any excuse for their sin, once they have been confronted with Christ (15$^{22-5}$), may be compared with John 3$^{18-21}$ and 3^{36}.

John 15^{25} quotes from Psalm 35^{19}.

John 16$^{8-11}$. The same Greek word is here given three different translations, *confute, convict,* and *convince.* It is a word which includes all these ideas, and *NEB* gives the best rendering of the passage. It is also possible, however, to translate *convince* in each case. Then the *parakletos* would not be regarded as a prosecuting counsel but as the defending counsel who convinces men of the truth of Christ's cause.

John 16$^{16-33}$—*The Future: Joy and Peace*

This assurance of Jesus to His disciples, that He will not long be absent from them, but will return again, points forward to His death and resurrection. Two main themes of this section are *joy* and *peace.* When Jesus returns, His disciples' grief will be transformed into joy, just as a woman forgets the pains of labour because of joy at her child's birth.

Through Jesus, who has overcome the world and all the evil in it, His disciples are able to have an inner peace in the midst of persecution. For the meaning of 'peace', see notes on John 14$^{27-31}$.

John 16$^{25-30}$. A contrast is made between *figures of speech* like verse 21 and the plain prediction of Jesus's future in verse 28.

John 16^{32}. For the scattering of the disciples, see also Mark 14^{27}.

John 16^{33}. In this verse *the world* is regarded as something evil to be overcome. Sometimes, however, the gospel regards the world as capable of being saved (for example, 3^{16}), but in this latter sense the world refers to the human race.

John 17$^{1-26}$—*The Prayer of Jesus*

The climax of the farewell discourse is Jesus's great prayer, which sums up much of the teaching of the earlier chapters of the discourse. It has often been claimed that this prayer depicts Jesus as the great High Priest praying for Himself and His people, but the evidence for this view is slight. The prayer is divided into three main sections.

(i) *A Prayer for Himself* (verses 1–5). When Jesus prays that God will glorify Him, He is referring to His crucifixion and probably also His resurrection. Included in this prayer is an important definition of eternal life as the knowledge of God and Jesus Christ (verse 3), a knowledge which is not so much a theoretical understanding as a personal relationship of love and trust (see p. 128). The passage also gives an insight into the gospel's teaching about the glory of Christ. In one sense He shares this glory eternally with the Father, but in another sense He will be glorified on the Cross and in the resurrection, because these events will show the true nature and power of His glory (verse 5 ; see notes on Jn 1^{14}).

(ii) *A Prayer for His Disciples* (verses 6–19). This section emphasizes that it is the Father who has chosen the disciples and given them to the Son (verses 6–10). The prayer for unity among the disciples (verse 11) shows that the unity of Christians ought to be as close as that of the Father and the Son. Because the disciples have a mission to the world, Jesus does not pray that they should be kept safe from the world but rather that they should be kept safe from the devil (verses 13–19). The reference to Jesus's consecration of Himself (verse 19) indicates that He is speaking of His death.

(iii) *A Prayer for All Disciples, Present and Future* (verses 20–6). The prayer is extended to cover all men and women in every age who put their trust in Christ. As in verse 11, the unity of the disciples is likened to the unity of the Father and the Son, but the additional point is made that they can have unity because they receive Christ's glory and dwell in Him as He dwells in them (verses 20–3). The prayer that the disciples may behold Jesus's glory and always be with Him, refers both to their communion with Him during their earthly life and to their final and eternal relationship to Him in the future.

John 17[12] refers to the fate of Judas Iscariot, and may see in it the fulfilment of Psalm 41[9].

John 17[14]. The idea that Christians are strangers in the world is also found in Philippians 3[20], Hebrews 11[13–16], James 1[1], 1 Peter 1[1], 2[11].

*　　*　　*

John 18[33]–19[37]—*The Passion and Death of Jesus*

In broad outline, John's account of these events (18[1]–19[42]) is similar to Mark's, but the sayings and many of the details are considerably different. This section of John's account will not be discussed paragraph by paragraph, but some of his special emphases will be mentioned.

(i) *The Indifference of Pilate.* Although John's gospel states that Pilate did not believe Jesus to be guilty of any crime (18[38], 19[4, 6, 12]), it also portrays him as a governor who was unprincipled and disillusioned. His lack of standards is shown by his cynical cry, 'What is truth?' (18[38]). It was to satisfy the Jews and not to maintain justice that he allowed Jesus to be crucified (19[16]).

(ii) *The Kingship of Jesus.* John's emphasis on the kingship of Jesus is consistent with his account of the crucifixion as the time of Jesus's glorification and exaltation. It was with claiming to be King of the Jews that Jesus was charged (18[33, 37]), and it was as King of the Jews that He was mocked by the soldiers (19[3]). When Pilate presented Him to the Jews, he said, 'Here is your king' (19[14]); and the inscription on the Cross, which Pilate refused to alter, was 'Jesus of Nazareth King of the Jews' (19[19–22]). This theme is present in the passion narratives of the other gospels, but John gives it special emphasis, implying that, whether the Jews liked it or not, Jesus was their king, and that His kingship could not be adequately accounted for by political ideas. The nature of His kingship is expressed in His words to Pilate : 'My kingdom does not belong to this world' (18[36]).

(iii) *Jesus, the Man.* When Pilate said, 'Behold the Man!' (19[5]), he was probably supposed to have spoken partly in scorn and partly in sorrow, but the words have a meaning which Pilate could never have intended. Jesus was the perfect man, a man of flesh and blood, experiencing human pain and death, and yet maintaining perfect obedience to God. He was also the heavenly Son of Man who had come to save the world.

(iv) *The Words of Jesus on the Cross.* Three sayings of Jesus on the Cross are recorded in this gospel, and none of them occurs in the synoptic gospels.

(a) 'Mother, there is your son.... There is your mother' (19^{27}). Jesus shows His concern for His mother even while He is being crucified, and commends her to the care of John, the beloved disciple.

(b) 'I thirst' (19^{28}). This is evidence of Jesus's natural human reaction to suffering. See Psalm 69^{21}.

(c) 'It is accomplished' (19^{30}). These words affirm that in His death Jesus's work on earth has been completed.

(v) *The Blood and the Water.* The comment that blood and water flowed from the side of Jesus's body (19^{34}) emphasizes the reality of His death—in answer to heretical teaching. John understands the incident as a fulfilment of Zechariah 12^{10}(19^{37}). He also regards it as symbolical: (a) The blood of Christ represents His life-giving power for men (see Jn $6^{53\,ff}$, and Lev 17^{14}), and the water stands for the Holy Spirit, who can purify the souls of men (see Jn 7^{38-9}). It was through His death that Jesus was able to give men life, sending the Spirit upon them. (b) The blood and the water have a sacramental meaning, the blood recalling the wine of the Lord's Supper, and the water recalling the water of baptism. Both sacraments point to the death of Jesus and derive their power from His self-offering on the Cross.

(vi) *The Date of the Crucifixion.* John's gospel dates the crucifixion to the afternoon of 14 Nisan when the Passover Lambs were being sacrificed (13^1, 18^{28}, $19^{14,\,31}$). The theological implication is that Jesus is the new Passover Lamb who delivers men from death and sin, rescuing them from captivity to the devil (see also Jn 1^{29}). For the conflict with the synoptic gospels about the date, see notes on Mark 14^{12-25}.

*   *   *

John 20^{1-9}—*The Empty Tomb*

John's story of the empty tomb follows a different pattern from the synoptic accounts. Mary of Magdala is said by John to have discovered the empty tomb on her own, and afterwards to have fetched Peter and 'the other disciple', presumably John, who confirmed the truth of her discovery.

The rest of John's resurrection narratives are not found in the synoptics, with the exception of the story of the Haul of Fishes which is similar to a narrative in Luke, who assigns it to the earlier part of Jesus's ministry.

John 20$^{10-18}$—*The Appearance of Jesus to Mary of Magdala*

There are two features of special interest in this story. The first is that Mary did not recognize the risen Jesus until He called her by name (verse 16; compare Jn 10^3). The second is that He said to her, 'Do not cling to me, for I have not yet ascended to the Father' (verse 17). This means that she must prepare herself for a new and spiritual relationship with Him after His ascension, when she would no longer perceive Him with her physical senses.

Luke records that Mary of Magdala had at one time been possessed with devils (Lk 8$^{2-3}$). She should not be confused with Mary of Bethany, the sister of Martha and Lazarus.

John 20$^{19-23}$—*The Appearance of Jesus to His Disciples*

Jesus's words to the disciples, 'Peace be with you!' (verses 19 and 21), were the usual Jewish form of greeting. They now acquired a special meaning, not just because Jesus's appearance quieted the disciples' fear of the Jews but because He had won for them peace with God (see also Jn 14^{27}, 16^{33}).

Like Luke and Matthew (Lk 24$^{46-9}$, Mt 28$^{16-20}$), John records the commissioning of the disciples by Jesus for their missionary work (verses 21–3). He describes it as the occasion when the disciples received the Spirit. Just as God breathed into man's nostrils the breath of life at the first creation (Gen 2^7), so Jesus breathed the Spirit into the men of the new creation. This gift of the Spirit was prophesied by the Baptist (Jn 1^{33}) and could only come after the death and resurrection of Jesus (Jn 7^{39}, 16^{17}).

Although the Acts dates the gift of the Spirit seven weeks later (Acts 2$^{1-4}$), there is no essential disagreement between the Acts and John. While John understands that the Spirit must have been active in the disciples from the very day of Jesus's resurrection, the Acts is concerned to show that at Pentecost the Spirit first led the disciples to go out and preach.

John also records that, when Jesus gave His disciples the Spirit, He authorized them to grant and withhold the forgiveness of sins (verse 23). Roman Catholics claim this as authority for the absolution of sins by priests (see also notes on Mt 16^{19}), but most Protestants regard it as a commission to proclaim forgiveness for the penitent and the impossibility of forgiveness for the impenitent.

John 20²⁴⁻³¹—*The Appearance of Jesus to Thomas*

This story is an answer to critics who claimed that Jesus had not really risen from the dead, and that it was only a phantom appearance which the disciples experienced.

The incident shows that even one of the original disciples could have doubts (for other evidence of Thomas's sceptical nature, see Jn 14⁵). The climax of the gospel, the original version of which probably ended with Chapter 20, is Thomas's acknowledgement of Jesus as Lord and God.

The saying of Jesus in verse 29 recognizes that future generations will be related to Him by faith and not by sight. This theme is elaborated in verses 30–1, in which the purpose of the gospel is summarized. For the meaning of 'signs', see p. 125.

John 21¹⁻¹⁴—*The Haul of Fish*

This narrative, which is similar to Luke 5¹⁻¹¹, shows the difference in character between Peter, who was the first to take action, and John, who was the first to recognize Jesus (verse 7). It also records that the disciples shared a meal with Jesus, an act which suggests an early form of the Lord's Supper, and which also emphasizes that Jesus really rose from the dead. The reference to 153 fish (verse 11) is perplexing, but probably indicates that every kind of fish was caught, and symbolizes the Church's ministry to the whole world (compare Mt 13⁴⁷⁻⁵⁰).

John 21¹⁵⁻²⁵—*Peter and John*

Like the previous incident, Jesus's conversation with Peter stresses the pre-eminence of Peter and John amongst the disciples. Three times Peter affirms His love for Jesus, and three times he is commissioned as a shepherd of the Christian flock, probably because he has denied Jesus three times. His death is predicted in language which suggests that he will be crucified (verses 18–19), a fate which, according to an ancient tradition, he met during Nero's persecution of Christians (AD 64).

The allusion to the beloved disciple John (verses 20–3) implies that a belief had arisen that John would never die. The gospel says, however, that it is not known whether John will live until the return of Jesus or not.

The final return of Jesus is not mentioned elsewhere in the gospel, but there are references to the resurrection and the last day (Jn 5^{28-9}, $6^{39-40, 44, 54}$).

For the importance of verse 24 see p. 124.

*　　　*　　　*

THE LETTERS OF ST JOHN

INTRODUCTION

Authorship and Date

None of the three letters of John in the New Testament actually claims to have been written by him, but all of them have been traditionally ascribed to him. Their teaching and literary style is similar to that of John's gospel, but the existence of important differences has led many scholars to believe that the author of the letters was not the same man as the author of the gospel. If he was not the evangelist, he clearly belonged to the same school of thought, and, like him, was probably a disciple of John the son of Zebedee.

The first letter of John makes no mention of its author's name, but the second and third letters claim to have been written by 'the elder', and this may be a reference to John the Elder (see p. 123). The letters seem to have been written about the end of the first century A D, either a few years after or a few years before the gospel.

The Purpose of the Letters

(i) The first letter is not addressed to a single church but to a group of churches, which were probably situated round Ephesus and were under the writer's authority. The letter was written to instruct its readers in some of the great themes of the gospel, but its immediate occasion was the rise of heretical teaching in the churches. False prophets had arisen, who claimed to be sinless, denied the reality of Christ's incarnation, and by their spirit of dissension flouted the law of love.

(ii) The second letter had a similar purpose to the first, but was addressed to one church only. 'The Lady chosen by God, and her children' (2 Jn 1) means the church and its members (see also 1 Pet 5^{13} for the description of a church as a woman). The writer's concern was to warn the church against heretics who taught that Jesus had not come in the flesh, and to remind its members of their duty to keep the commandment of love (2 Jn 5–8).

(iii) The third letter was written because the writer's authority over a particular church had been challenged. Diotrephes, one of the members of the church, had made false accusations against him and had tried to prevent the church from receiving some of his friends. He wrote this letter to Gaius, another member of the church, asking him to care for his friends and to remain loyal to him. The letter was sent with a trusted disciple called Demetrius.

The Teaching of the First Letter

The first letter is by far the most important of the letters of John, and its doctrines resemble those of John's gospel, although there are important differences. Before selected passages of the letter are examined, its main teaching will be summarized.

(i) *God the Father: Love and Light*. The title 'Father' is used frequently of God both in the gospel and the letter. But while both writings say that 'God loved' (Jn 3^{16}, 1 Jn 4^{11}), the letter also says that 'God is love' (1 Jn $4^{8, 16}$), and while the gospel describes Jesus as 'the light of the world' (Jn 8^{12}, 9^5), the letter says that 'God is light' (1 Jn 1^5).

(ii) *Jesus Christ, the Son of God*. Both the gospel and the letter regularly describe Jesus as the Son of God, and the letter's account of Him as 'the word of life' recalls the teaching about the Word in the gospel (1 Jn 1^{1-2}, Jn 1^{1-18}). Great emphasis is laid by both writings on the fact that Jesus has really come in the flesh (Jn 1^{14}, 1 Jn 1^{1-4}, 4^2) and that He is the Christ or the Messiah (Jn 1^{41}, 4^{25-6}, 1 Jn 2^{22}, 5^1). The letter also describes Jesus as an Advocate (see notes on Jn 14^{15-26}).

(iii) *The Spirit*. Although the letter does not have as much teaching about the Spirit as does the gospel, its teaching on this theme is important. The Spirit is active in those who confess that Jesus Christ has come in the flesh, and the inner presence of the Spirit is proof that God dwells in us and we in Him (1 Jn $4^{2, 13}$). The function of the Spirit is to bear witness to the the truth about Christ (1 Jn 5^{6-8}; see also Jn 14^{26}, 15^{26}, 16^{13-14}). When the letter speaks of the Spirit's witness, it refers not only to the preaching and corporate life of the Church but also to the inner experience of the individual.

(iv) *The Work of Christ*. The letter does not repeat the gospel's teaching about the Lamb of God and the glorification and exaltation of Christ. It does, however, stress that the work of Christ was the result of God's love for men (1 Jn 4^{8-9}, compare Jn 3^{16}). Jesus is described in sacrificial language as 'the remedy for the defilement of our sins' (1 Jn 2^2, 4^{10}), and the purpose of His coming is to destroy the devil's works

(1 Jn 3^8; compare Jn 12^{31}, etc.), to cleanse men from sin (1 Jn 1^7–2^2; compare Jn 1^{29}) and to give them eternal life (1 Jn 4^9; compare Jn 3^{16}). It is made clear that His work culminated in His sacrificial offering on the Cross (1 Jn 1^7, 2^2, 4^{10}).

(v) *Eternal Life, Judgement, and the Appearing of Christ.* Like the gospel, the letter teaches that men can possess eternal life here and now (1 Jn 5^{11-12}; compare Jn 3^{36}) and be children of God in this present life (1 Jn 3^2; compare Jn 1^{12-13}). Both writings refer also to a future coming of Jesus and a day of judgement, but, while the gospel does not say when these events will take place, the letter teaches that they are very near (Jn 5^{27-30}, $6^{40, 44, 54}$, 21^{21-3}, 1 Jn $2^{18, 28}$, 3^2, 4^{17}).

(vi) *Sin, and Antichrist.* The letter teaches that all men are sinners, and that those who confess their sins, keep Christ's commands, and dwell in Him, have eternal life (1 Jn 1^8–2^5). There is, however, one sin, the 'deadly sin', for which there is no forgiveness. The letter never says what this deadly sin is, but it is the complete rejection of Christ by some-one who has previously believed in Him (see also Hebrews 6^{4-6}). The letter also speaks of Antichrist. Whereas there was a general expecta-tion of the rise of a supremely wicked man, the letter claims that false prophets are themselves antichrists (1 Jn 2^{18-23}, 4^{1-3}).

(vii) *The Christian Life.* That Christians are children of God is a main theme of the letter. The marks of God's children are that they do right, do not commit sin, love each other, and believe that Jesus is the Messiah (1 Jn 2^{29}, 3^9, 4^7, $5^{1, 18}$). The letter, however, does not link this theme, as the gospel does, with the activity of the Spirit (Jn 3^5).

The Christian life is lived in the light of God's guidance and power (1 Jn 1^{5-7}, 2^{9-11}; compare Jn 1^9, 8^{12}, 9^5). It is also a life in accordance with the command of love, a life which actually dwells in love (1 Jn 4^7–5^4, 3^{9-20}; compare Jn 15^{10-13}). It is a life in which a man is honest about his own sinfulness (1 Jn 1^{8-10}), and in which a man dwells in God and God in him (1 Jn 4^{16-18}; compare Jn 17^{21}).

(viii) *The Church and Sacraments.* The letter speaks of 'the common life' which Christians share with each other and with the Father and the Son (1 Jn $1^{3, 6-7}$), but it has no developed doctrine of the Church. Its references to the sacraments are extremely ambiguous. 'Initiation' (the Greek means literally 'anointing') may refer to baptism (1 Jn $2^{20, 27}$), and 'water and blood' may mean baptism and the Lord's Supper (1 Jn 5^{6-9}).

*   *   *

COMMENTS ON SELECTED PASSAGES FROM THE FIRST LETTER OF JOHN

1 John 1$^{1-4}$—*The Word of Life*

This description of Jesus as the 'word of life' resembles John 1$^{1-18}$ (on which see notes). In answer to false teaching it stresses the reality of the incarnation.

1 John 1^3. *common life.* The Greek can also be translated *fellowship* or *communion.* It describes a fellowship of Christians with the Father and the Son as well as with each other. See also Acts 2^{42}.

1 John 1$^{5-10}$—*The Light of God, and the Sinfulness of Men*

The idea that God is light (verse 5) is found in the Old Testament (Ps 27^1) and in Greek thought. Light stands for the eternal glory of God and the guidance which He gives to men. In John's gospel Jesus is called 'the light of the world' (Jn 8^{12}, 9^5; compare Jn 1^4).

The 'blood' of Jesus (verse 7) refers to His sacrificial death and to His risen life. A sacrificial victim's blood stood for life offered to God and given back to men in renewed form as life-giving power (see Lev 17$^{11-12, 14}$, Mk 14^{24}).

The emphasis on the universal sinfulness of men (verses 8–10) is an answer to heretics who claim to be sinless.

1 John 2$^{1-2}$—*The Advocate*

The word *paraklētos* (see notes on Jn 14$^{15-26}$) is here used to describe Jesus as an Advocate who pleads for men with God (compare Rom 8^{34}, Heb 9^{24}).

1 John 2^1. *My children* suggests that the author had pastoral oversight of the churches to which he was writing.

1 John 2^2. *remedy for the defilement.* In pagan usage the Greek word meant *propitiation*, but in Jewish and Christian usage it referred to the removal or expiation of sins. A similar word is translated *means of expiating sin* in Romans 3^{25}.

*   *   *

1 John 2^{28}–3^3—*What we shall be*

A distinction is made between the present state of Christians, who are already children of God, and their future state, when they will be like Jesus.

1 John 3^2. *when it is disclosed.* A better translation, *when he is disclosed*, shows the verse to refer to the return of Jesus.

1 John 3^3. Men purify themselves by obedience to God's commands.

1 John 3⁴⁻¹²—*Without Sin*

This section, with its assertion that the child of God does not sin, appears to contradict 1 John 1⁸⁻¹⁰, where the man who claims to be sinless is condemned as a liar. One solution of the difficulty is that 1 John 3⁹ means that a child of God does not habitually sin, though he may sometimes sin. Another more likely solution is that 1 John 3⁹ states what a Christian ideally is, by contrast with 1 John 1⁸⁻¹⁰, which speaks of a Christian as he actually is. The reference to his ideal condition is an answer to false teachers who claim that moral standards no longer apply to the children of God. The apparently conflicting statements in the letter represent the tension between what a child of God is and what he ought to be.

1 John 3⁵. For the sinlessness of Christ, see also 2 Corinthians 5²¹, Hebrews 4¹⁵, 1 Peter 2²².

1 John 3⁸. For the description of a sinner as a *child of the devil*, compare John 8⁴⁴. The idea of Christ's work as a conflict with the devil is found also in John 12³¹ and 16¹¹.

*   *   *

1 John 4¹⁻⁶—*The Spirit of Truth and the Spirit of Error*

In the early Church were many prophets who claimed to be directly inspired by the Spirit in their utterances. According to this passage, the marks of a true prophet are his confession of the reality of Christ's incarnation (verse 2) and his readiness to give a hearing to the writer of the letter and his friends (verse 6). A prophet is not so much a foreteller of the future as a man who speaks for God. For the existence of false prophets, see Mark 13²¹⁻³, Matthew 7¹⁵.

'Antichrist' (verse 3) was one of the names given to the supremely evil being who was expected to arise in the last days, and is called elsewhere 'the abomination of desolation' (Mk 13¹⁴), 'that wicked man' (2 Thess 2⁸⁻⁹), and 'the beast' (Rev 13¹⁻¹⁸). The distinctive teaching of 1 John is that there is not just one antichrist but many, and that they have already appeared. Everyone who denies the reality of the incarnation or the Messiahship of Jesus is an antichrist (verse 3; see also 1 Jn 2¹⁸⁻²²).

1 John 4⁷⁻²¹—*Love*

Although John's gospel affirms that God loves men (Jn 3¹⁶), this letter is the only biblical writing which states that 'God is love' (verses 8 and

16). This love is a self-giving love (see notes on Mk 12$^{28-34}$), which has been supremely revealed in God's act of sending His Son for the salvation of men (verses 9–10). Love has its origin in God, and men's appropriate response is to love each other, a response which is itself evidence that they are children of God, who love Him and have a deep and intimate fellowship with Him (verses 7, 11–12, 19–21). Love reaches its perfection when a man can appear before God without fear at the last judgement (verses 16–19). Further evidence for the reality of men's fellowship with God is the gift of the Spirit (verse 13), which is an inner experience of certainty as well as the power of prophetic speech. And yet more evidence is found in the attestation of the Church to the truth of the gospel message and in the individual's own confession that Jesus is the Son of God (verses 14–16).

1 John 4^{10}. *remedy for the defilement of our sins.* See notes on 1 John 2^2.

QUESTIONS

(1) Discuss the meaning of the story of the Washing of the Disciples' Feet.
(2) What does John's Gospel teach about the Holy Spirit?
(3) Why was the First Letter of John written?
(4) Comment on: John 15^1, 19^5, 20^{29}, 21^{17}; 1 John 3^9, 4^{10}.

CHAPTER EIGHT

THE ACTS OF THE APOSTLES

THE ACTS of the Apostles is a sequel to Luke's gospel, written by the same author, and dedicated, like the gospel, to Theophilus. The date of its composition is uncertain, but it was probably written between AD 75 and 90.

The book, which begins with an account of the ascension of Jesus and the appointment of a successor to Judas, describes the gift of the Spirit at Pentecost, the struggles and achievements of the Church in Jerusalem, and the spread of Christianity through Palestine, Syria, Asia Minor, Macedonia, and Greece. First the leading figure in the story is Peter, and later Paul. The book ends with Paul a prisoner in Rome about AD 62.

The Sources of the Acts

Luke must have received much of his information from the local churches and also from the apostles themselves, but his reliance on Paul is obviously limited, because his account of events sometimes conflicts with Paul's. Certain sections of the narrative include the words 'we' and 'us', and are generally called the 'We-sections' (Acts 16^{10-17}, 20^{5-15}, 21^{1-18}, 27^1-28^{16}). They may well be excerpts from Luke's own diary, describing events in which he himself participated.

The Historical Value of the Acts

We cannot be sure that the Acts, any more than the gospels, always gives a literally accurate account of everything which was said and done. The comments which have already been made about the historical reliability of the gospel records and of the miracle-stories in particular (see pp. 30–2) apply also to the Acts of the Apostles. When the evidence of Paul's letters conflict with that of the Acts (see notes on Acts 9^{20-30}), then Paul's evidence must be regarded as the more reliable. It must be recognized that the Acts does not claim to give a comprehensive account of the history of the early Church and therefore cannot be criticized for omitting to mention some of the events recorded in Paul's letters (see notes on Acts 11^{27-30}). Although the book was not intended primarily to be a detailed work of history, it is, together with Paul's letters, the main source of information about the Church's history for the first thirty years after the resurrection. When the evidence of Paul is combined with that of the Acts, it is possible to form a picture of the early Church's development in Palestine and Syria, and along the northern coasts of the Mediterranean. But some important events, like the beginning of Christianity in North Africa and the foundation of the church in Rome, neither of which is recorded in the New Testament, remain shrouded in obscurity.

The Purpose of the Acts

The Acts does not claim to be a detailed history of the early Church or a complete biography of Peter and Paul. It seems to have been written for a variety of reasons.

(i) It stresses the unity of the early Church, and shows that Peter and Paul were in essential agreement, even though their work lay in different spheres. It also claims that there was no fundamental disagreement between Paul and James, the brother of Jesus.

(ii) It was written to prove that the early Christians were not disloyal to the Roman emperor and were not persecuted at the instigation of the Roman authorities but because of Jewish plots.

(iii) It describes the activity of the Spirit in the early Jerusalem Church, and shows how the gospel spread to other lands. Its climax is reached with its record of the preaching of the gospel in Rome, the capital of the empire.

COMMENTS ON THE ACTS OF THE APOSTLES

Acts 1^{1-14}—The Ascension

This narrative, which is the only detailed account of the ascension in the New Testament, has caused difficulty to many readers because it presupposes the outmoded belief that heaven is a place above the sky. The important truth conveyed by the story, however, does not depend on the literal accuracy of the description of Jesus's ascent into the sky. This truth is that, although the resurrection appearances of Jesus have ended, men can have fellowship with Him through the Spirit. He is the glorified Lord, who sends the Spirit to His disciples, enabling them to proclaim His Lordship throughout the earth, which He will finally claim as His own domain (verses 5–8, 11). Other references to the ascension agree that it was the occasion of Jesus's exaltation as Lord (John 6^{62}, 20^{17}, Acts 2^{33}, 3^{21}, Eph 4^{8-10}, 1 Tim 3^{16}, Heb 4^{14}, 7^{26}, 9^{24}), and the letter to the Hebrews also links it with His heavenly ministry of intercession for men and women. The scarcity of references to the ascension in the New Testament is probably explained by the tendency to see the resurrection and the subsequent appearances of Jesus as a unity and therefore to connect the Lordship of Christ with the resurrection.

It is interesting to compare Acts 1[1-14] with the account of the ascension of Elijah, whose spirit fell on Elisha (2 K 2[1-15]).

The references to Jesus's ascension in Mark 16[19] and Luke 24[51] are not found in the most reliable manuscripts.

Acts 1[1]. *Theophilus*. See notes on Luke 1[1].

Acts 1[3]. *forty days*. This was a conventional way of saying 'a period of time' (compare Lk 4[1-2]). Luke 24[50-3] gives the impression that Jesus's final appearance took place on the day on which He rose from the tomb. John's gospel, however, claims that Jesus continued to appear to His disciples for some time after His resurrection, and in this respect agrees with the Acts.

Acts 1[6] expresses the Jewish hope that Israel would become a kingdom again as a prelude to the establishment of God's reign over all the earth.

Acts 1[7]. For the assertion that the time of the end is not known, see also Mark 13[32].

Acts 1[11]. *will come in the same way* refers to the return of Jesus at the last day, not, as is sometimes argued, to the gift of the Spirit recorded in Acts 2[1-4].

Acts 1[15-26]—*The Appointment of Matthias as a Twelfth Apostle*

It was important that a twelfth apostle should be appointed to fill the vacancy created by the death of Judas, because, as the new Israel, the Church must have twelve leaders (see notes on Mk 3[13-19]).

The word 'apostle' means 'one who is sent', and the apostles were sent by Christ to lead the missionary work of the Church and to preside over its affairs. At this stage an essential qualification for an apostle was that he should have been a disciple of Jesus during His ministry and should have been a witness to the resurrection (verses 21–2). It was only later that others, who did not possess this qualification, were called apostles.

This period between the ascension and Pentecost was a time of preparation in which the disciples waited in faith for the gift of the Spirit (see Lk 24[49, 52-3], Acts 1[14-15]).

Acts 1[18-19]. For a different account of Judas's death see Matthew 27[5]. It is difficult to harmonize the two accounts, but even though they disagree about the details of the event, they agree that he met a sudden death.

Acts 1[20] refers to Psalms 69[25] and 109[8].

Acts 1[23-6]. The method of election was partly democratic, two names being selected by the assembled Church, and partly a reliance on direct divine choice, which was believed to operate through the drawing of lots.

Acts 2$^{1-13}$—*The Gift of the Spirit at Pentecost*

It is not surprising that Pentecost was the occasion when the Church emerged from its brief period of waiting and confronted the world with its message. Pentecost, which was the next feast after the Passover in the Jewish year, provided the disciples with their first opportunity after the resurrection to speak to large crowds of people.

The immediate consequence of the gift of the Spirit was that the disciples spoke in tongues. According to the Acts, they spoke in many different languages, but it is likely that Luke misunderstood the exact nature of what happened. Since most, if not all, of the onlookers were Jews, who would be able to speak either Aramaic or Greek, there was no need for the disciples to use a great variety of languages. They seem to have spoken in tongues in the sense that they uttered cries of wonder and ecstasy which were unintelligible to most people but which expressed deep and powerful religious emotions. This type of ecstatic speech, which is mentioned in 1 Corinthians 14$^{1-19}$, Acts 10^{46}, and 19^6, could certainly have given rise to the accusation that the disciples had been drinking (verse 13). It is possible that some of their cries resembled words in other languages, and thus helped to create the impression that they were speaking in foreign tongues. The disciples, of course, were not limited to ecstatic speech, but were able also to preach with great coherence and clarity.

The Meaning of the Event

(i) The gift of the Spirit is understood by Luke as the fulfilment of the Baptist's prophecy of one who would baptize men with the Holy Spirit (Mk 1^8, Lk 3^{16}, 24^{49}, Acts 1$^{4-5}$, 2^{33}). There is no essential contradiction between John's gospel, which dates this event to Easter Day, and the Acts, which dates it to Pentecost. Whereas John rightly understands that the risen Jesus gave the Spirit to His disciples when He appeared to them, the Acts is concerned to describe how the Spirit first empowered the disciples to go out and preach to others (see Jn 20^{22}).

(ii) The event is regarded by the Acts as a sign that the gospel is to be proclaimed to all nations. Even though Luke misunderstands the exact nature of speaking in tongues, he rightly sees that Pentecost was the beginning of the Church's world-wide mission. Because many

Jewish pilgrims would return from Jerusalem to other countries, the message was soon likely to spread beyond Palestine.

(iii) Since Pentecost was the festival at which the wheat harvest was dedicated to God, the gift of the Spirit on this occasion was a sign that the harvest of the Spirit had come.

(iv) Pentecost was also the festival at which the Jews remembered the giving of the Law on Sinai. When therefore the disciples received the Spirit at Pentecost, it was a sign that a new covenant had been established to supersede the covenant of the Law.

Acts 2^1. *Pentecost* is from a Greek word meaning 'fiftieth' and signifies that the feast began on the fiftieth day after the beginning of the Feast of Unleavened Bread. Pentecost was also called the Feast of Weeks.

Acts 2^{14-41}—*Peter's Sermon at Pentecost*

One of the results of the outpouring of the Spirit was the preaching of the apostles. This sermon of Peter's, like the other sermons in the Acts, can hardly be a verbatim report of what was said, but gives an idea of the content of early Christian preaching. The sermon has three main themes :

(i) *The Time of Fulfilment*. The coming of Christ and the gift of the Spirit mark the arrival of the Messianic age and are the fulfilment of prophecy. The gift of the Spirit (verses 16–21) fulfils Joel 2^{28-32}, the resurrection of Jesus (verses 24–32) fulfils Psalm 16^{8-11}, and His exaltation (verses 34–6) fulfils Psalm 110^1.

(ii) *The Work of Jesus and the Gift of the Spirit*. All these events were part of God's deliberate plan. God appointed Jesus to His ministry on earth. By God's will He was given up to be crucified. God raised Him from the dead and exalted Him as Lord and Messiah. And God gave Him the Holy Spirit to send upon the disciples (verses 22–4, 32–3, 36).

(iii) *The Appeal*. Men and women are invited to repent of their sins and be baptized. When they receive baptism, which signifies their acceptance of forgiveness and their confession of the Lordship of Christ, they will be given the Holy Spirit. The promise of the Spirit in Joel 2^{32} is extended to everyone whom God chooses to call, wherever he may live and to whatever nation he may belong (verses 38–9).

This account of Peter's sermon is followed by the record of the conversion of a large number of people (verse 41), a process which is said to have continued (see also Acts 2^{47}, 4^4, 5^{14}).

Acts 2^{36} need not mean that Jesus only became Lord and Messiah after His resurrection. Christian doctrine was in an early stage of development, and this statement was not intended to deny the unique status of the earthly Jesus but to stress the glory and authority of the exalted Jesus.

Other Speeches in the Acts

Other utterances of Peter and the rest of the apostles (Acts 3^{12-26}, $4^{8-12,\ 19-20,\ 24-30}$, 5^{30-2}, 10^{34-43}) and one speech of Paul's (Acts 13^{16-41}) repeat some of the teaching of Peter's sermon at Pentecost, and also include references to the final judgement and a universal restoration (Acts 3^{19-21}, 10^{42}). Jesus is given the titles of Prophet, Servant, Holy and Righteous One, the Stone rejected by the builders, Leader, Saviour, and Judge (Acts $3^{14,\ 22-4,\ 26}$, 4^{11}, 5^{31}, 10^{42}). The Spirit is described as a witness of Jesus's death, resurrection and ascension (5^{32}). According to 10^{43} and 13^{39}, forgiveness or acquittal (traditionally translated 'justification', see notes on Gal 2^{15-21}) is given to those who have faith in Christ.

These speeches in the Acts give an outline of the preaching (Greek, *kērugma*) of the early Church, and are evidence of the basic message common to New Testament writers.

Acts 2^{42-7}—*The Corporate Life of the Church*

One of the first results of the outpouring of the Spirit was that the early Christians lived a disciplined corporate life. They met for worship and prayer, went regularly to the Temple, and took meals together in their homes. The breaking of bread (verses 42 and 46) may refer to the earliest form of the Lord's Supper, which would include a real but simple meal.

At first the members of the Church shared their possessions and gave to each person according to his need (verses 44-5; see also Acts 4^{32-5}). This readiness to share possessions was exemplified by Barnabas, who sold his estate and gave the proceeds to the common fund (Acts 4^{36-7}). That not all of them were as honest as Barnabas is shown by the story of Ananias and Sapphira (Acts 5^{1-12}). The Christians seem eventually to have discontinued the practice of sharing goods, which is only mentioned in these early chapters of the Acts.

Acts 2^{42}. *the common life.* See notes on 1 John 1^3.

Acts 3^{1-26}—*The Healing of a Lame Man*

Through the gift of the Spirit the apostles were empowered not only to preach the gospel and organize the Church but also to continue Jesus's work of healing. 'Signs, marvels, and miracles' were regarded as proofs of the genuineness of an apostle (2 Cor 12^{12}; see also Acts 2^{43}), and 'gifts of healing' and 'miraculous powers' are described by Paul as spiritual gifts (1 Cor 12$^{9-10}$).

The story of the healing of the lame man emphasizes that Peter did not perform the miracle through any power of his own. The name of Jesus awakened in the man a faith which made it possible for him to be healed (verses 12 and 16). There is a vivid contrast between the man's expectation of a financial gift and the healing which he received (verses 5–6).

For the content of Peter's speech (verses 12–26), see notes on Acts 2$^{14-41}$ and also p. 165.

Acts 3$^{13, 26}$. *Servant*. This title may be derived from Isaiah 42^1 and 52^{13}.
Acts 3^{14}. *righteous*. There may be an allusion here to Isaiah 53^{11}.
Acts 3$^{22-3}$. This is a quotation from Deuteronomy 18^{15}. See notes on Mark 8^{28}.
Acts 3^{25} quotes from Genesis 22^{18}.

Acts 4$^{1-31}$—*Boldness in the face of Persecution*

One of the most conspicuous gifts of the Spirit was the 'boldness' (verses 13, 29, and 31) with which Christians spoke when they were threatened with persecution (compare Mk 13^{11}). Trouble arose when Peter used the healing of the lame man as an occasion for preaching about the resurrection of Jesus. Peter and John were arrested, and released with a caution against speaking in public about Jesus. That the motive of the apostles' action was obedience to God rather than men, is forcibly stated in verses 19–20. A similar example of persecution is recorded in Acts 5$^{17-41}$.

For the content of the prayer (verses 24–30) see notes on 'Other Speeches in the Acts' (p. 165).

Acts 4$^{25-6}$ quote Psalm 2$^{1-2}$. See notes on Luke 23$^{6-12}$.

Acts 4$^{32-7}$—*The Corporate Life: Barnabas*

For the corporate life of the Church (verses 32–5), see notes on Acts 2$^{42-7}$.

Barnabas, who is first mentioned in this passage (verses 36–7), was a Jew from Cyprus, a member of the tribe of Levi, and a cousin of Mark (Col 4^{10}). He befriended Paul in Jerusalem (Acts 9$^{26-7}$), and was later sent to supervise work in Antioch, to which he brought Paul as a colleague (Acts 11$^{22-6}$). He visited Jerusalem with Paul first to take famine-relief to the Church and later to champion a liberal attitude to the Law at the Jerusalem Council (Acts 11^{27-30}, 15^{1-35}, see also Gal 2^{1-14}). He was Paul's colleague on the missionary journey recorded in Acts 13^1-14^{28}, but because of a dispute did not accompany him on his second journey (Acts 15^{36-41}). He is described as an apostle in Acts 14^{4-14}, although there is no evidence that he knew Jesus in His earthly ministry or was an eye-witness of the resurrection (see notes on Acts 1^{15-26}).

Acts 5^{1-12}—Ananias and Sapphira

The honesty and generosity of Barnabas (Acts 4^{36-7}) is contrasted with the duplicity of Ananias and Sapphira who attempted to disguise the fact that they were not giving all their possessions to the Church. The difficulty of this story is not that Ananias dropped down dead, apparently through shock at Peter's denunciation of him, but that Peter told Sapphira that she would also die, as she promptly did. Peter's behaviour, as recorded here, was amazingly harsh for an apostle of Jesus. It is unlikely that the Acts gives a full account of what happened.

Acts 5^{12-42}—More Persecution

This passage records how the apostles, after having been arrested, freed, and later brought for trial, were finally released in answer to the plea of the rabbi Gamaliel. For the Christians' behaviour in persecution, see notes on Acts 4^{1-31}, and for Peter's speech (verses 29–32), see notes on Acts 2^{14-41} and also p. 165.

Acts 5^{19}. *an angel of the Lord*. Luke obviously regards this as a miracle. But *angel* means literally *messenger*, and it is possible that the apostles were set free by human help.

Acts 5^{20}. *this new life and all that it means*. A literal translation of the Greek is *the words of this life*.

Acts 5^{34}. *Gamaliel* was a famous rabbi, under whom Paul had studied (Acts 22^3). He was a member of the school of Hillel (see notes on Mk 10^{1-12}).

Acts 5^{36-7}. According to the Jewish historian Josephus, *Theudas* rebelled in A D 44 and *Judas* in A D 6. Because Josephus mentions the revolt of Judas in a paragraph which follows the account about Theudas, it has been thought that Luke misread Josephus and assumed that Judas's revolt was later than that of Theudas. This suggests that the Acts was written after A D 93, when Josephus's book was published. Since, however, Luke may have had access to one of Josephus's sources or may have heard Josephus lecturing, the Acts may well have been written before A D 93.

Acts 6[1-15]—*Stephen and the Seven*

The growing Church was joined by many Jews whose language was Greek and whose origin was in the Jewish communities outside Palestine. Trouble arose between these Greek-speaking Christians and those who spoke Aramaic, 'the language of the Jews' (verse 1), because the Greek-speaking members of the Church complained about the neglect of their widows in the daily distribution of goods. The apostles therefore called an assembly at which seven men were elected to deal with the problem. All these men had Greek names, which suggests that they were Greek-speaking Christians, and their leader, Stephen, was soon to make his mark on the Church's life (verses 1–6).

Stephen was not content to deal with the daily distribution, and soon became known for his outspokenness as a preacher. He provoked opposition from Greek-speaking Jews (who were not, of course, Christians), and was brought before the Sanhedrin, the Jewish Council, on a charge of speaking against the Temple and the Law (verses 8–15). The charge was based on teaching similar to parts of Stephen's speech, in which he implied that the man-made Temple, where many of the legal observances were enacted, was not essential to true religion (Acts 7[44-50]).

Acts 6[1]. *widows* could easily be left destitute in a country where no provision was organized for them. This incident shows that even in the Christian Church there was a tendency to neglect them.

Acts 6[2]. *to wait at table* refers to the organization of the daily distribution of goods, which was part of the Church's communal life.

Acts 6[3]. *seven men*. Traditionally these men are supposed to have been the first 'deacons' of the Church, but they are not called by this title in the Acts.

Acts 6[9]. *Freedmen* means liberated slaves. *Asia* refers not to the whole continent of Asia but to a part of what we now call Turkey. *Cilicia* is also in Turkey, and *Cyrene* and *Alexandria* are towns on the north coast of Africa.

Acts 7[1]-8[1]—*Stephen's Trial and Death*

Most of Stephen's speech at his trial was an account of God's dealings with the Israelites (verses 1–43), and could have aroused no opposition. At the end of his speech, however, are two sections which angered the audience. In the first of these sections (verses 44–50) he asserted that God 'does not live in houses made by men', and, although this statement was derived from 1 Kings 8[27], it irritated his accusers, who had an excessive veneration for the Temple. In the second section (verses 51–3)

he denounced the Jews for killing Jesus, and accused them of disobedience to the Law, presumably because they had rejected and killed
the Messiah. To crown it all, as the fury of his accusers mounted, he
claimed that he could see Jesus, the Son of Man, at the right hand of
God (verses 54–6). This was too much for his audience, who threw him
out of the city and stoned him to death (verses 57–60). His prayer that
Jesus would receive his spirit, and his plea for the forgiveness of his
murderers, recall the words of Jesus on the Cross (Lk 23[34, 46]).

Stephen is chiefly remembered as the first Christian martyr, but his
importance is not confined to the manner of his death. His Greek-
speaking background helped him to understand the world-wide nature
of the Christian religion, and his preaching made it clear that Christianity was not tied to the Temple or to the Jewish legal system. His
courage and vision made him the forerunner of Paul, who was the companion of his murderers and on whom his death must have made a lasting impression (Acts 7[58]–8[1]).

Acts 7[52]. *the Righteous One*. See notes on Acts 3[14].
Acts 7[56]. *the Son of Man*. See notes on Mark 2[1–12].
Acts 7[58]. *stoning*. The trial broke up in confusion, and the death of
Stephen was not legally authorized. He was in fact murdered.
Saul was also called Paul. See notes on Acts 9[1–19].

Acts 8[1–40]—*The Missionary Work of Philip*

After the death of Stephen the Christians were scattered over Judaea
and Samaria because of the intensive persecution which was carried out
against them. The eighth chapter of the Acts describes the work which
was done at this time by Philip, one of the seven men who had been
chosen to look after the distribution of goods (Acts 6[5]).

Samaria. Because the Samaritans were not regarded as genuine Jews,
Philip's work in Samaria was the beginning of the Church's mission to
non-Jewish lands. The Acts records that the baptized converts did not
receive the Spirit until Peter and John had laid hands on them (verses
14–17); perhaps Luke is thinking of outward manifestations of the
Spirit like ecstatic speech.

Simon the Magician. One of the converts whom Philip baptized was
Simon, a highly successful wonder-worker. When Simon tried to buy
from the apostles the power to bestow the Spirit, Peter denounced him
and called upon him to repent. The story ends with Simon begging the

apostles to pray for God's mercy on him (verses 9–13, 18–24). The word 'simony' is derived from this Simon.

The Ethiopian. The story of Philip's encounter with a eunuch, who was finance minister to the Queen of Ethiopia (verses 26–40), is important because it records the conversion of a man who seems to have been a Gentile by origin, and also because it shows the influence of Isaiah 53 on Christian thought. Since the eunuch had been on a pilgrimage to Jerusalem and was reading the scriptures, he was obviously sympathetic towards Judaism.

Acts 8²⁶. *the angel of the Lord* seems in this passage to refer to the Spirit (see verse 29).

Acts 8²⁷. *Kandake* was the official title of the Queen of Ethiopia.

Acts 8³²⁻³ quotes from Isaiah 53⁷⁻⁸.

Acts 8³⁷. The additional words in the *NEB* footnote are not in the most reliable manuscripts and may have been added later. They are evidence for the existence at a comparatively early date of the simple Christian creed, 'Jesus Christ is the Son of God'.

Acts 8³⁸ is evidence for the practice of baptism by immersion.

Acts 9¹⁻¹⁹—*The Conversion of Paul*

Paul's conversion is described three times in the Acts (9¹⁻¹⁹, 22¹⁻²¹, 26⁴⁻²³), and although there are discrepancies of detail between the accounts, there is general agreement about the broad outline of events. Paul had obtained authority to go to Damascus to arrest any Christians who were active there. As he drew near the city, he was dazzled by a blinding light, and fell to the ground. He heard the voice of Jesus asking why he was persecuting Him, and was led sightless into Damascus. When a Christian, called Ananias, laid hands on him, his sight was restored, and he was baptized.

This was the most spectacular conversion in the history of the early Church. The leading persecutor of Christianity became its leading missionary. The opponent of Stephen became the man who ultimately won acceptance for Stephen's emphasis on a Christianity which was free from the shackles of Jewish legalism. Paul himself described his conversion as the occasion of a resurrection appearance of Jesus (1 Cor 15⁸⁻⁹). It was a 'monstrous' birth, because he was in no way fit to be called an apostle (1 Cor 15⁹). At this time, he said, God 'chose to reveal his Son to me and through me, in order that I might proclaim him among the Gentiles' (Gal 1¹⁶).

Paul's birthplace was Tarsus in Cilicia, a province in the south-east corner of what is now called Turkey. He was born and bred a Jew, and studied the Law in Jerusalem under Gamaliel (Acts 22³, see note on Acts 5³⁴). He was a Pharisee, who tried with utmost zeal to keep the whole of the Jewish Law and traditions, and his first reaction to Christianity was one of hatred and relentless opposition (see Gal 1¹³⁻¹⁴ and Phil 3⁵⁻⁶). But an inner struggle was going on within him, because, although he wanted to keep the whole of the Law, he found himself unable to do so. He had no difficulty in keeping the commandments about outward actions, but his troubles were caused by his failure to control his inner attitude. It was the commandment 'Thou shalt not covet' which he was unable to obey (Rom 7⁷⁻⁸).

Although the martyrdom of Stephen, an event in which Paul himself assisted (Acts 7⁵⁸–8¹), probably raised questions in his mind, he vigorously asserted his loyalty to Judaism by organizing the persecution of Christians (Acts 8³, 9¹⁻²). On the road to Damascus his crisis came. Like a stubborn horse kicking against the goad (see Acts 26¹⁴), he had resisted Christ, but in the end he submitted.

In the earlier chapters of the Acts he is called Saul, his Jewish name, but in Acts 13⁹ he is called Paul, the name which is used of him in the rest of the book. Paul is a Roman name, which may have been chosen for its similarity to Saul. Indeed he may have been called by both names from childhood. It was as Paul that he wrote his letters and it is as Paul that he has always been remembered.

Acts 9². *Damascus*, which lay to the north of Galilee, had a mixed population of Jews and Gentiles.

In addition to the High Priest's authority, Paul would need the permission of the local synagogues before he could arrest anyone.

the new way. The Greek could be translated literally *the way*.

Acts 9⁷ shows a discrepancy from Acts 22⁹, but both statements imply that only Paul was able to understand what had happened to him.

Acts 9¹⁰. According to Acts 22¹², Ananias was a Jew. He should, of course, be distinguished from the Ananias whose death is reported in Acts 5¹⁻¹², and from the Ananias of Acts 23².

Acts 9¹⁵. In this narrative Ananias is told that Paul will be the apostle to the Gentiles. According to Acts 22¹⁴⁻¹⁵ Ananias commissioned Paul for the task, but according to Acts 26¹⁷⁻¹⁸ Paul was made aware of his vocation at the very moment of his conversion.

Acts 9²⁰⁻³⁰—*Paul's life immediately after his conversion*

According to the Acts, Paul remained in Damascus and preached in the synagogues, until he was forced to escape from the city to avoid becoming the victim of a Jewish conspiracy. He went to Jerusalem, and at first met with a suspicious reception from the Christians. When Barnabas, however, introduced him to the apostles, he felt that he was accepted, and began to preach the gospel openly in Jerusalem, until he left for Tarsus because of another plot against his life.

Paul's own account of these events in Galatians 1¹⁵⁻²⁴ agrees that he preached in Damascus, visited Jerusalem, and finally went to Cilicia. But there are important differences from the account in the Acts. He says that he went to Arabia immediately after his conversion, and later returned to Damascus. The Acts, on the other hand, makes no mention of Arabia, and says that after his conversion he stayed in Damascus and preached there. Paul also records that, when after three years he went to Jerusalem, he stayed there only a fortnight and saw none of the apostles except Peter and James, the brother of Jesus. The Acts implies that he remained longer in Jerusalem, became known to the apostles as a whole, and moved about freely in the city. In cases of disagreement like these we must follow Paul's own account rather than the later version which is given by the Acts.

Paul left Damascus, according to Acts 9²³⁻⁵, because of a Jewish conspiracy against him. In 2 Corinthians 11³²⁻³, however, he claims that it was the hostility of Aretas which drove him to escape from the city. There is no contradiction between the two accounts, since both the Jews and Aretas may well have plotted against him. Aretas was the king of the Nabataean Arabs, who lived in the territory east of the Jordan. The Arabia which Paul visited after his conversion (Gal 1¹⁷) was this area and not the peninsular now known as Arabia. Paul would use his time in Arabia as a period of preparation for his ministry, but the reaction of Aretas suggests that he also seized the opportunity to preach to the inhabitants of the area. Aretas would not have been hostile if Paul had remained silent during his residence there.

Acts 9³¹⁻⁴³—*Peter's Ministry in Judaea*

The story is told of two miracles which Peter performed during a tour of the Christian communities of Judaea. At Lydda he healed a man who was paralysed, and at Joppa he raised a dead woman, named Tabitha or Dorcas.

Acts 10¹–11¹⁸—*The Conversion of Cornelius*

While he was at Joppa, Peter had a vision in which he was instructed to kill and eat creatures of every kind, both clean and unclean (10⁹⁻¹⁶).

He was still trying to understand the vision, when messengers came from Cornelius, a Gentile centurion, who had been told in a vision to send for him. So Peter went to visit Cornelius at Caesarea ($10^{1-8, 17-23}$). When he talked with Cornelius, he understood the meaning of his vision. As a Jew he had been taught that it was wrong to associate with uncircumcised Gentiles, but God had shown him in the vision that he 'must not call any man profane or unclean' (10^{24-9}; see also 10^{15}). While Peter was expounding the gospel to them, Cornelius and his friends received the Holy Spirit and began to speak in tongues. Peter then ordered them to be baptized (10^{30-48}).

When Peter returned to Jerusalem, he was criticized for taking meals with uncircumcised Gentiles, but, after he had given an account of his vision and the subsequent events, the Jerusalem Christians accepted his explanation, and acknowledged that 'God has granted life-giving repentance to the Gentiles also' (11^{1-18}).

This story represents an important development in the Christian attitude to Gentiles. Philip had baptized Samaritans and also an Ethiopian. Now Peter had not only baptized the Gentile Cornelius and his friends but had also eaten meat with them; and there is no evidence that he required them to be circumcised. Some time, however, was to elapse before the Church finally recognized that the Jewish laws about circumcision and eating with Gentiles no longer applied under the new covenant which had been established by Christ (see notes on Acts 15^{1-35}).

Acts 10^1. *Caesarea*, a port on the Mediterranean coast, was the official residence of the governor of Judaea.

a centurion was an officer who was similar in rank to a modern army captain.

A *Cohort* was an army unit of about 600 men.

Acts 10^2. Cornelius seems to have been one of those Gentiles who were called 'worshippers of God' or 'Godfearers' (Acts 16^{14}, 17^4, 18^7), and who joined in synagogue worship without becoming circumcised Jews.

Acts 10^{34-43}. For the contents of this speech see p. 165.

Acts 10^{44-8}. Cornelius and his friends received the Holy Spirit before they were baptized. In the Acts there is no rigid attitude about the precise relationship of the gift of the Spirit to baptism. On other occasions the Spirit was given at baptism or even later (Acts 2^{38}, 8^{14-17}, 19^{5-6}).

Acts 10^{46}. *tongues of ecstasy*. See notes on Acts 2^{1-13}.

Acts 11^{19-26}—*Developments in Antioch*

Some of the most important events in early Christian history are recorded in this short section, and the brevity of the account must not deceive us into passing over the events as if they were a mere interlude.

(i) *The Gospel for pagans* (verses 19–24). A sign that the Church was becoming more conscious of its world-wide mission is this record that some of the Christians who came to Antioch preached to pagans as well as Jews. They made many converts, and Barnabas was sent from Jerusalem to supervise their work. These unknown evangelists were responsible for one of the great pioneer ventures in Christian history.

(ii) *The arrival of Paul in Antioch* (verses 25–6). When Barnabas brought Paul from Tarsus to Antioch, it was an important move, because Antioch became the base from which Paul set out on his missionary journeys. Antioch, the capital of the Roman province of Syria, was the first great Gentile city in which Christianity obtained a strong foothold. In this city, which was the meeting-place of Greek and Oriental religions and the home of a large Jewish population, the Christian Church had to mould its presentation of the gospel. Paul was the man for the moment and the man for the place.

(iii) *The name 'Christians'* (verse 26). It was in Antioch too that the disciples were first called Christians. We do not know whether the name was given to them by one of their own number or by their opponents. But it was a clear recognition that as a community the Christians had an identity of their own and that their faith was firmly centred in Christ.

Acts 11²⁷⁻³⁰—*Paul's Second Visit to Jerusalem after his Conversion*

There are two accounts of Paul's second visit to Jerusalem after his conversion, one in the Acts and the other in Galatians 2¹⁻¹⁴. According to the Acts, Paul and Barnabas were sent from Antioch to give relief to the Jerusalem Christians because of famine. Galatians does not mention the famine, but says that Paul's purpose in making the visit was to explain his refusal to insist on the circumcision of male converts. According to Galatians, the leaders of the Jerusalem church acknowledged the right of Paul and Barnabas to preach to the Gentiles, and did not insist that circumcision should be practised or that Jewish Christians should abstain from eating with Gentile Christians (Gal 2⁹⁻¹⁰). When Paul and Barnabas returned to Antioch, Peter visited them, and took meals with Gentile Christians. But when representatives of James, the Lord's brother, came to the city, Peter began to hold aloof from the Gentile Christians, and even Barnabas followed his example. Paul, who was not to be daunted, opposed Peter before the whole congregation. He was convinced that, if men and women had faith in Christ, they would be accepted by God without having to fulfil all the requirements of the Jewish Law. His conviction arose out of his own conversion crisis, when he realized that he could never fully keep the Law but depended entirely on the mercy of God. His beliefs are expressed in his teaching about justification through faith (see notes on Gal 2$^{15-21}$ and Rom 3$^{21-6}$).

The accounts given by the Acts and Galatians of this visit to Jerusalem are consistent with each other, and the view is accepted here that they are descriptions of the same visit. It is surprising, however, that the Acts does not mention the question of circumcision and Galatians does not mention the famine. For these and other reasons many scholars believe that the visit recorded in Galatians is identical with that which is described in Acts 15$^{1-35}$. The main difficulties of this alternative view are that Galatians claims to be describing Paul's second visit and not his third, and that Galatians refers to an informal discussion whereas Acts 15 describes a formal council. Other scholars argue that Acts 11$^{27-30}$ and 15$^{1-35}$ are based on two separate accounts of the same visit, and that Luke has mistaken them for accounts of two different visits.

Acts 11^{28}. *Agabus* is mentioned also in Acts 21^{10}.

a severe and world-wide famine. This was probably a famine which was dated by the historian Josephus to A D 46.

Acts 12$^{1-25}$—*Further Persecution in Jerusalem*

The first of the apostles to be martyred was James, the son of Zebedee, who was beheaded during a persecution organized by Herod Agrippa I (verses 1–2). In the same persecution Peter was imprisoned and eventually released (verses 3–19).

This chapter shows that James, the brother of Jesus, had become leader of the Jerusalem church (verse 17). It also provides evidence of the early Church's practice of holding religious meetings in private houses (verse 12).

Herod Agrippa I, whose painful death from an internal disorder is regarded by Luke as a divine judgement (verses 20–3), was a grandson of Herod the Great and ruled over Judaea, Samaria, Galilee, and other neighbouring territories. His death took place in A D 44, one of the few certain dates in early Church history. The events in Acts 12, therefore, must have preceded Paul's famine visit to Jerusalem (Acts 11$^{27-30}$).

Acts 12^7. *an angel of the Lord.* The Acts regards this, like 5^{19}, as a miraculous divine deliverance. But it is possible that the angel may have been a friend who obtained Peter's release.

Acts 12^{12}. *John Mark* was the author of the gospel.

Acts 12^{17}. *elsewhere.* It has been claimed that Peter went to Rome at this stage, but it is more likely that he went to Antioch (see Gal 2$^{11-14}$).

Acts 12^{25}. This verse is linked to 13^1 rather than to Chapter 12.

Acts 13^1–14^{28}—*Paul's First Missionary Journey*

After the Church in Antioch had set them apart for missionary work, Paul and Barnabas sailed for Cyprus, and, having preached in the island, crossed to the mainland of Asia Minor (a land roughly equivalent to the Asiatic part of modern Turkey). They toured through Pamphylia, Phrygia, and Lycaonia, and eventually returned to Antioch. Among the towns which they visited were Salamis and Paphos, which were in Cyprus, Pisidian Antioch, which was in Phrygia, and Iconium, Lystra, and Derbe, which were in Lycaonia. John Mark, who accompanied them in Cyprus, left them in Pamphylia (see 13$^{5,\ 13}$, 15$^{37-8}$).

Since the story is plainly told in the Acts, there is no need to trace it in detail, but certain points should be noted :

(i) *Teaching in the Synagogue.* It was the policy of Paul and Barnabas to begin their work in each town by teaching in the local Jewish synagogue (13$^{5,\ 14-16,\ 44}$, 14^1).

(ii) *Conversion of Jews and Gentiles.* Although many of their converts were Jews, it is recorded that at Pisidian Antioch and Lystra, Gentiles were converted (13^{48}, 14^1). Many of these converts were probably people who attended the synagogue without having been received into Judaism (see note on Acts 10^2). Sergius Paulus, the governor of Cyprus, is said to have become a believer (13^{12}), but, since there is no mention of his baptism, he may have done no more than show respectful interest in the teaching of Paul and Barnabas.

(iii) *Jewish Opposition.* The real opposition to the two missionaries came from Jews. The sorcerer, Bar-Jesus, who tried to turn Sergius Paulus against Christianity, was a Jew (13$^{6-12}$). It was because of Jewish agitation that Paul and Barnabas were driven out of Pisidian Antioch (13$^{50-2}$) and had to escape from Iconium (14$^{1-7}$). In Lystra, the very place where they had been greeted as gods, Paul was stoned and left for dead because of Jewish opposition (14$^{19-20}$). It was with justice that Paul and Barnabas warned their converts 'that to enter the kingdom of God we must pass through many hardships' (14^{22}).

(iv) *The Authority of Paul and Barnabas.* The two missionaries, who are first called apostles in 14$^{4,\ 14}$, were in a position of special authority over the communities which they had gathered together, and they made provision for the orderly conduct of affairs by appointing elders in each congregation (14^{23}).

Acts 13^{1}. *Barnabas* : see notes on Acts 4^{32-7}.

Acts 13^{2}. Their decision was made under the guidance of the Spirit.

Acts 13^{3}. *laid their hands*. This was not an act of ordination to ministerial office but a commissioning for a particular task.

Acts 13^{14}. *Pisidian Antioch* was near Pisidia but actually in Phrygia. It must be distinguished from the more famous Antioch in Syria.

Acts 13^{16-41}. For the content of this speech, see n. 165.

Acts 14^{12}. *Jupiter* (in Greek, Zeus) was the ruler of the gods, and *Mercury* (in Greek, Hermes) was their messenger.

Acts 14^{14-17}. This speech about God and creation may be compared with Paul's speech at Athens (Acts 17^{22-31}).

Acts 14^{23}. *elders*. See notes on Acts 20^{17}.

Acts 15^{1-35}—*The Council of Jerusalem*

The controversy about the Jewish Law had not yet ended (see notes on Acts 11^{27-30}), and trouble arose when people came from Judaea to Antioch and taught that circumcision was necessary for salvation. The dissension became so great that Paul and Barnabas were sent with other representatives to raise the matter in Jerusalem. At a Church council, in which Peter supported Paul and Barnabas, it was finally decided at James's suggestion to impose no restriction on Gentile converts except a rule against fornication and against certain kinds of food. This decision was formulated in a decree sent to the Gentile Christians in Antioch, Syria, and Cilicia.

The great importance of this decree was that it allowed Gentile converts to remain uncircumcised and to eat meals with Jewish Christians. It was a clear victory for Paul and confirmed the undertakings which had been given to him privately during his previous visit to Jerusalem (see Gal 2^{9-10}, and notes on Acts 11^{27-30}), except that on that occasion there had been no mention of food restrictions.

The Council of Jerusalem did not end the controversy about the Jewish Law. When Paul returned to Jerusalem for the last time, he was warned that there were Jewish Christians, 'staunch upholders of the Law' (Acts 21^{20}), who were highly indignant about his attitude to circumcision. Old prejudices die hard, and time was needed before the Church as a whole revised its opinions about the Law. Paul's views had been accepted officially, but it was probably not until after the fall of Jerusalem in A D 70 that the more conservative of Jewish Christians ceased to maintain the necessity of circumcision.

The views which Paul championed about the Christian attitude to the Law are forcibly expressed in his letters to the Galatians and the Romans (see notes on Gal 2^{15-21}, Rom 3^{21-6}), in which he argues that men are justified through faith and not by the performance of the works of the Law. In his dispute with Peter at Antioch (Gal 2^{11-14}) and in his second and third visits to Jerusalem after his conversion he acted with great tenacity in upholding these views. His firm and courageous behaviour helped to ensure the future of Christianity both as a universal religion and as a religion of personal faith in Christ.

Acts 15^2. For the view that this visit of Paul to Jerusalem is the one which is described in Galatians 2^{1-10}, see notes on Acts 11^{27-30}. The view which is accepted here is that Galatians 2^{1-10} records the visit mentioned in Acts 11.

Acts 15^{13}. *James*, the brother of Jesus, was at this time leader of the Jerusalem church (see also Acts 12^{17}), a position which he continued to hold until his death in A D 62. Although his action in sending men to Antioch (Gal 2^{12}) suggests that he was reluctant to support Paul's views, he gave public support to Paul at the Jerusalem Council. There is no clear evidence for the view, which is sometimes put forward, that he was Paul's chief opponent in the controversy about the Law.

Acts 15^{14}. *Simeon* refers to Simon Peter.

Acts 15^{16-17} are a quotation from the Greek version of Amos 9^{11-12}. Since James is likely to have spoken in Aramaic, this confirms the view that the Acts is not giving a verbatim report of his speech.

Acts 15^{20}. The decree refers to food dedicated to pagan idols, or strangled, or mixed with blood. Some manuscripts omit the reference to *anything that has been strangled* here and in Acts 15^{29} and 21^{25}. The decree would then be concerned not with food laws but with moral laws. It would forbid idolatry, fornication, and murder (such could be the meaning of *blood*).

Acts 15^{22}. *the apostles and elders*. James was by no means the absolute ruler of the Jerusalem church. The final decision was taken by the apostles and elders (for *elders* see notes on Acts 20^{17}) and was ratified by the whole church.

Acts 15^{36}–18^{23}—*Paul's Second Missionary Journey*

After he had been preaching and teaching for some time in Antioch, Paul decided to set out on another missionary tour. Because Barnabas wanted to take with them John Mark, whom Paul did not think reliable, the two apostles had a dispute, and Barnabas went with Mark to Cyprus, while Paul took Silas as his companion on a tour of Asia Minor.

On this journey Paul revisited some of the towns in which he had preached on his first missionary journey. Eventually he crossed to

Europe and preached in the cities of Macedonia and Greece, including Philippi, Thessalonica, Beroea, Athens, and Corinth. On his return journey he made a brief visit to Ephesus, sailed to Caesarea, and then travelled to Antioch.

The story will not be traced in detail, but important features of it will be mentioned.

(i) *The Mission to Macedonia and Greece.* On this tour Paul extended his activity to Europe. He had a vision in which a Macedonian asked him for help (16⁹), and he crossed as soon as possible to Macedonia.

(ii) *The Conversion of Jews and Gentiles.* Paul kept to his practice of teaching first in the local synagogues (17², ¹⁰, ¹⁷, 18⁴, ¹⁹); and at Philippi, where there was no synagogue, he went to a place where the Jews gathered for prayer (16¹²⁻¹³). Many of his converts on this European journey were Jews (17¹⁻⁴, ¹¹), among whom was Crispus, who had been an officer of the synagogue at Corinth (18⁸). Other converts, like Lydia, whom he met at Philippi, and Titus Justus, with whom he stayed in Corinth, were Gentiles who sympathized with Judaism and were called 'worshippers of God' or 'Godfearers' (16¹⁴, 17⁴, 18⁷; compare 10²). Some converts, however, were neither Jews nor sympathizers with Judaism, and they included the Philippian jailer and his household, Dionysius, who was a member of the Athenian court of the Areopagus, and Damaris, an Athenian woman (16³⁰⁻⁴, 17³⁴; see also 17⁴, ¹², 18⁸).

(iii) *The Encounter with Pagan Religions and Philosophies.* Paul was brought face to face with paganism in all its strength and glamour. In addition to the traditional Greek religion and the Oriental mystery cults, there were the Greek philosophies, two of which, Epicureanism and Stoicism, are mentioned in the account of his visit to Athens (17¹⁸). The Acts describes how Paul was brought before the the Court of the Areopagus in Athens, because he had been teaching about strange gods, Jesus and Resurrection—it seems that some of the Athenians thought that he believed the resurrection itself to be a goddess (17¹⁶⁻²¹). The speech in 17²²⁻³¹ is an impression of what Paul is likely to have said rather than a verbally accurate report. But it underlines Paul's concern to interpret the gospel in terms which his Greek audience could understand. Much of the address would commend itself to Stoic philosophers, who would agree with the proclamation of God as the universally present creator. It even includes a quotation, 'We are also his offspring', from the works of Aratus, a Stoic poet (17²⁸). But the idea that

Jesus has been raised from the dead and will return as judge, which is included in the second part of the speech, would appear ludicrous to most Greek philosophers. However much Paul adapted his language and ideas to his audience, sooner or later he had to present the distinctive teaching of Christianity, even though most of the seed was sown on stony ground. But, according to the Acts, not everyone in Athens laughed at Paul. Some asked to hear him again, and others were converted (17^{32-4}).

(iv) *Opposition from Jews and Gentiles.* Most of the opposition to Paul and his companions was still aroused by Jews. At Thessalonica the Jews stirred up a riot against the missionaries, and they tried to cause trouble at Beroea ($17^{5-9,\ 13-14}$). In Corinth they brought Paul before Gallio, the Roman governor, and accused him of preaching an illegal religion, but Gallio refused to take action (18^{12-17}). Gentiles, however, were also responsible for persecution of the missionaries. At Philippi Paul and Silas were flung into prison as a result of complaints by the owners of a slave-girl who ceased to be of profit to them after Paul had driven out a spirit from her (16^{16-24}). In Athens Paul encountered opposition from Greek philosophers, though it did not take the form of persecution (17^{18-21}).

Acts 15^{40}. *Silas* was Paul's chief companion on this second tour, and stayed with him until they reached Beroea (17^{14}). Later he joined Paul at Corinth (18^{5}). Silas was one of the delegates who had been appointed to take the decree of the Jerusalem Council to Antioch ($15^{22,\ 32}$). He was probably the same person as the Silvanus who preached with Paul at Corinth (2 Cor 1^{19}), was his companion when he wrote to the Thessalonians (1 Thess 1^{1}, 2 Thess 1^{1}), and is said to have written 1 Peter at Peter's dictation (1 Pet 5^{12}). He is described in Acts 15^{32} as a prophet.

Acts 16^{1}. *Timothy,* who joined Paul at Lystra and was circumcised by him in order to avoid trouble with the Jews, was the son of a Jewish Christian mother and a Greek father. He accompanied Paul on his second tour as far as Beroea (17^{14}), and was with him later in Athens, from which he went as his representative to Thessalonica (1 Thess 3^{1-2}). He then joined Paul again in Corinth (18^{5}). He was Paul's emissary and companion during his third missionary tour (19^{22}, 20^{4}), and is often mentioned in his letters as his representative, colleague, and fellow-preacher (Rom 16^{21}, 1 Cor 4^{17}, 16^{10}, 2 Cor 1^{19}, Phil 2^{19}, 1 Thess $3^{2,\ 6}$). He is named as Paul's companion in the introductory greetings of 1 and 2 Thessalonians, 2 Corinthians, Philippians, Colossians, and Philemon. Paul regarded him as one of his most trusted friends, of whom he could say : 'There is no one else here who sees things as I do' (Phil 2^{20}). Though the Pauline authorship of the two letters to Timothy is seriously disputed (see p. 238), the letters show that Timothy was believed to have had oversight of a number of churches.

Acts 16[9]. *a Macedonian*. The conjecture that this man was Luke has little to support it except the fact that a 'We-passage' begins in the next verse.

Acts 16[10-17] is the first of the 'We passages' which may have come from Luke's diary (see p. 160).

Acts 16[21]. Judaism was an officially permitted religion in the Roman Empire, but Christianity had not been granted this status.

Acts 17[1]. *Thessalonica* was the capital of Macedonia.

Acts 17[5]. Jason's house was being used for Christian meetings. If Jason was the person mentioned in Romans 16[21], he was a Jew.

Acts 17[16]. *Athens*, which had been formerly a great cultural centre of Greece, was now to a great extent living on its past. It was still, however, a meeting-place for philosophers.

Acts 17[18]. *Epicurean and Stoic philosophers*. The *Epicureans* believed that the gods were not interested in human affairs and that there would be no life after death. They advocated the pursuit of pleasure, but preferred the pleasure of a careful and moderate life to that of luxury and indulgence. The *Stoics* believed that a man's duty was to do what was right, whatever pain he had to endure. They had no strong or consistent beliefs in life after death, but they believed in a god whom they regarded as the basic principle of the universe. It is not surprising that members of these two famous schools of philosophy were offended by Christian teaching about Jesus and the resurrection.

Acts 17[19]. *The Court of Areopagus*, which had once been the Athenian equivalent of a House of Lords, was now responsible for the oversight of education and religion.

Acts 18[1]. *Corinth* was a great port, which was the seat of the Roman governor of Achaia. It was the meeting-place of many religions and philosophies, and was notorious for its immorality.

Acts 18[2]. *Aquila* and *Priscilla* had been forced to leave Rome in A D 49, when the emperor Claudius expelled the Jews from the city. A Roman historian says that Jews were expelled because of disturbances instigated by 'Chrestus', which suggests that the trouble may have arisen because of Christian preaching.

Because Aquila and Priscilla practised Paul's own trade of tent-making, he lodged with them and worked with them at Corinth. They accompanied him to Ephesus (18[18-19]) where they later gave instruction to Apollos (18[26]). They were in Ephesus when Paul wrote 1 Corinthians (1 Cor 16[19]), and, if Romans 16 was actually written to Rome, they returned eventually to Rome (Rom 16[3]; see p. 219). At some time they incurred great risks for Paul's sake (Rom 16[4]). In Paul's letters Priscilla is called Prisca.

Acts 18[8]. *Crispus* is mentioned also in 1 Corinthians 1[14].

Acts 18[12]. *Gallio* belonged to a distinguished Roman family. He was brother of the Stoic philosopher Seneca, who was Nero's tutor.

Acts 18[13]. See notes on 16[21].

Acts 18[18]. It was a custom for Jews to take vows, under which for a specified period they lived a strictly disciplined life and did not cut their hair (see Num 6[1-21]). Paul must have taken this vow in gratitude for escape from some danger or in anticipation of future troubles.

Acts 18[24-8]—*Apollos at Ephesus*

Before Paul returned to Ephesus, an Alexandrian Jew called Apollos came to the city. The Acts says that Apollos 'knew only John's baptism', implying that, although he was acquainted with the life and teaching of Jesus, he did not know that the baptism of the Spirit had been imparted to believers. After Priscilla and Aquila had given him instruction, he crossed to Corinth where he preached the gospel and continued the work which Paul had begun. 'I planted the seed', Paul wrote, 'and Apollos watered it' (1 Cor 3[6]).

Apollos was an independent-minded man who went his own way (see 1 Cor 16[12]). Nothing is said in the New Testament about the nature of his teaching. Since he was born in Alexandria, he may have been influenced by the allegorical method of interpreting the scriptures, which was practised by Philo, the Jewish theologian of Alexandria. Apollos was in Corinth again, when Paul wrote 1 Corinthians (1 Cor 16[12]).

Acts 19[1]–21[17]—*Paul's Third Missionary Journey*

After a period in Antioch, Paul set out on his third tour, and passed once more through Asia Minor (see 18[23]). He stayed for many months in Ephesus, and then crossed to Macedonia and Greece, from which he went to Troas and Miletus. He returned by sea to Caesarea, and travelled from there to Jerusalem.

It was during his residence in Ephesus that trouble flared up in the church at Corinth, but, since nothing is said about this in the Acts, it will be discussed in the notes on the Corinthian letters.

Some of the special features of the narrative of this third journey will now be mentioned.

(i) *Problems of Church Discipline*. At Ephesus, Paul found some men who did not know that the gift of the Spirit was available, though they had received John's baptism and claimed to be Christians.

When Paul baptized them and laid hands on them, they received the Spirit and began to prophesy and to speak in ecstatic language (19[1-7]). The Church's attitude to baptism was not uniform at this time, since Apollos, whose situation was like that of these men of Ephesus, was not baptized by Priscilla and Aquila. (18^{24-8}; see also note on 10^{44-8}).

Another problem was the rise of people who used the name of Jesus but had no allegiance to the Church. Acts 19^{13-20} tells of the seven sons of Sceva, who invoked the name of Jesus to drive out evil spirits and on one occasion were beaten up by the man whom they were trying to cure. The story is told in contrast with an account of Paul's successful work of healing (19^{8-12}).

(ii) *Opposition to Paul at Ephesus.* The Acts contains a graphic narrative of an agitation stirred up at Ephesus by Demetrius, a silversmith, whose trade had been affected when the growth of Christianity caused a drop in the demand for silver shrines of the local goddess Diana. The town clerk quelled the riot, and Paul decided to leave for Macedonia (19^{23-41}). The incident is an illustration of the way in which selfish interests can lead men to oppose the work of Christ.

(iii) *The Worship and Ministry of the Church.* The story of Eutychus (20^{7-12}) provides evidence of the nature of Christian worship. The members of the Church met at a private house on Saturday evening for the breaking of bread, which was a normal meal, centred on the sacrament of the Lord's Supper. The meeting, which included preaching, lasted until early on Sunday morning. The story shows that Sunday, the day when Jesus rose from the dead, was regarded by Christians as a special day for worship (compare 1 Cor 16^2).

There is a certain amount of information in this section of the Acts about the ministry of the Church. Paul had authority of an undefined nature over a whole group of churches, and was assisted by men like Timothy and Erastus (19^{22}). Although it was his policy to appoint elders in new churches (14^{23}), there was probably no fixed order of ministry at this time. In his speech at Miletus the elders are called bishops (20^{28}; *NEB* translates 'shepherds'), and in his letters there are references to various kinds of church leaders (1 Cor 12^{28}; Eph 4^{11}; Phil 1^1) including bishops (Phil 1^1), but there is no mention of elders (see notes on 1 Cor 12^{28}).

Acts 19^1. *Ephesus* was the capital of the province of Asia (see notes on Acts 6^9).

Acts 19^6. *tongues of ecstasy.* See notes on Acts 21^{1-13}.

Acts 19^{13}. *exorcists* were men who drove out evil spirits.

Acts 19^{22}. *Erastus* may be the man mentioned in Romans 16^{23} and 2 Timothy 4^{20}, who was city treasurer of Ephesus.

Acts 19^{24}. *Diana*, whose Greek name was Artemis, was traditionally the goddess of hunting, but was worshipped in Asia Minor as a goddess of fertility.

Acts 19[29]. *Aristarchus* came from Thessalonica, and was eventually imprisoned with Paul, probably at Rome (Acts 20[4], 27[2], Col 4[10], Philem 24).

Gaius should not be confused with Gaius of Derbe (Acts 20[4]) or Gaius of Corinth (Rom 16[23], 1 Cor 1[14]).

the theatre was an open-air amphitheatre, which was used for large civic assemblies.

Acts 19[31]. *dignitaries of the province.* RV translates *Asiarchs.* The Greek word *asiarchai* refers to delegates from the cities of Asia who presided over games and festivals, and had special responsibility for emperor-worship.

Acts 20[4]. *Tychicus* was a trusted helper of Paul (Eph 6[21], Col 4[7], 2 Tim 4[12], Tit 3[12]). *Trophimus* was an Ephesian, who is mentioned in Acts 21[29] and 2 Timothy 4[20].

Acts 20[5-15] is a 'We-passage'; see note on 16[10-17].

Acts 20[17]. *elders* was the title given by the Jews to the leading officials of synagogues. It was also a title used for the officers of guilds in Asia Minor. The elders at the Jerusalem church (see 11[30], 15[4, 6, 22-3], 21[18]) exercised authority under James and the apostles. The elders of other churches had general oversight of local church affairs. The Greek for *elder* is *presbuteros*, from which 'presbyter' is derived, and in the New Testament there is no essential difference between a presbyter and a bishop (see Tit 1[5-9], and notes on Acts 20[28]). In the second century the threefold order of bishops, presbyters, and deacons arose, but there was no fixed and universal pattern of ministry in the first century.

Acts 20[28]. *shepherds* is used by *NEB* here to translate *episkopoi*, which means *overseers* or *bishops.* This verse, which is from a speech to the elders of the church at Ephesus, shows that at this stage there was no real difference between elders and bishops.

Acts 20[35]. This saying of Jesus is not found in the gospels.

Acts 21[1-18] is another 'We-passage'; see note on 16[10-17].

Acts 21[8]. *Philip.* See 6[5] and 8[4-40].

Acts 21[10]. *Agabus.* See 11[28].

Acts 21[18]–26[32]—Paul's Arrest and Questioning

When Paul reached Jerusalem, he was warned that many Jewish Christians were disturbed by his attitude to the Law. He was persuaded to make a gesture of respect to the Law by paying the expenses of four men who had taken a vow, and by sharing with them the ritual of purification. But when some Jews from the province of Asia accused him of introducing a Gentile called Trophimus into the Temple, the crowd seized him. Troops came to his rescue, and he was taken into custody (21[18]–22[29]).

After an appearance before the Jewish Council, in which he divided the Sadducees and the Pharisees against each other by a reference to the resurrection, he was taken to Caesarea, and, in spite of a Jewish plot to ambush him, arrived safely before the governor Felix. He was kept under open arrest for two years until Felix relinquished office (22^{30}–24^{27}).

When the new governor, Festus, gave Paul the choice between a trial in Jerusalem and a trial in Rome, Paul chose Rome. The Acts records that about this time Paul spoke to Herod Agrippa II, who formed a high opinion of him and said that he did not deserve punishment (25^1–26^{32}).

The main impression of this section of the Acts is that, while the Jews were responsible for the arrest and imprisonment of Paul, the Romans were his protectors, rescuing him from the angry mob and making sure that he received a fair hearing. Nevertheless, the behaviour of the Roman officials was far from exemplary. Claudius Lysias, the commandant of the soldiers in Jerusalem (23^{26}), only just refrained from having Paul flogged (22^{22-9}). Felix kept Paul under arrest to please the Jews, although he knew that he was innocent (24^{27}). Festus's suggestion that the trial should take place in Jerusalem was made to win favour with the Jews and would have endangered Paul's safety (25^9). And Herod Agrippa II, who must be classed with the Roman officials, washed his hands of the matter, although he believed Paul to be innocent (26^{30-2}).

Emphasis is laid in these chapters on Paul's rights as a Roman citizen (21^{39}, 22^{25-9}, 23^{27}, 25^{10}; see also 16^{37-8}), which entitled him to privileged treatment, including the option of a trial in Rome. The fact that Tarsus, a Roman city, was his birthplace, did not itself entitle him to Roman citizenship, and he probably had this status because his father also possessed it.

Acts 21^{23}. *a vow*. See notes on 18^{18}.

Acts 21^{29}. *Trophimus*. See notes on 20^4.

Acts 21^{38}. The *Egyptian* had promised that the walls of Jerusalem would miraculously collapse and his followers would seize power from the Romans. His revolt, however, was suppressed, and he himself escaped into hiding. The *terrorists* who had supported him were members of the Sicarii (literally, dagger-men), a group of fanatical Jewish nationalists who during the governorship of Felix carried out political assassinations.

Acts 22^{1-21}. For this and other accounts of Paul's conversion, see notes on 9^{1-19}.

Acts 23^{24}. *Felix* was governor of Judaea from A D 52 to 60.

Acts 25^{13}. *Agrippa* was Herod Agrippa II, who at this time ruled over part of Galilee and other areas. He had oversight of the Jerusalem Temple and the right to nominate the High Priest. He was the son of Herod Agrippa I (see notes on 12$^{1-25}$).

Acts 26$^{1-29}$. For this speech, see notes on 9$^{1-19}$.

Acts 27^1–28^{31}—*Paul's Journey to Rome and his Ministry there*

Paul was sent by Festus to Rome. His voyage and shipwreck, his safe landing in Malta, and the final stages of his journey, are vividly described in 27^1–28^{15}. Having reached Rome, he met the leaders of the Jewish community and explained his position. When he expounded the gospel to them, some believed and others did not. The Acts ends with an affirmation that salvation is for the Gentiles (28^{28}) and with the statement that Paul remained two years in Rome, proclaiming the gospel 'quite openly and without hindrance' (28$^{30-1}$).

The narrative leaves Paul in Rome about A D 62, awaiting his trial. Until someone appeared to accuse him, the trial could not proceed; and we do not know if anyone emerged. It is possible that he was released and made a further missionary journey (see p. 239), but it is more likely that he remained for the rest of his life in Rome. Although the circumstances of his death are not known for certain, he was probably executed by the emperor Nero during the persecution of Christians in A D 64.

Acts 27^1–28^{16} is a 'We-passage'; see note on 16$^{10-17}$.
Acts 28$^{26-7}$ quotes from Isaiah 6$^{9-10}$.

QUESTIONS

(1) What was the importance of the gift of the Spirit at Pentecost?
(2) Show how first Peter and then James, the Lord's brother, gave leadership to the Church in Jerusalem.
(3) Give an account of the Council of Jerusalem and its consequences.
(4) Comment on: Acts 2$^{45-7}$, 7^{58}, 8^{30}, 9$^{4-6}$, 10^{15}, 11$^{25-6}$.

CHAPTER NINE

ST PAUL: HIS TEACHING; AND THE LETTERS TO THE GALATIANS, THESSALONIANS, AND CORINTHIANS

INTRODUCTION

MUCH OF Paul's life has been described in the previous chapter, and now we turn to his letters, in which he reveals his beliefs and thoughts, his spiritual experience, and his attitude to the problems he encountered in the Church. These letters are the earliest Christian writings which have survived. They were written before the first of the gospels, and for this reason alone would deserve serious attention. But they are not merely first-rate historical sources. They are intensely human documents, which give an insight into the personality of a man who is second only to Jesus Himself in importance for his influence on the growth of Christianity. They show this man immersed in the practical problems of the Church and working out the implications of his faith in his daily conduct. They are a testimony to the power of the risen Christ both in the life of an individual and in the life of the Church.

The genuineness of most of the Pauline letters has been questioned at one time or another, and a very large number of scholars have come to the conclusion that Paul did not write the letters to Timothy and Titus. Serious doubt has also been cast on the Pauline authorship of 2 Thessalonians and Colossians, and even more on that of Ephesians. It is impossible to discuss here the reasons for and against the Pauline authorship of the letters. Many of the arguments are concerned with the Greek vocabulary and style, and in recent years use has even been made of a computer to examine Paul's language. Those who question the Pauline authorship of a letter generally argue that the style and vocabulary betray the hand of an imitator, that the thought shows important differences from Paul's, and that the situation for which the letter was written could only have existed after his death. Even if the Pauline authorship of a letter is rejected, however, its message continues to have value and authority as an important presentation of the gospel.

In the following summary of the teaching of Paul no mention will be made of the letters to Timothy and Titus, which are assumed to have been written by a disciple of Paul. Reference will be made to the other

Pauline letters, but it should be remembered that the genuineness of Ephesians is widely disputed.

THE TEACHING OF ST PAUL

None of Paul's letters was intended as a systematic doctrinal treatise, and most of what he wrote was specially designed to meet the particular problems of the churches to which he was writing. But the letters show that he had thought deeply and comprehensively about the meaning of the gospel. His teaching has such power and insight that no subsequent Christian thinker has been able to neglect it. Anyone who attempts to present a systematic account of the Christian faith has sooner or later to come to terms with Paul.

(1) *The Sinfulness of the Human Race*

Paul teaches that the whole of the human race, both Jews and Gentiles, is sinful. This sinfulness began with Adam's disobedience in the Garden of Eden, and its consequence was death (Rom 3^{23}, 5^{12}, 1 Cor 15^{21-2}). Jews are made aware of their sinfulness through the law of Moses (Rom 7^{7-8}), and Gentiles ought to be made aware of it through their consciences (Rom 2^{11-16}). But although men know that they are sinners, they cannot set themselves free from the power of sin. Even the Mosaic law had only a temporary value as a tutor to God's people until the time of Christ, and was unable to liberate them from sin (Gal 3^{23-5}). When the sinner knows what is right, he has not the strength of will to do it. Two laws struggle within him, the law of God and the law of sin, and he becomes a prisoner to the law of sin (Rom 7^{14-25}).

A sinner is a man who lives on the level of 'the lower nature', or, according to a more literal translation, of 'the flesh' (Rom 8^5). The lower nature is not in itself evil, as long as it is kept in its place. But a man who lives on the level of the lower nature is a man who has no real allegiance to God and is dominated by selfish and materialistic desires and by bodily appetites. He is in fact an enemy of God and needs to be reconciled to Him (Rom 5^{10}, 8^7).

(2) *Salvation through Christ*

There is only one way in which a man can be rescued from sin and death and from servitude to the Jewish Law, and that is through Jesus Christ, whom God sent for this very purpose (Rom 3^{25}, 7^{24-5}, Gal 4^4). Although men were God's enemies, in Christ He was 'reconciling the world to himself' (2 Cor 5^{19}). Jesus was a 'means of expiating sin'

(Rom 3[25]; compare Rom 8[3]), and though he was not a sinner, He was made 'one with the sinfulness of men' in order that men might be made 'one with the goodness of God himself' (2 Cor 5[21]). By becoming subject to the curse of the Jewish Law at His crucifixion, He 'bought us freedom from the curse of the law' (Gal 3[13]). His death was a means of redemption which set men free from captivity to sin (Rom 3[24], 1 Cor 1[30], Gal 3[13], 4[5], Eph 1[7], Col 1[14]), and on the Cross He decisively overcame all supernatural powers which opposed Him (Col 2[15]; see also Col 1[13], Gal 4[3-5]).

The benefits of Christ's work are obtained through faith. It is impossible for a man to be 'justified' (i.e. acquitted of guilt for sin and reckoned as righteous) because of the good works which he has done, since it is impossible to fulfil all the demands of the Law. But if a man has faith in Christ, then God will 'justify' him, and receive him as a son (Rom 5[1], Gal 3[23-6]). This 'faith' of which Paul writes is not a mere acceptance of doctrinal pronouncements about Christ but a complete trust in Him and reliance upon Him. It is belief *in* Christ, not merely belief *about* Him.

Faith does not itself justify men. It is God who justifies them by His grace (Rom 3[24]; compare Eph 2[8]), that is by His undeserved, forgiving love. Faith is not a special kind of good works but the means by which a man accepts the grace of God.

(3) *Life in Christ*

The man who is accepted as righteous is at peace with God and lives in hope of future glory (Rom 5[1-5]). His present life on earth is lived 'in union with Christ'.[1] The Christian dies to sin and becomes alive to God 'in union with Christ Jesus' (Rom 6[5 11]). He is 'crucified with Christ' (Gal 2[20]) and is 'raised to life with Christ' (Col 3[1]). The sacrament of baptism, with its symbolism of a descent into the waters of death and a rising to new life, signifies both the death and resurrection of Christ and the Christian's entry into a new life. Men are 'baptized into union with Christ' (Rom 6[3], Gal 3[27]).

Paul regards the whole of his life as lived in union with Christ. When he suffers he shares Christ's sufferings (2 Cor 1[5], Phil 3[10]), and when he is weak he shares Christ's weakness (2 Cor 13[4]). Because he is united to Christ, he belongs to a new world (2 Cor 5[17]) and can say, 'To me life is Christ' (Phil 1[21]).

[1] Where the Greek is literally 'in Christ' *NEB* prefers to translate 'in union with Christ'.

(4) *The Life of the Spirit*

The Christian life is lived according to the Law of the Spirit, not according to the letter of the Jewish Law (Rom 8^{1-2}, 2 Cor 3^6, Gal 5^{2-6}). A Christian is an adopted son of God and enjoys the liberty which belongs to a son (Gal $4^{5, 31}$). He lives within the sphere of the new covenant of the Spirit (2 Cor 3^{1-6}), and 'where the Spirit of the Lord is, there is liberty' (2 Cor 3^{17}).

The Spirit dwells in the believer (Rom 8^9) and guides him (Gal $5^{16, 25}$). Virtuous actions and dispositions are the 'harvest of the Spirit' (Gal 5^{22}), and under the Spirit's influence men confess Jesus as Lord (1 Cor 12^3). The Spirit testifies that we are God's children, assuring us of this inwardly (Rom 8^{14-16}, Gal 4^{6-7}). Amid the imperfections and tensions of this life the Spirit is a foretaste of future blessedness, like the firstfruits of a harvest to come, or a pledge of immortality (Rom 8^{23}, 2 Cor 1^{22}, 5^5, Eph 1^{14}).

(5) *Ethical Teaching*

Because Christians are under the new covenant and have the liberty of the Spirit, they do not need a detailed code of ethics. The law which governs their conduct is the Law of Love, which sums up all the other commandments (Rom 13^{8-10}, Gal 5^{14}).

This does not mean that Paul has no place for ethical teaching. He gives it great prominence in many of his letters. Christians must offer their 'very selves' to God, as 'a living sacrifice, dedicated and fit for his acceptance, the worship offered by mind and heart' (Rom 12^1). They must aim at the greatest of spiritual gifts, faith, hope, and, above all, love (1 Cor 13^{13}). They must avoid 'the kind of behaviour that belongs to the lower nature: fornication, impurity, and indecency; idolatry and sorcery; quarrels, a contentious temper, envy, fits of rage, selfish ambitions, dissensions, party intrigues, and jealousies; drinking bouts, orgies, and the like'; and they must let the Spirit bring forth in them its harvest of 'love, joy, peace, patience, kindness, goodness, fidelity, gentleness, and self-control' (Gal 5^{19-22}). In their struggle against the supernatural powers of wickedness they need the spiritual armour of truth, integrity, faith, sobriety, hope, and love (Eph 6^{10-17}, 1 Thess 5^8). They must not think themselves better than other people (Rom 12^{16}, Gal 6^3). They must be ready to sympathize with others, 'call down blessings' on their persecutors, and 'never pay back evil for evil' (Rom $12^{14, 15, 17}$).

Sex, Marriage, and Divorce. Paul denounces fornication, adultery, and homosexual perversion (Rom 1^{26-7}, 1 Cor 6^9), and teaches that the body is 'a shrine of the indwelling Holy Spirit', which belongs to God and should be treated with honour (1 Cor 6^{18-20}, 1 Thess 4^{2-5}).

His attitude to marriage changes. In 1 Corinthians he regards marriage as a second-best alternative for those who lack the self-control which is needed for a celibate life (1 Cor $7^{1-9,\ 25-35}$), and he advises widows not to remarry (1 Cor 7^{39-40}). In his later writings, however, he says nothing to belittle the estate of marriage, and even describes Christ's love for the Church as a pattern for a husband's love for his wife (Eph 5^{22-33}; see also Col 3^{18-19}). His change of attitude is caused by his growing realization that the end of the world will not necessarily come in the immediate future.

Paul is opposed to divorce, and in a mixed marriage between a Christian and a heathen he permits a separation only if the heathen partner wishes it (1 Cor 7^{10-16}).

He also gives teaching about parents and children. Even in a mixed marriage the children 'belong to God' (literally 'are holy') (1 Cor 7^{14}). Children, he says, must obey their parents, and fathers must not exasperate their children (Col 3^{20-1}, Eph 6^{1-4}).

Although he stresses a husband's duty to love and care for his wife, he clearly accepts the subjection of women, and argues that the man is head of the woman, and that woman was created for man (1 Cor 11^{2-12}, Col 3^{18-19}, Eph 5^{22-33}). But his affirmation that in Christ there is neither male nor female (Gal 3^{28}) contains the seeds of more enlightened development.

Work and Slavery. Paul teaches men that it is their duty to do their daily work well (1 Thess 4^{11-12}). He accepts the institution of slavery, and exhorts owners of slaves to be just and fair to them, remembering that they themselves have a Master in heaven. He tells slaves to obey their masters and to do their work as slaves of Christ (Eph 6^{5-9}, Col $3^{22}-4^1$). Although he believes that slaves should be treated with kindness and regarded as brothers, he does not expect a Christian owner to release them (Philem 11–20). But his statement that there is neither slave nor freeman in Christ Jesus, is in advance of his detailed teaching on the subject (Gal 3^{28}, 1 Cor 12^{13}, Col 3^{11}).

The State. Paul regards secular rulers as divinely appointed. It is the Christian's duty to submit to them, and to pay taxes (Rom 13^{1-7}). But

Paul never let the secular rulers force him to compromise his Christian principles and was prepared to suffer flogging and imprisonment for Christ's sake (2 Cor 6^{4-5}, 11^{23-6}, Phil $1^{7, 13}$).

Wealth. Paul does not object to men owning property and money, but expects them to be generous in their giving : 'Each person should give as he has decided for himself; there should be no reluctance, no sense of compulsion; God loves a cheerful giver' (2 Cor 9^7). Christians must remember the generosity of Christ Himself : 'he was rich, yet for your sake he became poor, so that through his poverty you might become rich' (2 Cor 8^9). But riches are a secondary matter to Paul. 'I have learned', he writes, 'to find resources in myself whatever my circumstances. I know what it is to be brought low, and I know what it is to have plenty. I have been very thoroughly initiated into the human lot with all its ups and downs—fullness and hunger, plenty and want. I have strength for anything through him who gives me power' (Phil 4^{11-13}).

Consideration for the Weak. An important piece of Paul's ethical teaching is about the Christians' attitude to those who are 'weak in faith' and therefore over-scrupulous. These men believe it to be their duty to abstain from various kinds of food and drink, especially that which has been consecrated to a heathen idol. Paul teaches that no one should be contemptuous toward people with these scruples and that it is desirable to avoid such food and drink, although there is no real harm in it, rather than damage their faith (Rom 14^1–15^6, 1 Cor 8^{1-13}, 10^{23}–11^1).

(6) *The Church, Its Worship, and Its Ministry*

Paul describes the Church as 'Christ's body' (1 Cor 12^{27}; see also Rom 12^{4-5}, Col 1^{24}, Eph 4^{12}), of which Christians are limbs and organs. In the later letters he completes the picture by calling Christ the head of the body (Eph 1^{22-3}, 4^{15-16}, Col 1^{18}, 2^{19}). Life in Christ is not just a relationship between Christ and the individual but a relationship which includes all believers. Within the Church different people have different functions and are supplied with different spiritual gifts to perform them (1 Cor 12^{4-31}, Rom 12^{4-8}, Eph 4^{11-16}), but the highest gifts, faith, hope, and love, should be aimed at by all (1 Cor 12^{31}–13^{13}).

The Church is also regarded as the new Israel, the successor to the Jews as the chosen people of God (Gal 6^{16}). Those who have faith in Christ, whether they are circumcised or not, are the true children of

Abraham and the true people of God (Rom 2^{28-9}, 9^{24-9}, Gal $3^{7-9,\ 26-9}$).
They are not bound to God by a written covenant of the Law but by a
covenant of the Spirit, established in the hearts of men (2 Cor 3^{3-6}). The
community of the Church has been formed by Christ, who by His
death broke down the barrier between Jews and Gentiles and created
'a single new humanity in himself' (Eph 2^{13-16}).

Another metaphor for the Church is the temple of God or the temple
of the Spirit (1 Cor 3^{16-17}, 2 Cor 6^{16}, Eph 2^{20-2}); and the Church is also
regarded as the bride of Christ (2 Cor 11^2, Eph 5^{25-33}).

Sacraments. Baptism is the sacrament of incorporation into Christ,
through which men become members of the Church, which is the body
of Christ. In baptism men die to sin and become alive to God. All
Christians, irrespective of race, sex, and social status, are baptized into
one body, the Church (1 Cor 12^{13}, Rom 6^{3-4}, Gal 3^{27-9}, Col 2^{12}). But
baptism does not itself bring men into the new life. This is done by God,
who makes men His sons through faith (Gal 3^{26}).

Baptism is mentioned by Paul more often than the Lord's Supper.
But it is clear that the Supper was the centre of the Church's worship,
and included a proper meal. Paul exhorted the Corinthians to behave
in an orderly fashion at the sacrament, for, if they participated in the
meal unworthily, they would be desecrating the body and blood of
Christ, and would bring judgement on themselves (1 Cor 11^{23-34}). The
sacrament declares the unity of Christians in the Church, because they
all share in the body and blood of Christ, and because the one loaf is a
sign that they are one body (1 Cor 10^{16-17}). For further comments, see
notes on Mark 14^{12-25}.

Worship. There was considerable informality in worship. Different
members of the congregation made their own contributions to the service, and Paul, while accepting this informality, counsels them to behave
in an orderly fashion, because he fears that some of their displays of
religious emotion may be uncontrolled and unintelligible (1 Cor 14^{26-40}).
He also rules that women should not appear bare-headed at worship
(1 Cor 11^{5-6}) and that they should not speak to the congregation
(1 Cor 14^{34-5}).

The Ministry. There was no universal and rigid form of Church organization in Paul's day. Paul himself had authority over many churches
as an apostle, but the letters provide ample evidence that this authority

did not go unchallenged. Paul regarded his apostleship as derived from none but Christ (Gal 1^1) and though many people were inclined to assign a supremacy to the Jerusalem church, Paul merely accepted the obligation to provide contributions for the poorer Christians there (Rom 15$^{25-31}$, 1 Cor 16$^{1-4}$, Gal 2^{10}).

He mentions a variety of officers in the Church, giving different lists in different letters, and conveying the general impression that Church order was in a state of transition (Rom 12$^{6-8}$, 1 Cor 12$^{27-31}$, Eph 4$^{11-12}$, Phil 1^1). Apostles held the chief position in the Church, and their authority was not confined to a single congregation. Prophets seem to have been travelling ministers, and the position of teachers is not clear. Pastors probably remained in the same congregation, and by the time that Philippians was written, the chief local officers were called bishops and deacons. But the nature of the ministry may have varied from one district to another.

(7) *The Future*

Paul always taught that Jesus Christ would return to men, but his emphasis on the doctrine altered. In 1 Thessalonians 4^{15} he expects the return of Jesus in his own lifetime, and in 1 Corinthians 15$^{51-2}$ he expects it during the lifetime of his contemporaries. In Romans and Philippians he teaches that the coming of Christ is near, but does not say that he will live till that time (Rom 13^{11}, Phil 3^{20}, 4^5). In Colossians he writes of the future manifestation of Christ (Col 3^4), but neither in Colossians nor Ephesians does he suggest that Christ will return in the near future.

When Jesus comes, the faithful will rise to meet Him (1 Thess 4$^{15-18}$, 1 Cor 15$^{22-3}$), but it will also be a day of judgement (1 Thess 5$^{1-11}$, Rom 2^{16}, 2 Cor 5^{10}). At this final resurrection men will be transformed, and will have spiritual 'bodies' (1 Cor 15$^{42-9}$, Phil 3^{21})—the word 'body' stands for the form of a person's being and does not necessarily mean a body of flesh and blood. Those who are condemned will suffer retribution (Rom 2$^{5-10}$).

During the interval between a man's physical death and his final resurrection he will be with Christ (2 Cor 5$^{6-8}$, Phil 1^{23}). But even the redeemed will have to come under judgement at the last day (2 Cor 5^{10}). All that is unworthy in them will be destroyed, but they themselves will live (1 Cor 3$^{10-17}$).

There are suggestions in Paul's letters that all men may ultimately be saved. 'God's purpose', he writes, 'was to show mercy to all mankind' (Rom 11^{32}). 'As in Adam all men die, so in Christ all will be brought to life' (1 Cor 15[22]). Even if these sayings need mean no more than that both Jews and Gentiles will be saved, it is difficult to explain away the statement that God chose to reconcile all things on earth and in heaven (Col 1[20]).

This leads to another important aspect of Paul's teaching about the future. He believes that God's purpose of redemption is not confined to the human race. The whole of the created universe is waiting 'to be freed from the shackles of mortality and enter upon the liberty and splendour of the children of God' (Rom 8[18-22]). Paul does not explain how this will happen, but it is consistent with his belief that God is not only Source and Guide but 'Goal of all that is' (Rom 11[36]), and that the whole universe has been created for Christ (Col 1[16]). In Christ 'God chose to reconcile the whole universe to himself' (Col 1[20]), and it is God's ultimate purpose that 'the universe, all in heaven and on earth, might be brought into a unity in Christ' (Eph 1[10]).

A final point to be noticed in Paul's teaching about the last things is the tension between present and future. The resurrection will take place in the future, but in the present men receive new life; they are in a sense risen from the dead, because they are in union with Christ. Just as the synoptic gospels speak of the Kingdom of God as both present and future, and just as John's gospel speaks of the present blessing of eternal life and the future blessing of the resurrection, so Paul describes new life and resurrection as a present gift and a future hope. The link between the present and the future is made by the Spirit, who is the 'firstfruits of the harvest to come' (Rom 8[23]) and 'a pledge of what is to come' (2 Cor 1[22]; see also 2 Cor 5[5], Eph 1[14]).

(8) *The Sovereignty of God*

A belief in the almighty power of God underlies all the teaching of Paul. God is the 'Source, Guide, and Goal of all that is' (Rom 11[36]; see also 1 Cor 8[6]). Just as He was responsible for the creation, so He will be responsible for the last judgement and the final resurrection. His present control of the world is shown by the retribution which falls on sinners even in this life (Rom 1[18-32]). But His sovereignty is shown especially in His choice of men for salvation.

Paul is aware that he owes the blessings of his transformed life entirely to God (1 Cor 15[10]). He has been justified by God's grace. He has been set apart by God from birth for his work as an apostle (Gal 1[15]; see also Rom 1[1], Gal 1[1]), and he regards other Christians as called and chosen by God (Rom 1[7], 8[33], Col 3[12]), a choice which was made before the foundation of the world (Eph 1⁴⁻⁵). Indeed, as the 'chosen of God', the Christians are the new Israel, the new people of God. Since God has called them, He will be faithful to them (1 Thess 5²⁴), and they can be sure that, while they are working out their own salvation, He is working in them (Phil 2¹²⁻¹³).

According to some theologians, Paul believes that God has predestined certain men to salvation and others to damnation. But this is by no means clear from Paul's writings. He says that some men have been called and foreordained by God to salvation (Rom 8²⁹⁻³⁰). And his statements in Rom 9¹⁰⁻²³ have given rise to the idea that certain men are predestined to damnation. But the section of Romans which includes this passage culminates in the assertion that ultimately God will have mercy on all men (Rom 11³²). Paul's thought about the fate of those who reject Christ has not been fully and finally worked out in his letters.

(9) The Lord Jesus Christ

Paul's teaching is Christ-centred. It is through Christ that men receive salvation and it is in union with Him that they live the new life. The Church is His body, and He will come to receive the faithful at their final resurrection. In Colossians, Paul describes Him as the agent in the creation of the world and the goal to which the created universe moves (Col 1¹⁵⁻¹⁷). And in other letters he teaches that Christ existed before His physical birth (1 Cor 10⁴, 2 Cor 8⁹, Phil 2⁶).

Paul regularly calls Jesus by the title 'Lord', which was used for God in the Old Testament. 'Jesus is Lord' is Paul's basic creed (1 Cor 12³, Rom 10⁹, Phil 2¹¹). 'God the Father and the Lord Jesus Christ' is a frequent phrase in his letters, especially in the introductory paragraphs. Although Paul sometimes implies that the Father is greater than the Son (1 Cor 8⁶, 15²⁸, Phil 2¹¹), he also implies that the Son is divine. Jesus is 'the image of God' (2 Cor 4⁴, Col 1¹⁵) and 'the wisdom of God' (1 Cor 1²⁴, ³⁰). In Him 'the complete being of the Godhead dwells embodied' (Col 2⁹) and He had the divine nature from the beginning (Phil 2⁶).

In only one place in Paul's letters is it possible that Jesus is called God: in Romans 9⁵, where, instead of the NEB translation, we can read '. . . the Messiah, who is God, supreme over all, blessed for ever'. Apart from this passage Paul hesitates to call Jesus God. His account of Him as creator, judge, saviour, and Lord is clear enough proof of his belief in His divinity. His hesitation to call Him God is probably the outcome of a desire to avoid creating the impression that there are two separate gods. He is already confronted with the problem that God is one, yet more than one.

Paul's emphasis on Christ's divinity does not obscure his understanding of the reality of His manhood. The main theme of his preaching is the crucifixion, and he describes how Jesus was 'born of a woman, born under the law' (Gal 4[4]; see also Rom 1[3]). He bore the human likeness, was revealed in human shape (Phil 2[8]), and suffered pain (Col 1[24,] 2 Cor 1[5], Phil 3[10]); but, unlike other men, He was innocent of sin (2 Cor 5[21]).

It is fitting that this brief summary of Paul's thought should end with an account of his teaching about Christ, who was both the theme of his preaching and the source of his new life. 'The life I now live is not my life', he wrote, 'but the life which Christ lives in me' (Gal 2[20]). 'I resolved', he told the Corinthians, 'that while I was with you I would think of nothing but Jesus Christ—Christ nailed to the Cross' (1 Cor 2[2]). His letters are evidence of the sincerity and persistence of his determination to keep this resolve.

*   *   *

THE LETTER TO THE GALATIANS

Destination

The letter was probably written to Christians in the southern part of the Roman province of Galatia who were not Galatians by race. Some scholars believe, however, that it was written to Christians in the neighbourhood of Ancyra in the north of the province who were Galatians by race.

Date

It seems to have been written from Syrian Antioch in AD 48 shortly before the Jerusalem Council of Acts 15. On this theory it is the earliest of Paul's letters that we possess, and was written soon after his first missionary journey, in which he had visited Pisidian Antioch, Iconium, Lystra, and Derbe, all of which were in the southern part of the province of Galatia (Acts 13[14]–14[23]).

This explanation assumes that Paul's visit to Jerusalem described in Galatians 2[1-10] was the famine-visit of Acts 11[27-30]. If, however, the visit of Galatians 2[1-10] was the visit of Acts 15, Galatians was written after the Jerusalem Council. See notes on Acts 11[27-30].

Occasion

The letter was written because the churches in Galatia were yielding to pressure from men who insisted that male Gentile converts should be circumcised. Opponents of Paul were challenging his position as an apostle, and he wrote to defend both his personal authority and his attitude to the Jewish Law.

Contents

The letter includes a defence of Paul's conduct and call as an apostle (Gal 1^1–2^{14}, 4^{12-20}), an explanation of his attitude to the Law and of his belief in justification through faith (2^{15}–4^{11}), and a contrast between servitude under the Law and freedom under the Spirit (4^{21}–6^{18}).

COMMENTS ON SELECTED PASSAGES FROM THE LETTER TO THE GALATIANS

Galatians 1^{1-5}—*Introduction*

It was the custom in the ancient world for the writer of a letter to begin with his own name, and then to give the name of the people to whom he was writing. Paul follows this practice and describes himself as an apostle (see notes on Acts 1^{15-26}), stressing that his commission is not from men but from Jesus Christ and God the Father. He makes this point in answer to the critics who challenge his authority.

The Greeks began their letters with the word *chairein*, which means 'greetings'. By using *charis*, which is translated 'grace' and means God's free, unmerited love for men, Paul Christianizes the very courtesies of letter-writing.

Paul also wishes 'peace' to his readers. 'Peace' is the normal Hebrew form of greeting, but, when Paul uses the word, he is thinking of the peace which a man can enjoy after he has been reconciled to God (see notes on Jn 14^{27-31}).

Galatians 1^2. *the group of friends.* A literal translation of the Greek is *brothers.* Because they were all sons of God through faith, they were brothers in Christ.

Christian congregations. The Greek can be translated *churches*; the Greek word *ekklēsia* can refer either to the universal Church or to a local congregation.

Galatians 1^4. *sacrificed.* The literal translation is *gave*, but *NEB* rightly understands that the idea of sacrifice is present (see also Rom 3^{25}, 8^3, 1 John 1^7).

this present age of wickedness. A contrast is implied with the Messianic age which has been inaugurated by Christ and will reach its consummation in the future.

Galatians 1[6-12]—*The True Gospel*

Paul expresses his astonishment that the Galatians have reverted from the gospel to a form of legalism. There is only one true gospel, and that is the gospel which Paul preaches.

Galatians 1[13]–2[14]—*The Source of Paul's Authority*

Much of this section has already been discussed in the previous chapter (see notes on Acts 11[27-30]), and nothing further need be said about the main historical problems which it raises. Paul is affirming that his call came from God, who set him apart from the day of his birth and gave him the gospel by a special revelation of Jesus Christ (1[11-16]). He emphasizes that he is not indebted to the other apostles either for his authority or for his message. So far was he from being subordinate to the rest of the apostles that he consulted them as little as possible and was even prepared to defy them (1[17]–2[14]).

Galatians 1[15]. *from birth.* Literally, *from my mother's womb.* (Compare Isa 49[1, 5], Jer 1[5], Lk 1[15]).

Galatians 1[18]. *Cephas,* the Aramaic name of Peter; see notes on Matthew 16[18].

Galatians 2[3-4]. *Titus.* It is not clear whether Titus was circumcised or not. Paul does not say that the course which was 'urged as a concession' was actually taken. *Titus* was later Paul's companion in Macedonia (2 Cor 7[6]; see also 2 Cor 2[13]) and his emissary to Corinth (2 Cor 7[13-14], 8[6, 16-18, 23], 12[18]). The existence of a letter to Titus, even if it was not written by Paul, shows that Titus was regarded as a person with authority over a group of churches.

Galatians 2[15-21]—*Justification through Faith*

Paul develops here one of his most important and distinctive doctrines, that of 'justification through faith'. *To justify* does not mean 'to make righteous' but 'to accept as righteous' or 'to reckon as righteous'. It also includes the idea of acquittal from guilt. Because they are sinners, men are guilty in the sight of God, but, when God justifies them, He acquits them of their guilt and accepts them as righteous. In so far as He treats them as righteous, they are no longer estranged from Him, and are capable of a positive relationship of fellowship with Him.

Faith does not mean merely the acceptance of certain beliefs about Christ, but a complete reliance upon Him and the acknowledgement of utter dependence on Him.

Paul's doctrine of justification arose from his own experience of inability to fulfil the Law, and was worked out in answer to those Christians who insisted that Gentile converts should be circumcised. He asserts that men are not accepted as righteous because of the works which they have done, but because of God's grace. The emphasis on grace is more obvious in Romans 3^{24} than in this passage, though the grace of God is mentioned in Galatians 2^{21}.

Grace, means God's free, undeserved love for men, which is active in Christ's sacrificial death for men (Rom 3^{24-5}). When a man has faith in Christ, God's grace becomes effective for him. The blessing which God confers is not a reward for faith any more than for works, but an act of unmerited love and mercy. Faith is the means by which a man accepts God's grace.

Paul goes on to speak about the new life into which he has entered through justification (verses 20–1). He shares in Christ's crucifixion and resurrection. He has died a death in dying to the Law, and lives a new life because Christ lives in him. This new life is his own, and yet it is Christ's. He retains his individuality, but at the same time he is utterly dependent on Christ.

For justification, see also notes on Romans 3^{21-31} and 5^{1-11}; and for the idea of participation in Christ's death and resurrection, see also notes on Romans 6^{1-14}.

Galatians 2^{16} quotes Psalm 143^2.
Galatians 2^{18} means that, if a Christian accepts the Jewish Law again after he has rejected it, he will once more become a transgressor of the Law.
Galatians 2^{19} means that, because the Law showed Paul his inability to live a life of good works, the Law itself helped him to abandon the Law and to begin a new life.

Galatians 3^{1-9}—*The Sons of Abraham*

The Galatians had foolishly turned back from the way of faith to the way of Law. The Jews prided themselves on being children of Abraham, from whom they were descended by race. It is the men of faith, however, whether they are Jews or not, who are the true children of Abraham, because Abraham was above all a man of faith, whose faith was counted to him for righteousness (see Gen 15^6). This recognition of Gentiles as Abraham's children fulfils the prophecy that in Abraham all nations will find blessing (Gen 12^3).

This theme is developed in Romans 4^{1-25}, where Paul argues that Abraham's faith was reckoned to him for righteousness before he was circumcised, and that therefore the dispensation of faith came before that of the Law.

Galatians 3^{10-14}—*The Curse*

Those who rely on obedience to the Law are under the curse of Deuteronomy 27^{26} because they cannot keep the Law perfectly. The Law is concerned with works and not with faith. Since a man cannot fulfil all the works of the Law, it is only through his faith that he can be justified. Christ submitted Himself to the curse of the Law by being 'hanged on a tree' when He was crucified (see Deut 21^{23}). In order to free men from the curse He had to take it upon Himself, and, when He did this, He not only shared the consequences of men's sin but showed the Law to be inadequate and discredited. His work on the Cross made the blessing of new life possible for all who had faith in Him, Gentiles as well as Jews. Since the new life is based on the covenant of the Spirit and not of the written Law, it is a life in which men receive the promised Spirit.

Galatians 3^{11} quotes Habakkuk 2^4.

Galatians 3^{12} quotes Leviticus 18^5.

Galatians 3^{13}. See also 2 Corinthians 5^{21}.

Galatians 3^{14}. That Christ's death and resurrection made the gift of the Spirit possible is also the theme of John 16^7 and Acts 2^{33}. For the promise of the Spirit, see Joel 2^{28-32} and Mark 1^8.

*   *   *

Galatians $3^{23}-4^7$—*Sons of God*

A contrast is made between the status of a man who is under the Law and that of a man who has faith in Christ. Under the Law a man is like a ward who is under the supervision of a tutor, but when a man has faith, he is set free (3^{23-5}). Men who have faith in Christ are sons of God, and through baptism they enter into 'union with Christ Jesus', who is like a garment which they wear, transforming them and marking them out from other men. In God's family, distinctions of race, social class, and sex are of no ultimate value, since Christians are all united with Christ (3^{26-8}). Under the Law men were like heirs to an estate, who were not of age and were in the same condition as slaves. By sending His Son Jesus Christ to buy their freedom, God enabled them to be liberated and to become His sons. To achieve this end Jesus had to have a human birth and submit to the authority of the Law (4^{1-5}). It is through the Spirit within them that men are assured of their position as God's sons and are able to call Him Father (4^{6-7}).

Galatians 3²⁷. A literal translation is : *For as many of you as were baptized into Christ, put on Christ.* See notes on Romans 6¹⁻¹⁴.

Galatians 3²⁸. Compare 1 Corinthians 12¹³ and Colossians 3¹¹.

Galatians 3²⁹. *the 'issue' of Abraham.* See notes on Galatians 3¹⁻⁹.

Galatians 4³. *elemental spirits of the universe.* Paul believed the Law to be controlled by superhuman powers.

Galatians 4⁵. *purchase freedom.* The Greek word is often translated *redeem.* See notes on Romans 3²¹⁻⁶.

attain the status of sons. Literally, *receive the adoption.* Paul regarded Christian believers as adopted children of God. See notes on Romans 8¹⁵ and Ephesians 1⁵.

Galatians 4⁶. See notes on Romans 8¹⁻¹⁷. For *Abba* see notes on Mark 14³⁶.

*   *   *

Galatians 5¹³⁻²⁵—*The Life of the Spirit*

The Christian life is one of liberty, because it does not bind men to obedience to a written law. A man's duty can be summed up in the single commandment that he should love his neighbour as himself. But, if Christians are free men, they must not abuse their freedom, or they can expect only destruction. Men who are guided by the Spirit will not yield to the desires of the 'lower nature', which are barriers to their entry into the Kingdom of God. Their lives will bring forth the harvest of the Spirit, which consists of the virtues of 'love, joy, peace, patience, kindness, goodness, fidelity, gentleness, and self-control'.

Galatians 5¹³. *lower nature.* The Greek word means literally *flesh.* Paul does not regard the lower nature as evil in itself. It becomes evil when it takes control of a man. When Paul speaks of *the desires of the lower nature* (Gal 5¹⁶), he is thinking not only of bodily appetites but of selfish and materialistic desires in general. He contrasts life on the level of the lower nature with life guided by the Spirit. See also notes on Romans 8¹⁻¹⁷.

Galatians 5¹⁴ quotes Leviticus 19¹⁸, which is used by Jesus as one of His two great commandments. See notes on Mark 12²⁸⁻³⁴.

*   *   *

THE FIRST LETTER TO THE THESSALONIANS

Date and Place of Writing

This letter was written about A D 50 when Paul was in Corinth on his second missionary tour. He had visited Thessalonica with Silas and Timothy earlier in the same tour (Acts 17¹⁻¹⁰), and when he wrote this letter, he linked them with himself in the greetings (1 Thess 1¹).

Occasion and Contents

The letter was written because Paul had received news, presumably through Silas and Timothy, of the state of the church in Thessalonica. Some of the news was good. The Thessalonian Christians were loyal in spite of persecution, and were well disposed towards Paul (1^{2-6}, 2^{13-16}, 3^{6-7}). But some of the news was disturbing. Paul's Jewish opponents had been trying to discredit him, and he felt obliged to defend his conduct (2^{1-13}, 2^{17}–3^{11}). There was a growing laxity in faith and conduct among some of the members of the church, and there were three groups into which the difficult people could be divided : 'the careless, the faint-hearted, and the weak' (5^{14}). The 'careless' were idlers, who thought that in view of the expected end of the world there was no need to have regular employment (4^{11-12}). Paul told them to do their work properly. The 'faint-hearted' were those who had grave doubts about the future life. They were uncertain about the fate of those Christians who died before the return of Jesus, and they were uncertain about their own fate also. Paul assured them that the Christians who had died would rise at the return of Jesus, and, while he warned them to be in a state of readiness, he affirmed that Jesus had power to save them (4^{13}–5^{11}). The 'weak' were people of lax sexual morality, and Paul told them that fornication was an offence against God, who had called them to holiness (4^{2-8}).

COMMENTS ON SELECTED PASSAGES FROM THE FIRST LETTER TO THE THESSALONIANS

1 Thessalonians 4^{13}–5^3—*The Coming of the Lord*

Paul answers the 'faint-hearted' (see 5^{14}) by assuring them that Chistians who have died will share in the resurrection, and by warning them that the Day of the Lord will come suddenly.

His reference to 'we who are left alive' (4^{17}) shows that he expects Christ to return in his own lifetime.

1 Thessalonians 4^{17}. The state of eternal blessedness is one in which *we shall always be with the Lord*. (See also 2 Cor 5^8 and Phil 1^{23}.)

1 Thessalonians 5^2. *a thief in the night*. Compare Luke 12^{39}.

1 Thessalonians 5^{4-11}—*The Children of Light*

Christians must be sober and watchful, living in faith, hope, and love, because they are children of light. The children of darkness will not be ready when Christ comes, but the children of light ought to be prepared for him, because they are destined for salvation and not for judgement.

1 Thessalonians 5[5]. *children of light.* See also Ephesians 5[8], John 12[36].

1 Thessalonians 5[6]. Compare Mark 13[33-8], Matthew 25[1-13].

1 Thessalonians 5[7]. *faith and love . . . hope.* Compare 1 Corinthians 13[13]. The idea of the Christian's armour is also found in Ephesians 6[10-17].

1 Thessalonians 5[10]. *awake or asleep* means 'alive or dead at the return of Christ'.

1 Thessalonians 5[12-13]—*Respect for Leaders*

These words were probably intended for the 'careless', who were idlers (see 5[14]) and despised the activity of their leaders.

1 Thessalonians 5[14]—*The Careless, the Faint-hearted, and the Weak*

Much of the letter deals with the problems created by these three different types of people in the church at Thessalonica. Reference should be made to the section on *Occasion and Contents* (p. 203) in which an account is given of these people. In this verse Paul is advising the members of the church to be helpful and patient in their attitude to them.

*   *   *

THE SECOND LETTER TO THE THESSALONIANS

The first letter to the Thessalonians was not wholly successful in its effects on the members of the church, and Paul wrote a second letter in which he dealt once again with idlers (3[6-12]), and answered further misunderstandings of the faint-hearted, who mistakenly supposed him to have taught that the Day of the Lord had already arrived. To these he said that certain events must precede the return of Christ. First the supremely lawless man, the incarnation of evil, must appear, but at present he was being held in check by the Restrainer. It is not clear who the Restrainer was, but he may have been the Roman Government, which preserved law and order, or he may have been a supernatural power (2[1-12]).

The second letter was probably written from Corinth a short time after the first letter, and Paul coupled the names of Silas and Timothy with his own in the greetings (2 Thess 1[1]).

Although some scholars doubt the Pauline authorship of this letter, and others believe that it was written before 1 Thessalonians, the above explanation of its origin is the most convincing.

*   *   *

THE FIRST LETTER TO THE CORINTHIANS

Paul's first visit to Corinth was during his second missionary tour in AD 50 (Acts 18$^{1-18}$). During his third missionary tour, when he visited Macedonia and Greece in AD 57, he presumably called again at Corinth (Acts 20$^{1-2}$). Between these two visits he had many important dealings with the Corinthian Christians, which are not recorded in the Acts of the Apostles, but are brought to light in the two letters to the Corinthians.

Date

The first letter to the Corinthians was written by Paul from Ephesus (see 1 Cor 16$^{8, 19}$) during his third missionary tour (AD 54–6).

Occasion and Contents

Paul had obtained information about the state of the church in Corinth from Chloe's people (1 Cor 1^{11}), from Stephanas, Fortunatus, and Achaicus (16$^{17-18}$), and from a letter which he had received (7^1). 1 Corinthians was written to deal with the problems which were brought to his notice.

There were divisions among the Christians at Corinth, and Paul insisted that the church should maintain unity (1^{10}–4^{21}). He also told them to excommunicate one of their members who had committed incest, and instructed them to settle their disputes among themselves rather than appeal to pagan courts (5^1–6^{20}). He outlined his attitude to marriage and divorce (7$^{1-40}$), and advised them to refrain from eating food consecrated to heathen deities, lest they should offend the consciences and disturb the faith of over-scrupulous Christians (8$^{1-13}$, 10^{14}–11^1). He then dealt with behaviour at worship, explaining that women should be veiled in church as a sign of their subjection to men, and warning the members of the church not to abuse the Lord's Supper by excessive eating and drinking (11$^{2-34}$). He discussed spiritual gifts, showing that different people had different gifts, but teaching that all should have faith, hope, and love. He dealt at length with the gift of ecstatic speech, regarding intelligible speech as far more valuable, and appealing for both tolerance and order in worship. He forbade women, however, to address the congregation (12^1–14^{40}). He then answered some of the Corinthians' problems about the future life, asserting his belief in Christ's resurrection and future return, and giving an account of the final resurrection (15^{1-58}). The letter also includes a vigorous defence of his rights and conduct as an apostle (9^{1-27}), an exhortation to his readers to be faithful (10^{1-13}), and instructions about the collection for Jerusalem and other practical matters (16^{1-24}).

More than any other letter of Paul's this first letter to the Corinthians gives an insight into the life of the early Church, its worship, its social life, and its problems of organization. Corinth was a large and prosperous city, the capital of the province of Achaia. It was a centre for traditional Greek religion, Oriental mystery-cults, Judaism, and Christianity. It was a highly immoral city, and Christians were continually exposed there to the temptation to compromise their beliefs about God and about ethical conduct. In this letter, with firmness, patience, understanding, and love, Paul attempted to purify and strengthen the life of the Corinthian Christians.

*　　　　*　　　　*

COMMENTS ON SELECTED PASSAGES FROM THE FIRST LETTER TO THE CORINTHIANS

1 Corinthians 1^{10-17}—*Divisions in the Church*

There was real danger of a split in the church at Corinth. Some men were claiming to be followers of Paul or Apollos or Peter, and others were claiming to be the only true followers of Christ. Paul assured his readers that Christ was not divided, and that it was Christ, not Paul, who had been crucified for them, and in whose name they had been baptized. Indeed Paul's chief task was to preach rather than to baptize.

Conjectures have been made about the views of the different factions which Paul mentions. It has been suggested that the 'Paul-party' supported Paul's liberal attitude to the Law, that the 'Apollos-party' practised the allegorical method of interpreting scripture which was fashionable in Apollos's native city of Alexandria, that the 'Peter-party' upheld a conservative interpretation of the Law, and that the 'Christ-party' advocated an excessively liberal understanding of morality. These are only guesses, and it is not really known what the parties stood for, or even whether they can correctly be described as parties. It is unlikely, however, that either Apollos or Peter, any more than Paul, supported these divisive movements. Their names were being used without their consent.

1 Corinthians 1^{10}. *my brothers* is a characteristic form of address to fellow-Christians. See notes on Galatians 1^2.

1 Corinthians 1^{11}. *Chloe's people* were the servants of a Corinthian lady named Chloe. It is not known whether or not Chloe herself was a Christian.

1 Corinthians 1^{12}. *Apollos* : see notes on Acts 18$^{24-8}$. *Cephas* is the Aramaic equivalent of Peter : see notes on Matthew 16$^{17-19}$.

1 Corinthians 1^{14}. *Crispus* had been a ruler of the synagogue, and his conversion is reported in Acts 18^8. *Gaius* must be distinguished from the men of the same name in Acts 19^{29} and 20^4. He is also mentioned in Romans 16^{23}.

1 Corinthians 1^{16}. *the household of Stephanas* were the first converts in Achaia (1 Cor 16^{15}). If 1 Corinthians 1^{16} refers to every member of the household, it is evidence for the practice of infant baptism. It is possible, however, that it refers only to people of maturer years. See also Acts 10$^{24, 48}$, 16$^{15, 33}$, 18^8. *Stephanas* was one of the men who brought Paul information about the state of the church in Corinth (1 Cor 16^{17}).

1 Corinthians 1$^{18-31}$—*Wisdom and Foolishness*

Paul now develops the theme that his life's work is to preach the gospel. The so-called wise men, who are on the road to ruin, have been made to look foolish by their failure to find God and by their contempt for the Cross of Christ. The Jews, who expect spectacular miracles from the Messiah, regard the crucifixion as a stumbling-block, because it brought Jesus under the curse of the Law (see notes on Gal 3$^{10-14}$). The Greeks, who look for wisdom, regard the crucifixion as folly, because it declares that God is made known to men through a suffering and dying Saviour rather than through human reasoning. The men who are on the way to salvation, however, understand that the Cross is a demonstration of God's power, and that the crucified Christ is Himself the power and the wisdom of God (verses 18–24).

Few of the members of the Church are wise, powerful, or noble by human standards, but God has chosen them in order to show that His standards are different. Christians have no cause to be proud of themselves. Their new life in Christ is the act of God, who has made Christ the source of their wisdom, their righteousness, their consecration, and their liberty. It is in God and not in themselves that they should glory (verses 25–31).

1 Corinthians 1^{19} quotes Isaiah 29^{14}.

1 Corinthians 1^{24}. *the wisdom of God.* In the Old Testament (Job 28$^{12-28}$, Prov 1$^{20-1}$, 8^1–9^6) and in the Old Testament Apocrypha (Ecclus 24, Wisd 7, 9, Bar 3^9–4^4) the Wisdom of God is described in language which suggests that it is itself a person. Like the Word of God (see notes on Jn 1$^{1-18}$), the Wisdom of God is treated as an extension of the divine

personality. Wisdom was active in the creation, reveals God to men, and gives them life. The idea is therefore very suitable to express the uniqueness and divinity of Christ. It is found also in 1 Corinthians 1[30] and has influenced Colossians 1[15-18], 2[3], Hebrews 1[3].

1 Corinthians 1[30]. The literal translation is : . . . *who was made for us wisdom from God, and righteousness, and sanctification, and redemption.* For *wisdom* see notes on verse 24; and for *redemption* see notes on Galatians 4[5], Romans 3[24], 8[2].

1 Corinthians 1[31]. See Jeremiah 9[23-4].

1 Corinthians 2[1-5]—*Paul's Preaching*

Paul does not use clever tricks of oratory. In spite of his nervousness his preaching carries conviction because he speaks in the power of God and is resolved to think only of the crucified Christ.

That Paul has been criticized for his manner of speaking is clear from 2 Corinthians 10[10], and that Christ crucified is the centre of his thought and preaching is emphasized in 1 Corinthians 1[17, 23], Galatians 6[14].

*　　　*　　　*

1 Corinthians 3[5-9]—*God's Fellow-workers*

Paul now returns to the theme of disunity. He and Apollos are merely agents of God, who perform different tasks for Him. Paul founded the church in Corinth, and Apollos helped to develop it (see Acts 18[27]–19[1]), but all the time God was working through them. They were the gardeners, but it was God who made the garden grow.

1 Corinthians 3[10-17]—*God's Building*

The metaphor changes, and the Church is likened to a building. Jesus Christ is the foundation, and Paul is the master-builder who laid the foundation. Those who follow Paul can erect a good or a faulty structure on the foundation, and they will be judged accordingly at the last day. But even those who have worked badly will be saved.

This passage is evidence that Paul believes in the salvation of all those who have faith in Christ.

1 Corinthians 3[15]. *a fire* refers to the fire of judgement rather than to the flames of purgatory.

1 Corinthians 3[16]. *you are God's temple.* A similar idea is found in Ephesians 2[20-2] and 1 Peter 2[4-5]. While 1 Corinthians 3[16-17] likens the Church to God's temple, 1 Corinthians 6[19] describes the body of an individual as a shrine or temple of the indwelling Spirit.

*　　　*　　　*

1 Corinthians 12$^{1-3}$—*The Test of the Spirit*

The true test of the Spirit's activity in a man is when he confesses Jesus as Lord. 'Jesus is Lord' was one of the earliest forms of Christian creed (see Rom 10^9, Phil 2^{11}).

Those who say 'A curse on Jesus!' (verse 3) may be the Jews who attacked Christianity.

The idea that a man's confession of Christ is proof of the Spirit's presence is found also in 1 John 4$^{1-3}$.

1 Corinthians 12$^{4-11}$—*The Gifts of the Spirit*

When Paul says that there is one Spirit, one Lord, one God, but different gifts of the Spirit, which are allotted to different individuals, he is correcting the view that men with certain gifts like ecstatic speech (1 Cor 14$^{1-19}$) are superior to other Christians.

For the instinctive way in which Father, Son, and Spirit are linked together, see also 2 Corinthians 13^{14}, 1 Peter 1^2, Matthew 28^{19}.

1 Corinthians 12$^{12-31}$—*The Body, Its Limbs and Organs*

Christ is like a body, the limbs and organs of which are members of the Church who through baptism have received the one Spirit. Their unity transcends the barriers of race and social class. They have essential but different functions to perform, and the fate of one member influences the fate of the rest. Although they have different gifts for their specialized functions, they should all aim at the higher gifts, which, according to 1 Corinthians 13^{13}, are faith, hope, and, especially, love.

1 Corinthians 12^{12}. *one body*. See also Romans 12$^{4-8}$. The idea that Christ is the head of the body is introduced in Colossians 1^{18}, 2^{19}, Ephesians 1$^{22-3}$, 4^{16}.

1 Corinthians 12^{13}. Compare Galatians 3$^{27-8}$, Colossians 3^{11}.

1 Corinthians 12^{28}. *apostles* (see notes on Acts 1$^{15-26}$) were the chief ministers of the Church, whose authority was not confined to a local congregation. As an apostle Paul had oversight over a large number of churches. The word *apostle* means 'one who is sent'.

prophets seem to have been travelling preachers. They were prophets not merely because they foretold the future but because they spoke the word of God. *prophet* means not only *foreteller* but also *spokesman*.

teachers. It is not known whether they travelled from church to church or remained in one congregation.

power to guide. This probably refers to the administrators of the local church, who were called elders or bishops (see notes on Acts 20$^{17,\,28}$).

ecstatic utterance. This gift of ecstatic but unintelligible speech is contrasted with the gift of intelligible prophecy (1 Cor 14$^{1-19}$). The pretensions of these ecstatic speakers were the reason for Paul's discussion for the gifts of the Spirit. See also notes on Acts 2$^{1-13}$.

Lists of the different functions in the Church are also found in Romans 12$^{6-8}$ and Ephesians 4^{11}. The impression is given that there was no rigid order of ministry, except that the apostles had general oversight. Eventually the leading local ministers were called bishops (or elders) and deacons (see Phil 1^1, Acts 20$^{17, 28}$; 1 Tim 3$^{1-13}$, Tit 1$^{5-9}$). In the second century, however, a bishop, as presiding officer of a church, was distinguished from the elders, and there were three orders of ministry: bishops, elders (or presbyters), and deacons.

1 Corinthians 13$^{1-13}$—*Love*

This chapter describes the greatest of all spiritual gifts, love.

(i) *The necessity of love* (verses 1–3). Spiritual gifts, like ecstatic speech, prophecy, knowledge, faith, the readiness to sacrifice possessions and suffer a martyr's death are nothing without love.

(ii) *The nature of love* (verses 4–7). Although Jesus is not mentioned by name in this chapter, the patient, self-effacing, courageous, and unlimited love described in this paragraph was shown by Jesus Himself and is a pattern for His followers.

(iii) *The permanence of love* (verses 8–13). Other spiritual gifts are of temporary duration, but faith, hope, and love are eternal, and the greatest of them is love.

1 Corinthians 13^1. *love*. The Greek word *agapē* refers to a self-giving love by contrast with *erōs*, which describes a desiring love. See notes on Mark 12$^{28-34}$ and 1 John 4$^{7-21}$.

1 Corinthians 13^2. *to move mountains*. See Mark 11^{23}.

1 Corinthians 13^{12}. *puzzling reflections in a mirror* refers to the dark and distorted reflections which were given by mirrors in Paul's day.

*   *   *

1 Corinthians 15$^{1-11}$—*The Resurrection of Christ*

The whole of the fifteenth chapter of this letter is about resurrection, and was written because some of the Corinthian Christians were teaching that believers would not ultimately be raised from the dead. Paul begins his answer to them by affirming that the death and resurrection of Christ is at the heart of the gospel. He repeats the tradition which he has received of Christ's resurrection appearances, and describes his own vision of Christ at his conversion as a special resurrection appearance.

1 Corinthians 15$^{3-7}$. This paragraph may well be derived from an early credal statement.

1 Corinthians 15$^{3-4}$. *in accordance with the scriptures.* Paul may be thinking of Isaiah 53 and parts of Psalm 22 for the crucifixion, and of passages like Psalm 16$^{10-11}$ and Hosea 6^2 for the resurrection (see notes on Lk 24$^{13-32, 44-7}$).

1 Corinthians 15$^{5-7}$. There is evidence in the gospels for appearances to *Cephas* (i.e. Peter) (Lk 24^{34}), to *the Twelve*, or, more accurately at that time, the Eleven (Mt 28^{16} ff, Luke 24^{36} ff, Jn 20^{19} ff), but there is no other record of a special appearance to *James* or to *five hundred of our brothers.* From the context *all the apostles* seems to indicate a larger group than the Twelve, and James seems to be the Lord's brother.

1 Corinthians 15^{10}. The emphasis that everything which he does is due to God's *grace* (see notes on Gal 1$^{1-5}$) is found often in Paul (see also Gal 2^{20}, 1 Cor 3^6, 2 Cor 3^5, 12^9, Phil 2^{13}).

1 Corinthians 15$^{12-34}$—*The Resurrection of the Dead*

Paul continues his answer to those who deny the resurrection of the dead. By implying that Christ has not risen, they make the faith of Christians vain (verses 12–19). The resurrection of Christ is the first-fruits of the harvest of the resurrection of the dead, and, just as Adam brought death for all men, so Christ brings life for all men (see notes on Rom 5$^{12-21}$). When Christ returns, those who belong to Him will be raised from the dead. The end will follow, and Christ will destroy all evil powers including, finally, death itself. Then He will hand over the Kingdom to God the Father, who will be all in all (verses 20–8).

If there were no resurrection of the dead, there would be no point in the practice of baptizing living people as proxies for the unbaptized dead, and Paul would have vainly endured dangers and persecutions like his troubles at Ephesus (verses 29–32). Lack of faith in the resurrection leads to a dissolute life, and the Corinthians ought to return to sober and disciplined conduct (verses 32–4).

1 Corinthians 15^{20}. *firstfruits of the harvest of the dead.* A literal translation is *firstfruits of those who sleep.* Paul uses this idea because Jesus rose from the dead on the very day when the firstfruits of the barley harvest were being offered in the Temple during the Feast of the Passover and Unleavened Bread. It is possible that Paul was writing his letter at this time of the year. This would explain his reference to Christ as a Passover sacrifice (1 Cor 5^7) and would be consistent with his mention of the approach of Whitsuntide (1 Cor 16^8).

1 Corinthians 15^{25} refers to Psalm 110^1.

1 Corinthians 15^{27} quotes Psalm 8^6.

1 Corinthians 15^{29} is evidence of the practice in the early Church of baptizing people as representatives of dead persons who had not been baptized.

1 Corinthians 15^{32}. *wild beasts*. This probably refers to the trouble at Ephesus recorded in Acts 19$^{23-41}$. There is no good evidence that Paul had literally to fight with wild beasts there. This verse quotes Isaiah 22^{13}.

1 Corinthians 15^{33} quotes some words of the Greek poet Menander.

1 Corinthians 15$^{35-58}$—*The Nature of the Resurrection of the Dead*

In this section Paul makes frequent use of the word *body*, not to refer exclusively to a body of flesh and blood, but as a more general term to describe the form of a man's being. The *spiritual body* is not a body of flesh and blood, because 'flesh and blood can never possess the kingdom of God' (verse 50); it is a form of being in which a man preserves his individuality.

In his account of the resurrection of the dead Paul says that, just as a seed is transformed when it becomes wheat, so the body is transformed when a man rises from the dead. It becomes imperishable, glorious, powerful, and spiritual (verses 35–44). The animal body is like that of the first Adam (Gen 2^{7}), made of dust, a body of flesh and blood. The spiritual body is like that of the last Adam, Jesus Christ, who is from heaven and gives life. When men rise, they will have spiritual bodies and be like Christ (verses 45–9). At the final resurrection they will suddenly be changed and clothed with immortality. God will give them victory over death and sin (verses 50–7). Because they are assured of this victory, they ought to work for the Lord in the knowledge that their labour will not be in vain (verse 58).

It is clear from his chapter that Paul does not believe, as some Greek philosophers did, that men are by nature immortal. He teaches that immortality is a gift of God to those who belong to Christ. He also teaches that the resurrection of the dead will take place at the end of history, an event which he expects during the lifetime of his contemporaries (verse 51), though he does not assert, as in 1 Thessalonians 4^{17}, that he himself will live to see it.

1 Corinthians 15^{36}. Compare Mark 4$^{26-32}$, John 12^{24}, Galatians 6$^{7-8}$.

1 Corinthians 15^{45}. For the contrast between Adam and Christ, see notes on Romans 5$^{12-21}$.

1 Corinthians 15^{54} refers to Isaiah 25^{8}.

1 Corinthians 15^{55} refers to Hosea 13^{14}.

1 Corinthians 15^{56}. The relationship between *death, sin*, and *law* is discussed in Romans 5$^{12-14}$, 7$^{7-13}$.

* * *

THE SECOND LETTER TO THE CORINTHIANS

Occasion

The first letter to the Corinthians did not settle all the church's problems. Further trouble arose, and there was bitter criticism of Paul. There are two main theories about the circumstances in which the second letter was written .

(1) *The traditional theory* is that Paul sent 1 Corinthians to Corinth with Titus. Some time later Titus met him in Macedonia with the news that while most of the Corinthians had done their best to set the church right, a group of them was fiercely attacking Paul. It was for this situation that 2 Corinthians was written.

(2) *The modern theory* is that after Paul had sent 1 Corinthians he discovered that there was still serious trouble in the church. He paid a second visit to Corinth, which is implied by 2 Corinthians 12^{14} and 13^{1-2}, but not recorded in Acts. This visit was unsuccessful, and, when Paul returned to Ephesus, he wrote 2 Corinthians 10–13 to rebuke his opponents. This is the letter which he sent with Titus, and, when Titus brought him good news in Macedonia, he wrote 2 Corinthians 1–9 to express his relief and joy.

According to this theory, the present 2 Corinthians was compiled by an editor who took a complete letter of Paul's (2 Cor 1–9) and added to it part of another letter (2 Cor 10–13). The theory points out that Chapters 10–13 are more severe in tone than the earlier chapters and have no obvious connexion with them.

Many supporters of this theory claim that 2 Corinthians 6^{14}–7^1, which does not easily fit into its context, is a fragment of a letter which Paul wrote before 1 Corinthians (see 1 Cor $5^{9\ ff}$).

Limitations of space forbid a discussion of the detailed arguments about the origin of 2 Corinthians. But the importance of the letter does not depend on the truth of either of these theories. Its contents are of exceptional value, whatever may have been the occasion for which it was written.

Contents

2 Corinthians 1–9. Paul answers the charge that because he has changed his plans he is untrustworthy and insincere (Chs. 1 and 2). His credentials are the members of the church themselves, and his qualification is from God, who has made him a minister of the new covenant of the Spirit.

In the performance of this ministry he has endured hardship and persecution, but he does not glory in these achievements. He glories only in God, who has given him new life in Christ (3^1–6^{13}). He tells the Corinthians to keep away from social contact with unbelievers (6^{14}–7^1). He asks for affection from his readers, and assures them that he is glad they have received his severe letter in good spirit (7^{2-16}). He urges them to complete the collection for the Jerusalem Christians and tells them of the fine example set by the congregations in Macedonia. He is sending Titus to supervise the taking of the collection (8^1–9^{15}).

2 Corinthians 10–13. Paul denounces the false apostles who attack him. He prefers to boast in the Lord rather than in himself. But if they want boasting from him, he can tell them of his sufferings for Christ, of special visions and revelations he has received, and of God's power in his life. He warns them that he may be harsh when he visits them again, and prays that they will establish peace in the church, so that he need not be severe with them.

*   *   *

COMMENTS ON SELECTED PASSAGES FROM THE SECOND LETTER TO THE CORINTHIANS

2 Corinthians 4^{16-18}—*The Eternal Glory*

In spite of all his sufferings (see 4^{8-12}) Paul never loses heart. Confident that he is being inwardly renewed, he sets his mind on that which is eternal and unseen. This contrast between the outward and the inward, the seen and the unseen, and the temporal and the eternal, is often found in Greek philosophy.

2 Corinthians 5^{1-10}—*The Immortal Life*

Paul knows that, if his earthly body dies, an eternal mode of existence awaits him. He hopes, however, that the final resurrection, when he will receive his heavenly body, will take place before his physical death, because he does not want to be without a body (verses 1–4). God has given Christians the Spirit as a pledge of the immortal life which will be theirs at the resurrection. Hence Paul is full of confidence. He lives in exile from heaven, by faith and not by sight, and he would prefer to leave the physical body and be with the Lord. But, wherever he is, he must please the Lord, because all men will be judged at the return of Christ (verses 5–10).

The reference to living 'with the Lord' (verse 8) is evidence that

Paul envisages the possibility of an interim state between physical death and the final resurrection (see also Phil 1[23]). Some scholars have argued that this interim state is one of unconsciousness, in which Christians 'sleep' in Christ (1 Thess 4[13], see notes on 1 Cor 15[20]). But the word 'sleep' refers to death rather than to literal sleep, and, since Paul looks forward eagerly to this interim state, he must regard it as a period of conscious fellowship with Christ.

2 Corinthians 5[4]. *old body . . . new body.* In Paul's writings *body* refers to the mode of a person's being, not necessarily to a body of flesh and blood. See notes on 1 Corinthians 15[35-58].

2 Corinthians 5[5]. *a pledge.* The Greek word can also be translated *guarantee* or *earnest.* (See also 2 Cor 1[22], Eph 1[14]). A similar idea is that the Spirit is the firstfruits of the future life (Rom 8[23]).

2 Corinthians 5[10]. A reference to the judgement which awaits even the faithful is found in 1 Corinthians 3[12-15].

2 Corinthians 5[11-17]—*Christ's Love and the New Order*

In answer to personal criticisms of him, Paul says that his whole life is lived for God and for the members of the Church. His way of life is forced upon him by the love which Christ has shown. The purpose of Christ's death was to enable men to die to the old selfish order of things and live for Him (verses 11–15). Worldly standards no longer count for Paul, and, although before his conversion he judged Christ by these standards, he does so no more. For men who are united to Christ the new world and the new order has begun (verses 16–17).

2 Corinthians 5[13]. *beside ourselves.* Probably Paul's opponents had said that he was beside himself.

2 Corinthians 5[14]. *all mankind has died.* This does not mean that all men have in fact died to sin, but that Christ has made it possible for them to do so.

2 Corinthians 5[15]. This theme is developed in Romans 6[1-11].

2 Corinthians 5[16] seems to refer to Paul's attitude when he was persecuting Christians.

2 Corinthians 5[17]. *new world.* The Greek can also be translated *new creation* or *new creature.* See also Galatians 6[15]. For the connexion with the idea of the Adam, see notes on Romans 5[12-21].

2 Corinthians 5[18]-6[2]—*Reconciliation in Christ*

By their sinfulness men were estranged from God, and it was God who took the initiative in reconciling them to Himself through Christ. In one sense the work of reconciliation was accomplished in the life, death, and resurrection of Christ. But in another sense it continues in the activity of Christian preachers, who appeal to men to be reconciled to God and to accept the benefit of Christ's work (5^{18-20}).

Although Christ was sinless, He became one with the sinfulness of men in so far as He underwent the consequences of sin, coming under the curse of the Law (see notes on Gal 3^{10-14}) and experiencing what it was like to be separated from God (see notes on Mk 15^{33-40}). Men can be one with God's goodness by being united with Christ, who has united Himself with them (5^{21}).

Paul urges his readers to accept this opportunity of reconciliation (6^{1-2}).

2 Corinthians 5^{20}. *Christ's ambassadors.* Compare Ephesians 6^{20} and Galatians 4^{14}.

2 Corinthians 5^{21}. *made ... one with the sinfulness of men.* The literal translation is *made to be sin.* This does not mean that Christ became a sinner, but that He shared with men the consequences of their sin.

made one with the goodness of God himself. The literal translation is *made the righteousness of God.* This does not mean that in Christ men become completely sinless but that they share in the life of Christ who is Himself perfect. (Compare Philippians 3^9.)

innocent of sin. See also Hebrews 4^{15}, 1 Peter 2^{22}, 1 John 3^5.

2 Corinthians 6^2 quotes Isaiah 49^8.

2 Corinthians 6^{3-10}—*The Servant of Christ*

Paul describes the sufferings which he endured as an apostle, and defends himself against those who accuse him of being an impostor (verse 8) and an unknown man (verse 9). In spite of all adversity he survives and rejoices. Although he is materially a poor man, he gives spiritual wealth to many people. Because he is united with Christ, who is Lord of all things, he owns the world.

2 Corinthians 6^3. *we.* The use of the first person plural in this passage implies that, although Paul is speaking primarily of his own experience, he is thinking also of companions like Silvanus, Timothy, and Titus (2 Cor $1^{1, 19}$, $7^{6-7, 13}$).

2 Corinthians 6^5. *flogged, imprisoned* : see Acts 16^{23}. *mobbed* : see Acts 17^5. A similar account of Paul's sufferings is found in 2 Corinthians 11^{21-33}.

2 Corinthians 6^{10}. *we own the world.* Compare Matthew 5^5.

*   *   *

2 Corinthians 11^{21-33}—*Paul's Boasting*

In reply to the false apostles, who have criticized him for his lack of courage and the feebleness of his oratory (see 2 Cor $10^{2, 10}$), Paul says that he has been weak but his very weakness is a cause for boasting—

though by his own standards he boasts only in God, and speaks as a fool when he boasts about himself. But, if necessary, he can boast about his Jewish origin, his service for Christ, his endurance of persecution and danger, and his acceptance of the burden of responsibility in the Church. An example of the suffering which he has endured and which could be called weakness is his escape from Damascus in order to avoid arrest.

2 Corinthians 11$^{23-7}$ show that Paul went through a much greater number of gruelling experiences than are recorded in the Acts. See also notes on 2 Corinthians 6^5.

2 Corinthians 11^{24}. *thirty-nine strokes.* The Jewish law prescribed a maximum of forty lashes for a criminal (Deut 25^3), but, to make sure that the law was not broken, it was customary to inflict only thirty-nine.

2 Corinthians 11^{25}. *beaten with rods.* This was a Roman form of punishment.

2 Corinthians 11$^{32-3}$. For comments on *Aretas* and Paul's escape from Damascus, see notes on Acts 9$^{20-30}$.

2 Corinthians 12$^{1-10}$—*Strength in Weakness*

Paul continues his boasting, and describes an ecstatic experience of rapture, which he underwent fourteen years earlier, when his soul seemed to be separated from his body and to be taken up into the innermost sanctuary of heaven (verses 1–4). He prefers, however, to speak of his weakness, and tells how he prayed to be freed from 'a sharp pain in my body', which must have been a form of disease. God did not answer his prayer by healing him, but by assuring him that 'My grace is all you need ; power comes to its full strength in weakness'. Paul therefore rejoices in his weakness, because it provides an opportunity for the power of Christ to give him strength to endure.

2 Corinthians 12^2. *the third heaven* is the inner court of heaven.

2 Corinthians 12^7. *a sharp pain in my body.* A literal translation is *a thorn* (or *stake*) *in the flesh.* It has been conjectured that this refers to eye-disease or to epilepsy. It certainly seems to mean a physical affliction.

2 Corinthians 12^9. For the way in which God answers prayer, see also notes on Mark 14$^{32-42}$ and Matthew 7$^{7-11}$.

2 Corinthians 12^{10}. See also 2 Corinthians 13^4.

QUESTIONS

(1) What does Paul teach in his letter to the Galatians about justification through faith?

(2) Examine Paul's teaching in 1 Corinthians about the different functions of Church members, and show its importance for an understanding of Church unity.

(3) What does Paul say in 1 Corinthians about (a) the return of Christ and (b) the resurrection of the body?

(4) Comment on : Galatians 1^1, 3^{26-7}, 1 Thessalonians 5^{1-2}, 1 Corinthians 1^{23-4}, 2 Corinthians 5^{21}, 12^{8-9}.

CHAPTER TEN

ST PAUL: THE LETTER TO THE ROMANS, THE CAPTIVITY LETTERS, AND THE PASTORAL LETTERS

THE LETTER TO THE ROMANS

THE CHURCH in Rome was certainly not founded by Paul, and there is no biblical support for the tradition that it was founded by Peter. Indeed the absence of Peter's name from the greetings in Paul's letter to the Romans suggests that he had no close connection with the church at the time when the letter was written. It is probable that this, the most famous of Christian churches, was founded by unknown persons.

In AD 49 the emperor Claudius expelled all Jews from Rome because of disturbances which probably arose between orthodox Jews and Christians. It was on this occasion that Priscilla and Aquila had to leave the city (see notes on Acts 18²), but by the time that Paul wrote his letter, about AD 57, Jews were in Rome again and an important Christian congregation was there.

The Early History of the Letter

At an early date the letter was issued as a circular letter, which could be sent to many different churches. This is proved by the omission of references to Rome in an early text, of the last two chapters in some texts, and of the last chapter in another. The likeliest explanation of these facts is that the letter was originally written to Rome, and then edited as a circular letter, which omitted all references to Rome and to people connected with it.

The Destination of the Last Chapter

Many scholars believe that Chapter 16 was originally intended for Ephesus, because the people to whom greetings are sent are more likely to have been in Ephesus than in Rome. It is quite possible, however, that these men and women had emigrated from Ephesus to Rome by the time that Paul wrote the letter.

Occasion

Paul was probably in Corinth during his final visit to Greece (Acts 20^{1-3}). Because he intended eventually to travel to Rome and from there to Spain (Rom 15^{22-3}), he wrote this letter to prepare the Roman church for his arrival. His plans were later upset by his arrest, and he arrived in Rome as a prisoner.

Since he had not yet visited the church in Rome, there are only a few references to its particular problems. There are hints of quarrels in the church (Rom 16^{17-20}), but for the most part the letter is a presentation of Paul's mature thought about some of the main themes of the gospel.

Contents

This letter is the most famous and most discussed of all Paul's letters, and although selected passages will be examined in detail, a brief outline of its argument will first be given.

(i) *Introduction* (1^{1-17}).

Paul stresses his debt both to Greek and to non-Greek, both to learned and to simple. He speaks of his desire to visit Rome, and affirms that the gospel is 'the saving power of God for everyone who has faith'.

(ii) *The Sinfulness of Mankind, and Justification through Faith* (1^{18}–5^{21})

All men, both Jews and non-Jews, are sinners (1^{18}–3^{20}). They can be freed from sin by Jesus Christ, who died that men might be justified. It is not by their works that men are justified but by God's grace, and they receive this blessing when they have faith (3^{21-31}). Abraham's faith was reckoned to him for righteousness before he was circumcised, and the true children of Abraham are not those who are descended from him by blood but those who are justified through faith (4^{1-25}). Justified believers are exhorted to remain in the state of grace into which they have entered, and to rejoice in God, to whom they have been reconciled through Christ (5^{1-11}). Through Adam sin and death entered the world, but through Christ has come remission of sins, righteousness, and life (5^{12-21}).

(iii) *Sanctification* (6^1–8^{39})

In their baptism Christians have been united to Christ, dying to sin and becoming alive to God. They must therefore yield their bodies to God and no longer be slaves to sin (6^{1-23}). They have died to the Law as well as to sin, and serve God under the new code of the Spirit. The Law is itself holy, but it acquainted Paul with sin, and thus led him to commit sin. Paul was a slave of sin, wanting to do right, but unable to refrain from doing wrong (7^{1-25}). Liberation comes to those who are united with Christ. They live in the power of the Spirit and are children of God. Their present sufferings are nothing compared with their future glory, which the whole universe will share. Their weakness is helped by the Spirit's intercession for them and by their knowledge that God will be faithful to those whom He has called. With God on their side nothing can separate them from the love of Christ (8^{1-39}).

(iv) God's Purpose in History (9^1-11^{36})

God has the right to choose some men and reject others. As a potter can do what he likes with his clay, so God can do what He likes with men. The right to be God's chosen people has been granted to Christians, who have a righteousness which is based on faith (9^{1-33}). The Jews looked for legal righteousness, and, in spite of the warnings of the scriptures, rejected the good news about Christ (10^{1-21}). Although they forfeited the right to be the chosen people, God has not utterly rejected them. The salvation of the Gentiles will stir the Jews to emulation, and the whole of Israel will be saved, like branches grafted on to an olive-tree from which they have previously been cut off. In the end God will have mercy on all men (11^{1-36}).

(v) Ethical Section (12^1-15^{13})

The whole of a Christian's life should be a sacrifice offered to God. Within the Church different people have different gifts, and these gifts should be rightly used. A Christian must love others and care for them. He should never ask for revenge, but leave it to God to mete out justice (12^{1-21}). He ought to obey the government and pay taxes, because the rulers are God's agents. If he loves his neighbour, he has fulfilled the law. Since the last day is near, men must be watchful, and behave like soldiers of the light (13^{1-14}).

Christians should not condemn each other, and should abstain from certain kinds of food and drink rather than disturb the faith of fellow-Christians who have tender consciences. They should accept each other, as Christ has accepted them (14^1-15^{13}).

(vi) *Conclusion* (15^{14}–16^{27})

Paul intends to visit Rome on his way to Spain, and asks for the help and prayers of the members of the church (15^{14-33}). He concludes the letter with greetings, advice, and a doxology (16^{1-27}).

*   *   *

COMMENTS ON SELECTED PASSAGES FROM THE LETTER TO THE ROMANS

Romans 3^{21-6}—*God's way of righting wrong*

In Romans 1^{18}–3^{20} Paul has argued that the whole of the human race is sinful and deserves punishment. Now he describes how God demonstrates His justice by providing a remedy for sin. Paul uses three ideas to develop his teaching: justification, which is taken from the law courts; redemption, which is linked with slavery; and expiation, which is connected with the sacrificial system.

(i) The idea of *justification by grace through faith* has already been discussed in the notes on Galatians 2^{15-21}.

(ii) The death of Jesus is called *an act of liberation* (verse 24). The Greek word can also be translated *redemption*, and normally describes the liberation of a slave or prisoner by the payment of a ransom. Paul believes that by the death of Jesus men are liberated from captivity to sin; it is a new and greater deliverance than the Exodus from Egypt. The word 'redemption' emphasizes that the liberation was achieved at great cost—the cost of Jesus's suffering and death. See also Galatians 4^5, 1 Corinthians 1^{30}, Mark 10^{45}.

(iii) The death of Jesus is described as *the means of expiating sin* (3^{25}). The Greek word was used in pagan religions for the propitiation or appeasement of an angry god, but in the Greek version of the Old Testament this and similar words refer to the removal or expiation of sin. The word can also mean the Mercy Seat, the place where sacrifices were enacted (Ex 25^{17-22}). Paul's use of the word implies that Christ has taken the place of the Jewish sacrificial system as the means by which the guilt of sin is removed. See notes on 1 John 2^{1-2}.

Romans 3^{21-5}. The word translated *righteousness* by *RV* is translated by *NEB* as *justice* (verses 21, 25) and *way of righting wrong* (verse 22). This last translation reflects the Jewish understanding of righteousness as a saving activity rather than an abstract quality.

Romans 3^{25}. *sacrificial death*. The Greek is literally translated *blood* (for its meaning, see notes on 1 Jn 1^{5-10}).

to demonstrate his justice. God might appear to have been falling below His own standards of justice by His postponement in the past of the punishment of sins. His justice, however, has been demonstrated by the action which He has taken through Christ to remove the guilt of sin and to set men free from its power.

Romans 3$^{27-31}$—*Justification for both Jews and Gentiles*

Men have no reason for pride, because they are justified through faith and not through obedience to the Law (verses 27–8). Since God is the God of all men, He will justify both Jews and Gentiles because of their faith (verses 29–30). Paul's teaching reveals the true significance of the Law, which itself contains God's assurance to Abraham of justification through faith (verse 31 ; see Gen 15^6 and Rom 4$^{1-25}$).

*   *   *

Romans 5$^{1-5}$—*The consequences of justification*

In the fourth chapter of the letter Paul has argued that Abraham was justified through faith long before the Law was established, and he uses this as evidence for his teaching about justification through faith.

In this fifth chapter he writes about the consequences of justification.

(i) *Entry into the sphere of God's grace* (verse 2). The Christian lives in a new order of being, and is under the dispensation not of the Law but of God's love and mercy. For the meaning of *grace* see notes on Galatians 1$^{1-5}$.

(ii) *Peace with God* (verse 1). As sinners men were estranged from God, but through Christ they have been reconciled to Him and are at peace with Him (see notes on 2 Cor 5^{18}–6^2). Paul encourages them to continue in this state of peace.

(iii) *Joy* (verses 2–3). Paul asks his readers to rejoice both in the hope of future glory and in the endurance of present sufferings.

(iv) *Certainty of Hope* (verses 4–5). They can be confident in their hope, because they themselves have been able to endure suffering and because the Holy Spirit has given them an inner awareness of God's love for them.

Romans 5$^{6-11}$—*Present Reconciliation and Future Salvation*

The consequences of justification are now outlined in another way.

(i) *Present Reconciliation.* God showed His love by sending Christ to die for men, even while they were His enemies. His sacrificial death made possible their present reconciliation to God.

(ii) *Future Salvation*. If men are united with Christ in a new life, they will be saved from final punishment.

Romans 5⁹. *Christ's sacrificial death*. A literal translation is *his blood*. See note on Romans 3²⁵.

final retribution. A literal translation is *the wrath*, implying that the last judgement is the result of God's hatred for sin.

Romans 5¹²⁻²¹—*Adam and Christ*

Through one man, Adam, sin and death entered the world. The whole human race is sinful and subject to death, but, before the Law was given, there was no conscious disobedience to God of the same order as Adam's. Nevertheless death was the lot of the human race, even before the Law was given to Moses (verses 12–14).

Through the obedience of one man, Christ, God has brought men freedom from condemnation and has given them righteousness and life (verses 15–19). Although sin, in so far as it is conscious disobedience to God, abounded with the coming of the Law, the grace of God exceeds the sinfulness of men, and brings righteousness and eternal life through Christ (verses 20–1).

Paul's contrast between Adam and Christ is found also in 1 Corinthians 15²², ⁴⁵⁻⁹. It belongs to the same sphere of ideas as his teaching that Christ is the image of God (2 Cor 4⁴, Col 1¹⁵), that image in which the first man had originally been created (Gen 1²⁶). It is also similar to the idea of the new creation in Christ (2 Cor 5¹⁷, Gal 6¹⁵) and to the idea that those who belong to Christ have put on 'the new man' (Col 3¹⁰, Eph 4²⁴).

Paul believed that Adam was a historical person, from whom sinfulness was inherited by the rest of the human race. But he also regarded Adam as representative of the corporate nature of mankind. 'Adam' means 'man' and stands for the whole of sinful humanity. Paul's doctrine of the universality of sin does not depend for its validity on the historical accuracy of the stories of Creation and the Fall in the first three chapters of Genesis. The contrast between Adam and Christ is not just a contrast between two individuals but a contrast between the sinful human race and the type of manhood represented by Christ.

Although Paul teaches that all men are sinful as a consequence of Adam's sin, he does not claim that the whole human race is guilty of the particular sin which Adam committed. This doctrine is a theological development which took place after biblical times. Paul never uses the words 'original sin', but he does teach a doctrine of 'original sin' in the sense that all men are sinful because of Adam. He does not teach a doctrine of 'original guilt', the doctrine that all men are guilty of Adam's sin.

A distinction is made between the men who lived before the giving of the Law and those who lived afterwards. The former did not consciously disobey God, as Adam did; but the latter, who were aware of God's Law, consciously sinned. Although the former were not condemned by God as guilty, sin nevertheless reigned in them and they were subject to death, which in Paul's thought is not merely physical death but spiritual death, a condition of estrangement from God and of defective spiritual and moral perception.

Romans 5[18]. *acquittal and life.* The Greek means literally *justification of life.* The words *for all men* may imply that all men *will* be saved, or that all men *can* be saved.

Romans 5[19]. *made righteous.* The faithful have already been pronounced righteous or 'justified'. In the end they will actually be made righteous.

Romans 6[1-14]—*Union with Christ*

Christians have no right to go on sinning in order that there may be more opportunity for the exercise of God's forgiving love. They are in union with Christ, and ought to live accordingly.

(i) *Baptism.* When he says that men are baptized into union with Christ (verses 3–4), Paul is thinking of baptism by total immersion. The descent into the water declares that men share in Christ's death and burial. The rising from the water declares that they share in His resurrection. Baptism is the sacrament of incorporation into the Church, the body of Christ (1 Cor 12[13]), and those who have been incorporated into Christ's body share in His death and resurrection. In Paul's teaching baptism not only symbolizes entry into the new life but is itself the moment of entry. There is, however, no suggestion that the ritual act of baptism itself effects any change in a man. The change is effected by God in response to a man's faith (Gal 3[26-7], Col 2[12]).

(ii) *Death to Sin.* Those who are united with Christ are united with Him in death. This does not mean that they die physically, but that they die to sin. Throughout His life Christ overcame temptation, and His death was a victory over the powers of evil. Those who are united with Him participate in this victory by ceasing to be slaves to sin (verses 5–11). Therefore, if a Christian sins, he is failing to be what his union with Christ declares him to be (verse 2). He is failing to be the righteous person God pronounced him to be when He 'justified' him.

(iii) *Life in union with Christ.* Those who are united with Christ have begun a new life (verse 4). They are alive to God (verse 11), and look to a future resurrection (verses 5 and 8). Paul does not say in Romans that men are already risen with Christ, although this idea is present in Colossians 3^1. In Romans he prefers to say that Christians are 'alive to God' in the present, and that they will share in Christ's resurrection in the future. They participate in Christ's triumphant life already, but they will participate in it even more fully at the final resurrection.

Paul's account of union with Christ shows that it is not merely an emotional state. It is true that the justified man experiences peace and joy (see notes on Rom 5^{1-5}), but the man who is in union with Christ has also been incorporated into the Church, which is the sphere of the new life. By being incorporated into Christ crucified and risen, he shares in Christ's victory over sin and in His triumphant life. He can regard his sufferings as part of Christ's sufferings (2 Cor 1^{5-7}, Phil 3^{10}, Col 1^{24}), and although he still faces temptation, he can regard his battle against it as part of Christ's death to sin and resurrection to life. This life of union with Christ reaches its climax in the future. The Spirit a man receives in this earthly life is a firstfruits of the harvest to come (see notes on Rom 8^{18-25}), and the condition of the man who is united with Christ is 'to know Christ, to experience the power of his resurrection, and to share his sufferings, in growing conformity with his death, if only I may finally arrive at the resurrection from the dead' (Phil 3^{10-11}).

*   *   *

Romans 7^{7-25}—*The Inner Struggle*

It has long been debated whether this passage refers to a man's condition before or after his conversion and whether it refers to Paul's own experience or to the experience of Christians in general. The most likely explanation is that it reflects Paul's own experience shortly before his conversion, when he had already begun to question his Pharisaic attitude to life and to doubt his ability to fulfil the Law completely. This passage, however, has a message not only for the unconverted but also for those Christians who have relapsed into a legalistic and moralistic attitude to religion and have lost their sense of dependence on God.

Paul describes his inner conflict when he lacked the strength of will to do what he believed to be right and to avoid what he believed to be wrong. This conflict was concerned with his desires as well as with his actions. Indeed, when he gives an example of his inability to fulfil the Law, he quotes the tenth commandment, which is concerned with coveting (verses 7–8). The inclination to sin was fighting within him against the Law of God. In his misery he cried for help, and acknowledged that only God could rescue him, through Jesus Christ.

The conflict in Paul was between the Law of God and the law of sin. The Law of God is in itself holy, but, because it made Paul aware of the nature of sin, it produced a situation in which he was tempted to commit sin. Instead of providing the means by which he could live a spiritual life, it led him to commit sin and to experience spiritual death (see Rom 5^{20}, Gal 3^{19-25}). The law of sin is not strictly speaking a law but the principle of sin or the inclination to sin, which conflicts with the commandments of God.

Romans 7^9. This refers to Paul's boyhood, when he had not yet been admitted as a 'son of the commandment' (see notes on Lk 2^{39-52}) and was neither fully instructed in the Law nor fully committed to it.

Romans 8^{1-17}—The Life of the Spirit

Having described the inner conflict of the man who tries to fulfil the Mosaic Law, Paul goes on to describe the life which is lived in accordance with the 'life-giving law of the Spirit'.

(i) *The Law of the Spirit.* The Law of Moses could not overcome sin, because of men's inability to observe it. But God has overcome sin through the work of Christ, who inaugurated the new covenant of the Spirit, in which men can fulfil God's Law not by the observance of a detailed code of conduct but by a whole life committed to Christ. Under this covenant men are united to Christ and are free from condemnation (verses 1–4).

(ii) *The Lower Nature and the Spirit.* Life on the level of the lower nature (the Greek, which is translated *lower nature*, means literally *flesh*) is life in accordance with sinful desires. This kind of life makes a man God's enemy. When, however, the Spirit dwells in a man, he lives a new kind of life which is eternal (verses 5–11). For the contrast between *the lower nature* and *the Spirit*, see also notes on Galatians 5^{13}.

(iii) *Sons of God.* A man who is led by the Spirit has been adopted as a son and heir of God, and will inherit God's glory. At present he shares Christ's sufferings, not just the sufferings of persecution but all the tensions imposed on a man who follows Christ in a materialistic society. In the future he will share the splendour of Christ's resurrection glory. The Spirit enables men to call on God as Father, and bears witness within them that they are God's children. Their own spirits are convinced of this by the witness of the Spirit of God (verses 14–17).

When Paul writes in this way about the testimony of the Spirit (verses 15–16; see also Gal 4[6]), he does not merely mean that a man's acknowledgement of God as Father is a sign of the Spirit's presence in him. He also means that a man can have an inner assurance that he is a son of God (see 1 Jn 4[13]). It is to this inner sense of certainty that he refers when he says that 'the Spirit of God joins with our spirit'.

Romans 8[2–3] refer to three laws; *the law of the Spirit* which is given through Christ, *the law of sin and death* which is the sinful principle within a man, and *the law* (verse 3) which is the Mosaic Law.

Romans 8[5–6]. The use of the small *s* in *spirit* by *NEB* implies that a reference is being made to the spirit of man and not the Spirit of God. Since the original Greek was written entirely in capital letters, the distinction is due to the translator. Even though Paul himself may have referred to the spirit of man in these verses, he was thinking of the spirit of man as guided by the Spirit of God.

Romans 8[15]. *a Spirit that makes us sons.* Literally, *a Spirit of adoption.* See notes on Galatians 4[5], Ephesians 1[5].

Romans 8[16]. *Abba.* See notes on Mark 14[36].

Romans 8[18–25]—*Suffering and Glory*

The present sufferings of Christians cannot be compared with their future splendour, which will be shared by the whole universe. At the moment the universe is frustrated, and agonizes to be set free, as also do Christians, who wait for their final redemption. They possess the Spirit, who is the firstfruits, and they live in hope of the future resurrection, which is the harvest.

It is clear from this passage that Paul believes in the redemption of the universe as well as the redemption of mankind. The idea of the ultimate redemption of the universe is found also in Colossians 1[20] and Ephesians 1[10], and is consistent with the belief that God and Christ are the goal towards which all things move (Rom 11[36], Col 1[16]).

Romans 8[18]. The word translated *splendour* can also be translated *glory*, and stands for the majesty and the moral and spiritual perfection of God. In the final state the redeemed will share in this condition. See also p. 132.

Romans 8[20] refers to Genesis 3[17], according to which the ground itself was cursed by God because of Adam's sin. The fall of the world was the consequence of man's sin, and the redemption of the world will follow the redemption of man.

Romans 8²³. *firstfruits.* Compare the idea of the Spirit as a pledge. See notes on 2 Corinthians 5⁵.

his sons. There is a contrast in this chapter between present sonship of God (verses 15–16) and future sonship (verses 19 and 23), which is typical of the contrast between present and future life in Christ. The words *while we wait for God to make us his sons* are the *NEB* version of Greek words which literally mean *waiting for adoption* or *waiting for sonship.*

to set our whole body free is the *NEB* rendering of Greek words which are literally translated *the redemption of our body.* For the meaning of *redemption* see notes on Romans 3²¹⁻⁶, and for the meaning of *body* see notes on 1 Corinthians 15³⁵⁻⁵⁸. According to Paul, the body is set free when at its resurrection it is transformed into a spiritual body. The redemption has been made possible by the work of Christ. There is a contrast between present redemption (Gal 4⁵, Rom 3²⁴) and future redemption.

Romans 8²⁶⁻⁸—*The Spirit's Help*

Sometimes our prayers, whether they are silent or spoken, are not fully articulate, and we do not know how to express ourselves. In these situations the Spirit prays for us even through our own 'inarticulate groans'. This is an example of the way in which God uses all situations for good in his dealings with those who love Him.

According to *NEB*, verse 28 means that the Spirit works with us for good. But *he* could refer to God instead of the Spirit. Whichever of these interpretations is adopted, the fundamental meaning of the passage is the same. The older translation, *all things work together for good . . .* should be rejected.

Romans 8²⁹⁻³⁰—*The Calling of God*

Paul is convinced of his complete dependence on God's grace, and believes that everything has happened to him according to God's plan. In these verses he says that God has foreknown, foreordained, and called those who are justified believers. The idea that God has a predestined plan for all men is not found here but may be implied by Romans 9¹⁰⁻²¹ (see also p. 196).

Romans 8³⁰. Although there is a future *splendour* (verse 18) there is also a present *splendour* which belongs to those who are in union with Christ.

Romans 8³¹⁻⁹—*The Assurance of Salvation*

The chapter ends with a great hymn of praise, in which Paul affirms that nothing, neither physical death nor the intervention of superhuman powers, can separate men from the love of Christ.

Romans 8[33]. *pronounces acquittal*. The traditional translation is *justifies*.

Romans 8[34]. *pleads our cause*. For the idea of Christ as a heavenly intercessor for men, see also Hebrews 9[24], 1 John 2[1].

Romans 8[36] quotes Psalm 44[22].

*　　　*　　　*

THE CAPTIVITY LETTERS

The letters to the Philippians, the Colossians, Philemon, and the Ephesians were written while Paul was in prison (Phil 1[7, 13, 17], Col 4[3, 18], Philem 1, 10, Eph 3[1], 4[1], 6[20]). Traditionally he is thought to have been a prisoner in Rome when he wrote them, but scholars have argued that he wrote them while he was a prisoner at Ephesus—an imprisonment not recorded in the Acts—or at Caesarea, when he was waiting to be sent to Rome (Acts 23[33]–27[1]). Some scholars believe that Philippians was written at Ephesus and the other captivity letters at Rome. The arguments cannot be entered into here, and, though the problem has by no means been finally settled, it will be assumed that the captivity letters were written from Rome between A D 61 and 63.

It is disputed whether Philippians was the first or the last of these letters. Because its style is more like that of the earlier letters, and the expectation of Jesus's return is more prominent in it than in the other captivity letters, the balance of the argument is in favour of its being the first of this group of letters.

The Pauline authorship of Colossians and Ephesians is widely questioned, because the literary style and nature of the teaching is in many ways different from that of the other Pauline letters. The authorship of Ephesians is that which is the more seriously doubted, and many scholars argue that it was written after Paul's death by one of his disciples, who wanted to give a summary of the essence of Paul's teaching. The arguments, many of which are linguistic, are too complicated to be examined here. The differences of literary style, however, may well be explained by the more tranquil existence which Paul enjoyed when he was forced to remain in one place, even though that place was a prison. The differences of thought may be the result of a natural development of the apostle's thinking. Whatever conclusion is reached about the authorship of the letter, it is generally agreed that Ephesians was written after Colossians, and Philemon at the same time as Colossians.

THE LETTER TO THE PHILIPPIANS

Paul wrote this letter to thank his friends in Philippi for a gift of money which they had sent through Epaphroditus (4^{10-20}). He also wrote to advise them to be united against their opponents (1^{27-30}) and to avoid petty rivalries (2^{1-4}). He denounced Christians who still tried to enforce circumcision on converts ($3^{2}-4^{1}$)[1], and he asked two women of the church, Euodia and Syntyche, to patch up a quarrel which had arisen between them (4^{2-3}).

This is a deeply personal letter, full of Paul's affection for his readers. Philippi was the first great city of Europe which he had visited, and, as he lay in prison, he thought of the Philippian Christians with special joy and love. Of all Paul's letters this is the warmest in tone, and its underlying theme is joy in the Lord.

The letter contains allusions to the Day of the Lord and the return of Christ ($1^{6, 10}$, 3^{20}, 4^{6}). There are hints too of the doctrine of justification through faith (3^{9}), and there are important sections about the person and work of Christ (2^{5-11}), union with Christ (3^{8-11}), and the Christian life (3^{12-14}).

COMMENTS ON SELECTED PASSAGES FROM THE LETTER TO THE PHILIPPIANS

Philippians 2^{1-4}—*The Common Life in Christ*

Paul appeals to the Philippians to give up rivalry, to consider each other, and to maintain unity.

Philippians 2^{5-11}—*The Example of Christ*

Paul uses the humility and obedience of Christ as an example which Christians ought to follow in their relationship with each other. Much of this section has the character of a hymn, and some scholars suggest that it was taken over by Paul from an earlier Christian writer. This is a disputed matter, and the teaching of the passage reveals a developed doctrine of the person of Christ, which is hardly characteristic of very early Christianity.

At any rate, the passage is evidence for Paul's own view about Christ. It teaches the divinity of Christ and His existence before His physical birth (verse 6). It tells of His self-humiliation in taking human nature and living a life of perfect obedience to God which culminated in

[1] Some scholars think that Philippians $3^{2}-4^{1}$ was originally part of another letter by Paul.

His death (verses 7–8). It affirms the exaltation of Christ as the Lord whom everything in the universe acknowledges (verses 9–11). The doctrine of Christ in this passage is more developed than any teaching on the theme in Paul's earlier letters.

Philippians 2[8]. *obedience*. That the death of Christ was a supreme example of His obedience to the Father is the theme of Mark 14[36], Hebrews 5[8].

Philippians 2[9]. *the name above all names* is *Lord*, which in the Greek Old Testament was used as a substitute for the divine name, *Yahweh*.

Philippians 2[10] recalls Isaiah 45[23].

Philippians 2[11]. *Jesus Christ is Lord* was an early form of creed. See notes on 1 Corinthians 12[1-3].

Philippians 2[12-13]—*Working out Salvation*

In Paul's absence the Philippians will have to work out their salvation for themselves. It will not be they themselves, however, who make their work effective, but God who is working in them (see 1 Cor 15[10], Gal 2[20]).

*   *   *

Philippians 3[8-11]—*The Knowledge of Christ*

Paul has been speaking about his excellent record in Judaism (verses 4–7), and now he says that he has given it all up for the sake of knowing Christ. The only righteousness which he desires is given by God in response to faith. His only concern is to know Christ, which means to experience His transforming power, suffer as He suffered, and die more and more to sin, in order to share in the final resurrection.

In verse 9 Paul refers to the doctrine of *justification through faith* (see notes on Gal 2[15-21]) and also to the idea of sharing the righteousness of Christ (see notes on 2 Cor 5[21]).

In verse 10 he speaks not only of sharing in Christ's death and resurrection (see notes on Rom 6[1-11]) but also of sharing in His sufferings. Paul sees his own sufferings on behalf of Christ as a participation in Christ's suffering (see also 2 Cor 1[5], Col 1[24]).

Philippians 3[12-16]—*Pressing on to Perfection*

Although Paul has not yet attained to perfection, he aims at it, as indeed should all Christians who have reached maturity. They should, moreover, make sure that they do not fall below the level which they have already reached.

Philippians 3[12]. *perfection* is described as *the prize which is God's call to the life above* (verse 14). It is not only a moral perfection but a state of perfect union with Christ.

Philippians 3[15]. *mature.* The Greek word can also be translated *perfect*, but *NEB* gives the correct translation in this context.

Philippians 3[17]–4[1]—*Citizens of Heaven*

Paul attacks those who pay no respect to moral standards. They are enemies of Christ, heading for destruction. True Christians are citizens of heaven, waiting for the return of Christ, who will transform their mode of existence (see 1 Cor 15[35–58]). With this end in view Paul exhorts his friends to be 'firm in the Lord'.

For the idea of heavenly citizenship, see also Galatians 4[26], Hebrews 11[10, 13–16], 13[14], 1 Peter 2[11].

*　　　*　　　*

THE LETTER TO THE COLOSSIANS

Colossae was a city in the west of Asia Minor, which Paul had not visited (2[1]), but where a church had been founded by Epaphras (1[7]). Paul's letter was written in answer to false teaching which was being given in the town.

The false teaching, which seems to have been a form of the later heresy of Gnosticism, claimed that there was a large number of intermediary powers between men and God. Paul replies that Christ alone is the intermediary. Everything apart from Him is a creature of God, and He is supreme over all things, even over supernatural powers. The complete being of God is embodied in Him (1[13]–2[15]).

Another aspect of this false teaching was its emphasis on ritual observances and angel-worship. Paul says that the ritual observances are only a shadow. The reality is Christ, and too much reliance on ritual can separate men from Him (2[16–20]).

A third fault of the false teaching was its advocacy of an extremely ascetic way of life, with a great deal of emphasis on abstinence from certain food and drink. Paul claims that true piety consists in victory over vicious appetites and desires, and in the practice of the Christian virtues (2[20]–3[17]). He gives instruction about relationships between husbands and wives, fathers and children, masters and slaves, which may have incorporated some early Church rules for converts (3[18]–4[6]; see notes on Eph 5[22]–6[9]).

COMMENTS ON SELECTED PASSAGES FROM
THE LETTER TO THE COLOSSIANS

Colossians 1[13-20]—*Christ and the Universe*

In his reply to the teaching that there were many intermediaries between men and God, Paul stresses the uniqueness of Christ.

(i) *Release, Forgiveness, and Reconciliation* (verses 13, 14, and 20). It was through Christ that God set men free from the power of evil and forgave their sins. This liberation is not only for men but for the whole universe, which God has reconciled to Himself through the death of Christ.

(ii) *Christ and God* (verses 15 and 19). Christ is *the image of the invisible God*, and *the complete being of God* dwells in Him. This idea of the image of God is connected with the idea that Christ is a second Adam. The first Adam was made in God's image, but the image was defaced. Christ is the true image of God, revealing God's real nature (see 1 Cor 15[22, 45-9], Rom 5[12-21]).

(iii) *Christ and the Universe* (verses 15–20). Christ is supreme over all the universe because He was active in its creation and continues to hold it together, and because He is the one for whom it has been created and the means by which it is reconciled to God. The pre-existence of Christ has already been mentioned in Philippians 2[5-11] (see also 2 Cor 8[9]), but this is the first passage in which Paul says that He actually took part in the creation, a doctrine also found in John 1[1] and Hebrews 1[2]. Moreover, there is no letter earlier than Colossians in which Christ is described as the goal of all things.

(iv) *Christ and the Church* (verse 18). In Romans 12[4-5] and 1 Cor 12[12-31] the Church is likened to the body of Christ. In Colossians the metaphor is developed and Christ is described as the head of the Church. He is the origin of its life, which stems from His resurrection and His Lordship (see also Col 2[19], Eph 1[22-3], 4[16]).

This passage from Colossians shows the influence of the idea of the Wisdom of God (see notes on 1 Cor 1[24]). The description of Christ as the image of God recalls the description of Wisdom as the image of God's goodness (Wisd 7[26]), and the idea that Christ was active at the creation is similar to the idea that Wisdom was present with God at the creation (Prov 8[30]). But although Paul describes Christ as 'the wisdom of God' in 1 Corinthians 1[24, 30], he does not use the title in Colossians. Probably he thinks that while the idea of the divine Wisdom can help him to expound his beliefs about Christ, it is not of itself adequate to express who Christ really is.

Colossians 1[14]. *release*. The Greek word can be translated *redemption*. See notes on Romans 3[21-6].

Colossians 1[15]. *image of the invisible God*. Compare 2 Corinthians 4[4], Hebrews 1[3].

his is the primacy over all created things. A literal translation is *he is the firstborn of all creation*, meaning that He was supreme over the creation and existed before it.

Colossians 1[16]. *thrones, sovereignties, authorities, and powers*. These are supernatural beings. Because the false teachers advocated the worship of angels, Paul asserts that Christ was an agent in the creation of the angels.

for him. In Romans 11[36] it is God who is 'Goal of all that is'.

Colossians 1[18]. *the first to return from the dead*. Literally, *the firstborn from the dead*. Compare 1 Corinthians 15[20], Revelation 1[5].

Colossians 1[19]. *the complete being of God*. Literally, *all the fullness*. The term *fullness* was used to describe the whole group of angelic mediators between men and God. Paul is saying that Christ Himself is the only mediator who is needed.

*   *   *

THE LETTER TO PHILEMON

In Colossians 4[9] Paul mentions that Onesimus is returning to Colossae. Onesimus was the run-away slave of a Colossian Christian called Philemon. Paul sent him back with this short letter, in which Philemon is asked to treat him gently and to receive him 'as more than a slave— as a dear brother . . . as man and as Christian' (Philem 16).

This letter does not condemn the institution of slavery but asks both owner and slave to make their relationship basically a Christian one (see Col 3[22]-4[1]).

*   *   *

THE LETTER TO THE EPHESIANS

This letter may have been written originally as a circular letter, since some of the earliest manuscripts omit the reference to Ephesus in 1[1]. It does not seem to have been written for any particular situation, and its message is of a general nature.

The first part of the letter (1[1]-3[21]) deals with God's purpose for the universe and for the Church. It is God's will that the whole universe should be 'brought into a unity in Christ'. He has brought unity between Jews and Gentiles through the sacrifice of Christ, and they are being built up in Christ into a spiritual dwelling for God.

The second part of the letter (4^1–6^{24}) deals with the life of Christians in the world. In many ways it is similar to the final sections of Colossians, listing the duties of Christians in worship, in family life, and at work. It also speaks of the different officers in the Church and gives general instruction about conduct.

COMMENTS ON SELECTED PASSAGES FROM THE LETTER TO THE EPHESIANS

Ephesians 1^{1-10}—*Unity in Christ*

After the introductory greetings Paul says that he and his readers have been destined before the creation to be sons of God. By His death Christ obtained forgiveness of sins for them, and they have discovered God's hidden purpose, which is for the whole universe to attain to unity in Christ.

This idea of the redemption of the universe is also found in Romans 8^{19-22} and Colossians 1^{20}.

Ephesians 1^2. For the greetings in Paul's letters see notes on Galatians 1^{1-5}.

incorporate in Christ Jesus : literally, *in Christ Jesus*.

Ephesians 1^5. *to be accepted as his sons*. Literally, *for adoption*. See notes on Galatians 4^5, Romans 8^{15}.

Ephesians 1^6. *Beloved*. On the use of this title for Christ, see notes on Mark 1^{11}.

Ephesians 1^7. *release*, or *redemption*. See notes on Romans 3^{21-6}, where is also a comment on *blood*.

Ephesians 1^9. *hidden purpose*. Literally, *mystery*.

Ephesians 1^{11-14}—*The Pledge of the Heritage*

Both those who preach and those who receive their message will enter into the future heritage when God's work of redemption is complete. The Spirit is a seal of their incorporation into Christ and a pledge of their future state. Although Christians are already 'in Christ', the future heritage is a life in which, according to Ephesians 1^{10}, the whole universe has unity in Christ.

Ephesians 1^{13}. *seal*. This may well refer to baptism.

Ephesians 1^{14}. *pledge*. See notes on 2 Corinthians 5^5.

*   *   *

Ephesians 5^{22}–6^9—*The Christian Household*

These instructions to wives, husbands, children, fathers, slaves, and masters are very similar to the instructions given in Colossians 3^{18}–4^1, and are not unlike the lists of duties in 1 Peter 2^{13}–3^7 and Titus 2^{1-10} (compare 1 Tim 2^{8-15}, 6^{1-2}). They seem to be based on teaching which was widely circulated in the early Church and which formed an agreed pattern for ethical instruction. There are parallels to this kind of teaching in both Stoic philosophy and Jewish writings of the period. It is important to notice how the New Testament teaching is based on the relationship between Christ and the Church. The woman must show obedience and respect to her husband and the husband must show a self-sacrificing love for his wife, just as Christ loved the Church and sacrificed Himself for it (5^{22-33}). Children's obedience to parents is enjoined by the Fifth Commandment (Ex 20^{12}), and fathers' treatment of children ought to be such as could come from Christ Himself (6^{1-4}). Slaves should act as slaves of Christ, and masters should remember that they have a Master in heaven (6^{5-9}).

These instructions about marriage, and those in the parallel passage in Colossians, reveal a far different attitude from that of 1 Corinthians 7. Whereas in 1 Corinthians Paul regards marriage as an inferior state to celibacy, in Colossians and Ephesians marriage is a sacred relationship which is accepted as part of the Christian order of society. The change in Paul's attitude was partly caused by his change of belief about the return of Christ. In 1 Corinthians he expects it in the near future but in Colossians and Ephesians he does not indicate when it will happen.

Paul's teaching about marriage in Ephesians emphasizes that women are subject to men, a view which is found also in 1 Corinthians 11^{2-12} and 14^{34-5}. Although in Galatians 3^{28} he affirms that men and women are one in Christ, he continues to accept the traditional Jewish belief that it is God's will for women to be subordinate to men.

The comparison between Christ's love for the Church and a husband's love for his wife is evidence of the belief that the Church is the Bride of Christ. The idea is also found in Mark 2^{19-20}, John 3^{29}, 2 Corinthians 11^2, Revelation 19^{7-8}, 21^9, 22^{17}, and may well be implied by Matthew 22^{1-14} and 25^{1-13}. It is derived from the Jewish description of the coming of the Messiah as a marriage-time and from the Old Testament idea of God as the husband of the nation Israel (Isa 54^5, 62^5, Jer 3^{1-4}, Hos 2^{20}).

Paul's instructions to slaves and masters show that, although he believes that slaves and free men are one in Christ (Gal 3^{28}), he accepts the institution of slavery (see notes on Philemon).

Ephesians 5^{23}. *the head of the church.* See notes on Colossians 1^{13-20}.

Ephesians 5[26]. *water and word* refers to baptism and the words which are spoken at baptism.

Ephesians 5[31] is based on Genesis 2[24]. See also Mark 10[7-8]. The word translated *body* by *NEB* would literally be translated *flesh*.

Ephesians 5[32]. *It is a great truth that is hidden here.* The literal translation is *This mystery is great.* Because the Greek *mustērion* (mystery) was translated *sacramentum* in Latin, some scholars use this as evidence that marriage is a sacrament. *NEB*, however, gives the correct interpretation of the Greek.

Ephesians 6[4]. A literal translation of the second half of the verse is: *nurture them in the correction and instruction of the Lord.*

Ephesians 6[10-20]—*The Christian's Armour*

In this passage an idea is expanded which is found in 1 Thessalonians 5[8]. The Christian must put on the spiritual armour, because his life is a warfare against superhuman powers. The armour which he must wear is truth, integrity, the gospel of peace, faith, salvation, and words given by the Spirit.

Then follows an exhortation to prayer, in which Paul asks his readers to pray that he will speak the right words with boldness and freedom. Even when he is in prison, he is Christ's ambassador.

Ephesians 6[12]. All superhuman powers have been subjected to Christ because of His death (Col 2[15], Eph 1[20-3]), but their defeat is not yet complete, and Christians need divine strength to continue their warfare against evil.

Ephesians 6[20]. *ambassador.* See 2 Corinthians 5[20].

* * *

THE PASTORAL LETTERS

The letters to Timothy and Titus are called the Pastoral Epistles or Pastoral Letters, because they claim to be written by Paul to two of his followers in order to give them pastoral advice in their work of oversight in the churches. The title 'Pastoral' was not given to the letters in early times and did not come into regular use until the eighteenth century.

Authorship and Date

The authorship of these letters has been questioned more than that of the other Pauline letters. Some of the reasons brought forward against the Pauline authorship are not very convincing in themselves. It is pointed out that both the Church order and the doctrine of the Pastoral

Letters would be well suited to a situation at the end of the first century or the beginning of the second. But it is not impossible that the order and the doctrine could belong to Paul's time. Another argument is that it is difficult to fit the historical information given in the letters into the known life of Paul. But it is possible that Paul was released from Rome after the events recorded in Acts 28, and that he made another missionary tour before he was finally imprisoned and put to death. It is noteworthy too that the Pastoral Letters treat Timothy and Titus as inexperienced young men, while the other Pauline letters give the impression that they were Paul's tried and trusted assistants. But an argument of this nature cannot decide the question of authorship. The most cogent reasons for doubting the Pauline authorship of the letters are based on a close examination of their vocabulary and style, which show important and striking differences from those of the other Pauline letters. It is chiefly on these linguistic arguments, which cannot be discussed here, that the question must be decided. The linguistic arguments against the Pauline authorship are so strong that the majority of modern scholars, apart from Roman Catholics and those who presuppose the inerrancy of the scriptures, believe that the letters were written some time after Paul's death by one of his followers, who wished to give the Church of his day the teaching which he imagined that Paul himself would have given, if he had been alive.

Many of the scholars who reject the Pauline authorship believe that Titus 3$^{12-15}$ and several parts of 2 Timothy are fragments of genuine Pauline letters which have been incorporated into the Pastoral Letters. These passages contain typically Pauline language and have a spontaneity and artlessness which suggest that they are genuine.

Some of the scholars who accept the Pauline authorship suggest that Paul was in prison when the letters were written, and dictated their main themes to an unknown companion who was responsible for their present form and style.

If Paul wrote the letters, they must have been written late in his life between AD 63 and 64. But if he did not write them, they could have been written at any time between AD 70 and 125. Many scholars argue that they were written early in the second century, but there can be no certainty about the matter.

The view which is accepted in this book is that Paul himself did not write these letters. Once the Pauline authorship is rejected, the question arises of the morality of composing a letter in the name of a man who has not himself written or dictated it. In modern times such a procedure would be regarded as morally wrong, but in the ancient world different customs of authorship prevailed. A modern author might write a book about the message of Paul for the twentieth century, and in it he might apply what he believed to be Pauline teaching to modern problems. This is what the writer of the Pastoral Letters was doing. He was trying to state what he believed to be Paul's message for a later generation, and, by the literary custom of his age, he put it into the form of letters by Paul. In a similar way, when the Greek philosopher Plato composed dialogues in which he claimed to report the teaching of Socrates, he put a great amount of his own teaching on to the lips of Socrates. The nearest modern parallel is the historical novel, in which the author uses a framework of historical events and personages but allows himself great liberties in stating what might have been done and said.

The question of the authorship of these letters is important, but not as important as the message which they convey. Whether they were written by Paul or not, they contain an interpretation of the gospel which is of lasting value. Indeed, if they were not written by Paul, they add to the number of New Testament witnesses to the power of Christ in the lives of men and women.

Occasion and Contents

The Pastoral Letters were written to strengthen the Church against heretical teaching, which included both a corrupt form of Judaism and a speculative belief in the existence of angelic intermediaries between God and men. The heretics taught that there was a superior type of Christian who had a higher kind of knowledge, and their doctrine of angelic mediators obscured the uniqueness of Christ. Their teaching resembles that of the Gnostics, who were a major problem to the Church in the second century.

The letters present some of the central truths of the gospel, proclaiming Christ as the Saviour, who by His death won freedom for mankind (1 Tim 2$^{5-6}$, Tit 2^{14}). Those who have faith in Him gain eternal life (1 Tim 1^{16}). He is both man and God, the mediator between God and men (1 Tim 2^5, Tit 2^{13}), the Saviour and Judge who will return at the last day (1 Tim 6^{14}, 2 Tim 4$^{1,\,8}$, Tit 1^4, 2^{13}, etc.). The letters contain a large amount of ethical teaching, which advocates sober and considerate behaviour and prescribes the qualities which are required in Church officers. There is no reference to the Lord's Supper, but baptism is regarded as the sacrament of rebirth (Tit 3^5).

The information which the letters give about Church organization is very instructive. Timothy and Titus have authority over a number of churches, and the local ministers are bishops, elders (or presbyters), and deacons. Titus 1^{5-9} shows that there is no essential difference between bishops and elders, but the very use of two different titles, bishop and elder, may be evidence that a distinction was beginning to be made between the presiding elder and his colleagues, a distinction which eventually grew so great that bishops and elders became two separate orders of ministry (see notes on Acts 20^{17} and 1 Cor 12^{28}). There is no indication about the function of deacons (1 Tim 3^{8-13}), but they probably cared for the poor. There seems to have been a special order of widows (1 Tim 5^{3-16}), and it is possible, but a matter of dispute, that 1 Timothy 3^{11}, instead of referring to wives, refers to deaconesses (the word translated *wives* can equally well be translated *women*).

COMMENTS ON SELECTED PASSAGES FROM THE PASTORAL LETTERS

1 Timothy 6^{3-10}—*False Teaching and False Ideals*

The letter denounces false teachers who expect financial profit out of religion. Money is of no use beyond this life; the love of money, but not money itself, is the root of all kinds of evil, and leads astray from the Christian faith.

1 Timothy 6^3. *what you are to teach and preach* refers to the instructions given in earlier sections of the letter.

1 Timothy 6^{10}. *the faith* means the Christian religion.

1 Timothy 6^{11-19}—*The Christian Way*

Timothy is exhorted to avoid false ideals and practices and to seek the Christian virtues. Life is like a race of faith, and its goal is eternal life. It is for this goal that Timothy should aim. He must continue to be loyal and to confess his faith until Christ appears. He must instruct men to hope in God, not in money. In this way they will receive eternal life.

1 Timothy 6^{12}. *confessed . . . before many witnesses* could refer to Timothy's baptism or ordination or to some occasion when he was put on trial. But it may well refer to the fact that his whole life was a confession of his faith before the world.

1 Timothy 6^{15}. There is no suggestion that Christ will appear in the immediate future. He will come in God's *good time*.

*   *   *

2 Timothy 4^{6-8}—*Paul's Destiny*

Many scholars who reject the Pauline authorship of the Pastoral Letters believe this to be a fragment from a genuine letter of Paul. It was written when Paul expected his life soon to end, and it likens him to an athlete who has run the race of a dedicated Christian life, and is ready, when the last day comes, to receive the prize of eternal life.

2 Timothy 4^8. The *garland* was a sign of victory in a contest. The *Judge* is Christ.

*   *   *

QUESTIONS

(1) Expound Paul's teaching in Chapters 6 and 8 of Romans about union with Christ.

(2) What does chapter 8 of Romans tell us about Paul's doctrine of the Holy Spirit?

(3) Give an account of Paul's teaching about Christ in Philippians 2^{5-11} and Colossians 1^{13-20}.

(4) Comment on: Romans 5^{1-2}, 5^{19}, 7^{21}, Philippians 3^{20}, Ephesians 6^{11}, 2 Timothy 4^8.

CHAPTER ELEVEN

OTHER NEW TESTAMENT LETTERS

THE LETTER TO THE HEBREWS

Authorship

THIS LETTER does not itself claim to have been written by Paul, and was not unanimously accepted as Paul's in the early Church, although it has been traditionally ascribed to him. Tertullian (about AD 200) suggested that Barnabas was the author. Later suggestions have been Luke, Clement of Rome, Silas, and Apollos. Its vocabulary, style, and theology show marked differences from that of Paul, and it is difficult to imagine that he could have written it. The final word rests with the third-century theologian Origen, who observed that only God knew who had written it.

Occasion

The letter may have been written from Italy (see Heb 13^{24}), but we cannot be sure. As for its destination, Rome, Palestine, and Egypt are three of the suggestions, but no certain conclusion can be reached. It is not surprising that there is a variety of conjectures about the letter's date, ranging from AD 50 to 95. And opinion is divided whether it was written for Jewish or Gentile Christians, or for both.

The Christians to whom it was addressed were in need of assurance that Christianity was superior to Judaism, and that Christ was the unique mediator, who was greater than the angels. They had suffered persecution, although none of their members had been martyred (12^4).

THE TEACHING OF THE LETTER

Our ignorance about the authorship of the letter and about the circumstances of its writing is not as serious a matter as might be imagined. The letter's importance depends on the value of its message, not on the identity of its author or on the situation in which it was written. It has a distinctive theological approach to the gospel, and contains an original presentation of the fundamental truths of Christianity.

(i) *The Son of God*

Jesus is the eternal Son of God, who was an agent in the creation of the universe and has been exalted above the angels. He is superior to Moses as the founder is superior to the household and the son to the servant (1^1–3^6). In 1^8 He even appears to be addressed as God. Alongside this emphasis on His divinity is an emphasis on His humanity. He calls men His brothers and has shared their flesh and blood and their suffering (2^{9-18}, 4^{14}–5^{10}).

(ii) *The High Priest*

The main section of the letter (4^{14}–10^{25}) expounds the idea that Jesus is the one effective High Priest, who by His self-offering has taken away men's sins and has freed them from death (see also 1^3, 2^{14-15}). He is called a priest 'in the succession of Melchizedek', because Melchizedek is supposed to be eternal, and to be greater than Abraham. This priesthood is superior to that of the Levites. Christ does not need to offer daily or even annual sacrifices, as other priests do. He has made one sacrifice, the offering of Himself on the Cross. He does not minister in a tent which is the copy and shadow of the reality, but in the real heavenly sanctuary. Whereas the priests offer dumb animals which have no choice about their fate, He offered Himself voluntarily. His death sets men free to enter into the heavenly sanctuary and to participate in the new covenant of which He is mediator. He has obtained for men forgiveness of sins and participation in a new life.

The letter seems to have in mind chiefly the sacrifices on the Day of Atonement and also the Covenant Sacrifice (see notes on 9^{11-15}), but there is a reference to the fact that Christ bore men's sins (9^{28}; see also 1 Pet 2^{24}), which seems to be linked with the sin-bearing of the Servant (Isa 53^{12}) and implies that Christ suffered the consequences of men's sins.

(iii) *Ethical Teaching*

Faith. The people to whom this letter was written had suffered persecution and were expecting to suffer more. They are encouraged to endure suffering and to show faith. The steadfast faith of the Hebrew patriarchs and heroes is quoted as an example for Christians. Above all, the example of Christ Himself is brought forward. Christians should live in faith, and should accept suffering as a discipline from God (10^{32}–12^{13}).

Love. Christians should love each other. They should give hospitality to others, remember prisoners and victims of ill-treatment, revere marriage, avoid sexual immorality, and show respect and obedience to their leaders (13^{1-17}).

Other Ethical Teaching. Christians should not live for money, but be content with their possessions, and rely on God. They should not make scruples about food a substitute for their reliance on God's grace ($13^{5-6,\ 8-9}$).

(iv) *The Heavenly Gift and the Limits of Forgiveness*

Christians have an inner awareness of God's goodness, and partake of His life through the Holy Spirit. But if they continue to sin after they have received this new life, they will not be able to repent, and the sacrifice of Christ will not avail for them ($5^{11}-6^6$, 10^{26-31}). Probably the sin of which the letter is thinking is the complete and deliberate rejection of Christ by someone who has previously believed in Him.

(v) *The Church*

A contrast is made between Mount Sinai, where the old covenant was given, and the heavenly Jerusalem, the home of the Church triumphant, of the angels and the redeemed, and of Jesus Himself, who is the mediator of the new covenant (12^{18-29}).

The Church on earth does not offer any sacrifice for sins—that has been done by Jesus once and for all—but it offers up a sacrifice of praise and kindness (13^{15-16}). It is a community in exile, and looks to the life of heaven ($11^{8-10,\ 13-16}$, 13^{14}).

(vi) *The Future*

The letter speaks of the future as the sabbath rest which God has promised for His people (3^7-4^{13}). Heaven is 'the city which is to come' (13^{14}), and the Christian has no permanent home on earth (see also $11^{8-10,\ 13-16}$). The last day is approaching (10^{25}), when Christ will return to save those who wait for Him and to bring God's judgement on the unfaithful (9^{27-8}, 10^{37-9}).

(vii) *The Shadow and the Reality*

The letter shows the influence of the kind of thought which was developed by Alexandrian Jews and especially by Philo. This thought owed a great debt to the philosophy of Plato and, although there is no evidence that the writer of Hebrews had actually read the works of

Greek philosophers or even of Philo, he certainly shows their influence in the contrast between the 'real sanctuary' and that which is 'only a copy and shadow of the heavenly' ($8^{2, 5}$). The earthly man-made sanctuary, he says, is 'only a symbol of the reality' (9^{24}), and the Law 'contains but a shadow . . . of the good things which were to come' (10^1). This contrast between the earthly things, which pass away, and the heavenly realities, which are eternal, is characteristic of Platonic philosophy, and is also found in 2 Corinthians 4^{18} and Colossians 2^{17}.

*   *   *

COMMENTS ON SELECTED PASSAGES FROM THE LETTER TO THE HEBREWS

Hebrews 1$^{1-4}$—*The Eternal Son*

This letter has no introductory greeting, but begins like a treatise rather than a letter. Its opening paragraph declares the uniqueness of Christ as the revelation of God. The fragmentary revelations through the prophets are contrasted with the final revelation through God's Son. Christ was the agent in the creation (compare Jn 1^3 and Col 1^{16}), and continues to sustain the life of the universe. Indeed all the universe belongs by right to Him. As the 'stamp of God's very being' He is the true incarnation and revelation of God. By His death He obtained the forgiveness of men's sins, and in His present state of exaltation He is superior to the angels.

Hebrews 1^2. *this the final age.* A literal translation would be *the end of these days.*

Hebrews 1^3. *the effulgence of God's splendour . . . the stamp of God's very being.* These words are reminiscent of the description of the Wisdom of God in the apocryphal Book of Wisdom (Wisd 7^{25-6}). For the idea of Christ as the Wisdom of God, see notes on 1 Corinthians 1^{24}.

Hebrews 1^4 is a prelude to a section in which the writer refutes those who give undue honour to angels.

*   *   *

Hebrews 4^{14}–5^{10}—*The High Priest*

A priest is a mediator between God and men, who represents God to men and men to God. In Jesus's time, however, the doctors of the Law had the function of interpreting God's will to men, and the priests offered sacrifices on behalf of men to God. In the letter to the Hebrews Jesus is the mediator between God and men. As the Son He is the representative of God to men, declaring God's nature and speaking God's word to them. As the High Priest He is the representative of men to God, offering Himself to God on their behalf as the perfect sacrifice for their sins.

In this passage Jesus is described as the great High Priest who is superior to all other high priests, yet shares their human nature. Like other high priests He can sympathize with men's weaknesses, because He Himself has endured the trials and temptations of life, although, by contrast with the rest of men, He has not committed sin (4^{15}). Like other high priests He has been called by God to His office (5^{4-6}). In Gethsemane He prayed to God for deliverance, and God answered Him by enabling Him to learn obedience through suffering, to complete a perfect life, and to be the source of salvation to others (5^{7-10}).

The theme of the High Priest's sacrifice is not developed here, but later in the letter. This section lays great emphasis on the life of Jesus, His temptations, His agony at Gethsemane, and His sufferings. It also implies (4^{14-16}) that He is the heavenly intercessor for men, but this is not explicitly stated until Hebrews 9^{24} (see also Rom 8^{34}, 1 Jn 2^{1}). The idea that He is a priest in the succession of Melchizedek ($5^{6, 10}$) is explained in Hebrews 7^{1-3}, where it is claimed that both Melchizedek and his priesthood are eternal, in contrast with the Jewish priesthood, which is of temporary duration.

Hebrews 4^{15}. *tested*. The word can also be translated *tempted*. It refers to all the human trials which Jesus had to endure, but in this context especially to the temptation to commit sin.

without sin. See also 2 Corinthians 5^{21}, 1 Peter 2^{22}, 1 John 3^{5}.

Hebrews 5^{3}. The rule that the priest must make an offering for himself is found in Leviticus $16^{6, 11}$.

Hebrews 5^{4}. The call of Aaron is recorded in Exodus 28^{1}.

Hebrews 5^{5} quotes Psalm 2^{7}.

Hebrews 5^{6} quotes Psalm 110^{4}.

Hebrews 5^{8}. For Christ's obedience see also Mark 14^{36}, Philippians 2^{8}.

*   *   *

Hebrews 9^{11-15}—*The High Priest and the One Sacrifice*

The background to these verses is the Jewish sacrificial system and especially the ritual for the Day of Atonement (Lev 16^{1-34}), when the High Priest went into the Holy of Holies to make atonement for the sins of the people. First he killed a bullock as a sin-offering for himself and then a goat as a sin-offering for the people. Finally he transferred the sins on to the head of a second goat, known as the scapegoat, and drove it out into the desert.

Jesus is contrasted not with the scapegoat, but with the animals which were sacrificially slaughtered; and the superiority of His priest-hood and sacrifice to that of the Jewish priests is asserted in various ways.

(i) The old sacrifices pointed to a better time in the future, but Christ is 'high priest of good things already in being' (verse 11) because the Messianic age has already begun.

(ii) The priests of the Jewish Law ministered in a tent which was man-made, but Christ ministers in the invisible sanctuary of heaven (verse 11), where He appears before God on men's behalf (see Heb 9^{24}).

(iii) The Jewish priests sacrificed animals which were physically perfect and able to purify men externally, but Christ has sacrificed Him-self, a victim without spiritual blemish (see also Heb 4^{15}), who by His sacrifice can cleanse men's consciences (verses 12–14).

(iv) The sacrifices of animals were repeated time after time, because they secured only temporary deliverance from sin. The sacrifice of Christ has been made once and for all, and has secured 'an eternal deliverance' (verse 12).

(v) The old sacrifices were made under the old covenant. Christ is the mediator of a new covenant under which each individual can know God (verse 15; see Jer 31^{31}).

The sacrifice of Christ is not merely interpreted against the back-ground of the sin-offering and the Day of Atonement. In Hebrews 9$^{19-22}$ it is contrasted with the covenant sacrifice of Exodus 24$^{1-8}$, and Jesus is shown to be both the mediator and the inaugurating sacrifice of the new covenant.

Hebrews 9^{11}. *The tent* or *tabernacle* was the Most Holy Place or Holy of Holies, the innermost sanctuary of the Temple (see Heb 9$^{1-5}$).

Hebrews 9^{12}. For the meaning of *blood* in sacrifice, see notes on 1 John 1^7.

Hebrews 9^{14}. *a spiritual and eternal sacrifice.* Literally, *through eternal spirit.*

Hebrews 9^{15}. The Greek *diathēkē* can be translated either *covenant* or *testament. NEB* gives both translations in this verse.

*   *   *

Hebrews 11$^{1-40}$—*The Faith of the Old Testament Heroes*

Faith is defined as that which 'gives substance to our hopes, and makes us certain of realities we do not see' (verse 1). This reminds us of Paul's statement that 'faith is our guide, we do not see him' (2 Cor 5^7). In the conditions of human existence it is inevitably by faith that a man must draw near to God. Faith, in the teaching of the letter to the Hebrews, means a firm and courageous trust in the unseen reality of God, and a hope of future triumph. Its meaning is not quite the same as Paul's (see notes on Gal 2$^{15-21}$), but it is sufficiently akin to it for the writer to be able to say that by faith men find life (10$^{38-9}$). Faith has an intellectual content, since by it men believe that God created the universe. But this intellectual content proceeds from trust in God, which is the fundamental aspect of faith (verse 3).

The eleventh chapter of Hebrews is devoted to an account of the faith of the great men and women of the past (verses 4–40). Special attention should be paid to the statement that Abraham and the other heroes were passing travellers on earth, whose faith was shown by their confident longing for the heavenly city which was their real home (verses 8–10, 13–16).

These men of faith, however, were unable to enter into their inheritance until the coming of Christ and the inauguration of a new convenant, when they would share the promised blessing with the followers of Christ (verses 39–40).

Hebrews 11^4. *Abel.* See Genesis 4$^{1-15}$. Hebrews probably implies that Abel's faith enabled him even before the time of the Law to understand that a true sacrifice needed shedding of blood.

continued to speak after his death. After his murder his blood cried out (Gen 4^{10}).

Hebrews 11$^{5-6}$. *Enoch.* See Genesis 5^{24}.

Hebrews 11^7. *Noah.* See Genesis 6$^{9-22}$.

Hebrews 11 $^{8-10}$. *Abraham.* See Genesis 12$^{1-9}$. Abraham is also described as a man of faith in Galatians 3$^{6-9}$, Romans 4$^{1-25}$, James 2$^{21-4}$.

Hebrews 11$^{11-12}$. *Sarah.* See Genesis 18$^{11-14}$.

Hebrews 11$^{13-16}$. The idea that the faithful are strangers on earth is found in Philippians 3^{20}, 1 Peter 2^{11}. See also Hebrews 13^{14}.

Hebrews 11$^{17-19}$. *Abraham* and *Isaac.* See Genesis 22$^{1-19}$.

Hebrews 11$^{20-21}$. *Isaac, Jacob,* and *Joseph.* See Genesis 27$^{27-9,\ 38-40}$, 48$^{1-22}$, 50$^{24-5}$.

Hebrews 11$^{23-9}$. *Moses.* See Exodus 2$^{1-10}$, 12$^{21-37}$, 13$^{17-18}$, 14$^{21-30}$. Verse 26 means that Moses regarded captivity in Egypt as part of *the stigma* to be borne by the Messiah and his people.

Hebrews 11$^{30-1}$. *Jericho* and *Rahab.* See Joshua 2$^{1-24}$, 6$^{15-25}$.

Hebrews 11$^{32-8}$. *overthrew kingdoms* probably refers to Joshua, David, and the Maccabees.

muzzled ravening lions refers to Daniel (Dan 6), and

quenched the fury of fire to Shadrach, Meshach, and Abed-nego (Dan 3).

The women who *received back their dead* were the widow of Zarephath and the Shunammite woman (1 K 17$^{8-24}$, 2 K 4$^{18-37}$).

tortured to death means literally *broken on the wheel* and was used to describe the death of the Maccabean hero, Eleazar (2 Macc 6[18-31]).

jeers and floggings also seem to refer to Eleazar and his friends.

fetters and prison bars could refer to several heroes, including Jeremiah (Jer 20[2], 37[15]).

stoned may refer to Zechariah (2 Chr 24[20-1]).

sawn in two probably alludes to the non-biblical tradition that Isaiah suffered this fate.

refugees ... seems to mean David and Elijah (1 S 23[14-29], 24[3], 1 K 19[4-9]).

Hebrews 12[1-2]—*The Faith of Christians*

Christians have the men of the past to encourage them in their race through life. They must fix their thoughts on Jesus, who both gave them their faith and will bring it to perfection. By His endurance of the Cross He is the supreme example of faith.

Hebrews 12[2]. *on whom faith depends from start to finish*. A literal translation is *the author and perfecter of our faith*.

*   *   *

THE LETTER OF JAMES

The letters of James, Peter, John, and Jude are often called the Catholic or General Epistles, meaning that they are not addressed to a particular congregation but to the Church as a whole. This is a misleading description of 1 Peter and 2 and 3 John, which are addressed to particular congregations. But the rest of these letters may well have been addressed to the Church in general.

Authorship

The author of the letter of James is described as 'James, a servant of God and the Lord Jesus Christ' (Jas 1[1]). According to tradition he was James, the brother of Jesus. The thought of the letter and its Greek style, however, do not suit a Jew of Jerusalem. It is unlikely too that the brother of Jesus would fail to mention his relationship to the Lord in the letter's introduction. James was a very common name—in Greek and Hebrew the same as 'Jacob'—and the author could have been a James who is otherwise unknown to us. Alternatively, he may have been a writer who wished to give the impression that the letter was written by the brother of Jesus, because he imagined that it was the kind of teaching which he would have given.

Date

Since the authorship of the letter is disputed, its date is also disputed. Those who believe that it was written by Jesus's brother date it between AD 40 and 62, because, according to the Jewish historian Josephus, James was martyred in AD 62. If it was the work of someone else, it could have been written at any time between AD 70 and 100.

Origin and Destination

Palestine, Rome, and Alexandria have all been suggested as places from which the letter was written, but there is no certainty about the matter.

The letter is addressed to the "Twelve Tribes dispersed through the world' (1^1), a description which could refer to the Jews of the Dispersion (i.e. the Jews outside Palestine) or to Jewish Christians outside Palestine, but is more likely to mean the whole Christian Church, which is the new Israel and is 'dispersed' through the world because it is in exile from heaven (see also 1 Pet 1^1).

Contents

The letter is composed mainly of instructions about endurance in temptation (1^{2-15}), the relationship between rich and poor (2^{1-13}, 5^{1-6}), the dangers of a sharp tongue (1^{26}, 5^{12}), the need for patience in waiting for the Lord's coming (5^{7-11}), and the power of prayer (5^{13-20}).

The most famous sections of the letter are those which teach the need for action as well as listening (1^{19-27}) and affirm the barrenness of faith without works (2^{14-26}). True religion is defined as 'to go to the help of orphans and widows in their distress and keep oneself untarnished by the world' (1^{27}).

Although the letter is mainly concerned with moral advice, it has some doctrinal content. God is the unchanging Father, who is the source of all good gifts (1^{17-18}). Jesus Christ is the exalted Lord (2^1), who will return as Judge (5^{7-11}).

The letter provides evidence of the anointing of the sick, and of the confession of sins by the sick to each other (5^{14-16}).

COMMENTS ON SELECTED PASSAGES FROM THE LETTER OF JAMES

James 2^{1-7}—Snobbery

In the early Church, as in the Church of modern days, there was a constant temptation to pay special deference to rich people who attended worship. The letter attacks this snobbery and affirms that God has chosen the poor to be rich in faith and inherit the kingdom (see also 1 Cor 1$^{26-8}$ and Mt 5^3).

James 2$^{8-13}$—*The Sovereign Law*

Snobbery is a transgression of the sovereign (literally, 'royal') law that men should love their neighbours as themselves (see notes on Mk 12$^{28-34}$). If a man breaks part of the law, he has broken the whole law. The Christian law is one of freedom, according to which a man must be merciful (see also Mt 5^7).

James 2$^{14-26}$—*Faith and Works*

Faith without works, says James, is dead. A man is 'justified by deeds and not by faith in itself'. The letter's teaching on this theme is vastly different from that of Paul, who says that men are justified by grace through faith, and not by works (see notes on Gal 2$^{15-21}$ and Rom 3$^{21-6}$). It was because of the letter's teaching about justification by works that Luther called it a 'right strawy epistle'. There is no doubt that the immediate impression which it gives is that it is opposed to Paul's teaching. It does not follow, however, that the letter is a direct attack on Paul himself. Its purpose was probably to correct what James believed to be false deductions from Paul's teaching.

The difference between Paul and James is partly a difference in the use of words. 'Faith' according to Paul is utter reliance on Christ, a faith from which good works naturally issue. 'Faith' for James is merely the acceptance of certain beliefs, and on this definition faith would certainly be barren without works. But the difference between Paul and James is not only about the use of words. It is a difference of outlook. In James the emphasis is on man's faith and man's works. In Paul the emphasis is on God's grace.

James 2$^{21-5}$. *Abraham* (Gen 15^6, 22$^{1-19}$) and *Rahab* (Josh 2$^{1-22}$, 6^{23}) were traditional heroes of faith (see Rom 4$^{1-25}$, Gal 3$^{6-9}$, Heb 11$^{8-19}$ for Abraham, and Heb 11^{31} for Rahab). It is noteworthy that James uses them as examples of justification by works.

James 2^{23}. *God's friend.* See 2 Chronicles 20^7, Isaiah 41^8.

*   *   *

THE FIRST LETTER OF PETER

Authorship and Date

The letter claims to have been written by Peter (1^1), a view which has been widely challenged in recent years on the grounds that the Greek style is too polished for a Jewish fisherman and that the situation for which it was written suggests a later date, probably the persecution in Bithynia in AD 112 during the reign of Trajan. Many scholars, however, continue to believe that it was written by Peter, and some of them argue that the Greek style is the work of Silvanus, alternatively known as Silas (see notes on Acts 15^{40}), who wrote the letter at Peter's dictation (5^{12}) and influenced its form of expression. If the letter is Peter's, it was probably written shortly before Nero's savage persecution of Christians in AD 64.

Occasion

The letter was written to a group of churches in Asia Minor (1^1) which were in danger of persecution (4$^{1-2,\ 12-16}$). It was written from Rome, where the church is called she 'who dwells in Babylon' (5^{13}). Some scholars claim that the letter includes part of a baptismal homily (1^3–4^{11}), but, whether this theory is accepted or not, the references to baptism and new birth (1$^{3,\ 23}$, 3$^{19-22}$) suggest that the letter may have been written to candidates for baptism or to recently baptized converts. Since the practice arose in early days of baptizing converts at Easter, it may have been written for that event.

Contents

The letter tells of the hope and joy which the readers share. They are God's people, whom Christ has died to redeem, and they must show this by their daily conduct (1^1–2^{12}). Instructions are given about their behaviour towards the State, and about the duties of servants, wives, and husbands. They must show brotherly affection to each other, and be patient under injustice (2^{13}–3^{12}). Jesus, who suffered for them, is now exalted, and baptism is the means by which men come to salvation (3$^{13-22}$). Christians should be ready to suffer as Christ did, since the end of the world is near. They should use their time in God's service and should not be discouraged when they are persecuted in Christ's name, because they are sharing His sufferings (4$^{1-19}$). Advice is given to elders and to younger men, and all are exhorted to be alert and on the defensive against the devil's attacks. After their brief suffering God will restore and establish them (5^{1-14}).

Much of the letter's teaching resembles that of the speeches in the first part of the Acts (see notes on Acts 2^{14-41}), with their simple statements about the fulfilment of prophecy, the death and resurrection of Jesus, and the gift of the Spirit, and with their appeal for repentance and baptism. These themes are developed more in 1 Peter than in the Acts. Jesus is clearly linked with the Servant of Isaiah 53, and His sufferings are seen as a pattern for the sufferings of His followers (2^{18-25}). His death is regarded as a sacrifice ($1^{2, 19}$) and He is said to have borne men's sins to the Cross (2^{24}). His resurrection is a victory over superhuman powers (3^{22}).

The letter's teaching about the Church is important. Christians are God's chosen people, a royal priesthood, who must offer the spiritual sacrifices of dedicated lives and be built up into a spiritual temple (2^{1-10}). They have been born again through God's word ($1^{3, 23}$), and, when they are persecuted, they share in Christ's sufferings (4^{13}).

The end of the world, which the letter regards as not far distant, will bring judgement for sinners and salvation for the righteous ($4^{7, 17-19}$), whose destiny is eternal glory, an inheritance which cannot be corrupted (1^{4-5}, 5^{10}).

A difficult passage in the letter tells how Jesus preached to the imprisoned spirits after His death (3^{19-20}). It is not clear whether they were angels or the spirits of men who had died before the time of Christ. Whoever they were, they were being given an opportunity to accept the preaching of Christ.

COMMENTS ON SELECTED PASSAGES FROM THE FIRST LETTER OF PETER

1 Peter 1^{1-2}—*Introductory Greeting*

The reference to Peter's apostleship and the prayer for grace and peace are similar to the opening of a typical Pauline letter (see notes on Gal 1^{1-5}). The recipients of the letter are 'those of God's scattered people who lodge for a while' (literally, 'the sojourners of the Dispersion'), which, like James 1^1, means that Christians are exiles on earth. They are 'aliens in a foreign land' (1 Pet 2^{11}), and heaven is their home.

The greeting emphasizes God's initiative in the process of redemption. The reference to sprinkled blood means that the death of Christ was sacrificial, and points especially to the covenant sacrifice of Exodus 24^8, implying that by His death Jesus inaugurated a new covenant.

Although there is no conscious trinitarianism in this letter, Father, Spirit, and Christ are grouped together in these opening greetings (compare Mt 28[19], 1 Cor 12[4-6], 2 Cor 13[14]).

1 Peter 1[3-5]—*The Christian Inheritance*
God has given new birth to Christians (compare Jn 3[1-8]), and they have been born into a condition of hope for future salvation. The new birth has been made possible by the resurrection of Christ, because the resurrection is the ground of hope and the beginning of new life.

1 Peter 1[6-16]—*Faith and Salvation*
Christians can rejoice, even amid the trials of persecution. Indeed trials are a test of the genuineness of faith, just as fire is a test of the genuineness of gold.

Salvation is the harvest of faith. Like the suffering of Christ, it was prophesied in the Old Testament, and now it is openly preached. With hopes fixed upon it, men must lead holy lives.

1 Peter 1[13]. The first part of this verse would be literally translated *Wherefore, girding up the loins of your mind, be sober*. In the ancient world a man wrapped his robe round his loins when he was preparing for vigorous physical activity. To 'strip for action' is the modern equivalent.

1 Peter 1[16] quotes Leviticus 11[45].

1 Peter 1[17-25]—*The Saviour*

'Freedom' (verse 18; the word can also be translated 'redemption': see notes on Rom 3[21-6]) was obtained through Christ, the sacrificial lamb (see also Jn 1[29]), who was predestined to perform His redemptive work, and has enabled men to have faith in God. Christians ought to love one another, because they have been born again through the word of God.

1 Peter 1[24-5] quotes Isaiah 40[6, 8].

1 Peter 2[1-3]—*Pure Milk*

They must turn from evil ways, and, since they have been born to a new life, they must drink the spiritual milk of the gospel. In 1 Corinthians 3[2] and Hebrews 5[11-14] 'milk' refers to the elementary teaching given to new converts and immature Christians in contrast with the more advanced teaching which is given to maturer Christians and is described as 'solid food'. Here in 1 Peter there is no such contrast, and the emphasis is that the nourishment given by the gospel is spiritual and free from deceit.

1 Peter 2[3] is adapted from Psalm 34[8].

1 Peter 2[4-10]—*The Living Stone, the Spiritual Temple, and the Royal Priesthood*

Jesus is described as 'the stone' in two senses. He is the corner-stone (Psalm 118[22], Isaiah 28[16]) of the Church, and He is the stone of stumbling which becomes an obstacle to unbelievers (Isa 8[14]).

The Church is a spiritual temple (see 1 Cor 3[17]), and its members are living stones. They are a holy and royal priesthood, who offer the spiritual sacrifices of consecrated lives and have succeeded the Jewish nation as the chosen people of God (verses 5, 9–10).

Although the Church's ministers are never called priests in the New Testament, the Church as a whole is a priesthood (see also Rev 1[6], 5[10]). The spiritual sacrifices which its members offer are the sacrifice of dedicated lives (Rom 12[1]) and sacrifices of praise (Heb 13[15]). There is nothing in these ideas which conflicts with the teaching of Hebrews that the one atoning sacrifice has been made by Christ Himself, who is the great High Priest.

1 Peter speaks of the spiritual sacrifices which the priesthood offers to God, but says nothing of the priesthood's ministry to men. It is possible, however, that the letter's instructions about loyalty and holiness are intended to show how the Church should perform its priestly ministry to the world. It is important to remember that 1 Peter does not say that every believer is a priest but rather that the Church as a corporate unit has a priestly function.

1 Peter 2[7]. *corner-stone*. See notes on Mark 12[10].
1 Peter 2[9] is partly derived from Exodus 19[6].
1 Peter 2[10] is based on Hosea 2[23].

*   *   *

THE LETTER OF JUDE

This letter claims to have been written by Jude (in Greek, 'Judas'), the brother of James and presumably of Jesus (see Mk 6[3]). It cannot have been written by this Jude, however, because it assumes that the age of the apostles is past (verse 17) and that a fixed body of belief has already been formulated (verse 3).

The letter was written to attack heretics who abused the liberty of the Spirit by leading immoral lives (verse 4) and claimed to be a special class of spiritual persons, although their lives were in fact wholly unspiritual (verse 19). It tells of the terrible punishment which awaits them on the Day of Judgement (verses 13–15). It also exhorts its readers to fortify themselves in the faith and to look forward to the return of Christ, who will give them eternal life (verses 20–1).

The heresy which is denounced in this letter is a type of Gnosticism —the false teaching which assumes that there is a specially privileged class of spiritual people, who have spiritual knowledge. It is impossible to identify the teaching attacked in Jude with that of any particular group of Gnostics. There were signs of this kind of teaching even when Paul wrote to the Corinthians, and it was probably fairly widespread by the time that the letter of Jude was written.

It is interesting to note that the letter quotes from the *Book of Enoch* (see verses 9, 14 and 15), an apocryphal book much of which was written in the first century before Christ and which may have influenced Jesus in His use of the title 'Son of Man'. The letter also mentions religious meals called love-feasts (verse 12), which in the early days were akin to the Lord's Supper, but continued to be proper meals even when the Lord's Supper itself was limited to token quantities of bread and wine.

Because the letter was written after the age of the apostles, it can be dated between A D 90 and 130. It is not addressed to any particular congregation but to the Church as a whole.

*   *   *

THE SECOND LETTER OF PETER

The second letter of Peter incorporates most of the letter of Jude, and is itself proof of Jude's acceptance in the early Church. Because it must have been written several years after the letter of Jude, during the first half of the second century, it cannot have been written by Peter. Its reference to the letters of Paul as scriptures (3^{15-16}) confirms the view that it was written during the second century, since many years must have elapsed before Paul's letters were accepted in this way. Its literary style is far different from that of 1 Peter, and it was late in being accepted by the Church.

The letter attacks the immoral teaching which is denounced in Jude (2^{1-22}). In answer to the heretics' claim that Jesus will not return to earth, it points out that a long time to human beings is only a short time to God, and that by God's standards the return of Jesus will be soon. It speaks of the coming of new heavens and a new earth and of a future reign of justice (3^{1-13}).

Great emphasis is laid on the grace of God, who is the sole source of 'everything that makes for life and true religion' (1^3), and has given men promises through which they can escape corruption and 'come to share in the very being of God' (1^4). If men accept God's choice and calling, they can enter His eternal kingdom (1^{10-11}).

COMMENT ON SELECTED PASSAGE FROM THE SECOND LETTER OF PETER

2 Peter 3^{8-13}—*The Day of the Lord*

The letter is answering false teachers who claim that, because all the first generation of Christians have died, the Day of the Lord is not going to come (see 3^{3-4}). It points out that God does not measure time as men do (verse 8; see Ps 90^4), and that He has delayed the last day because He wants everyone to be saved (verse 9). Nevertheless, the day will come suddenly like a thief (see 1 Thess 5^2, Mt 24^{43}), and men must prepare for it by holy lives. On that day the whole universe will disintegrate, and there will be new heavens and a new earth (verses 10–13).

The expectation of new heavens and a new earth is found in Isaiah 65^{17}, 66^{22}, Revelation 21^1.

QUESTIONS

(1) Give an account of the teaching of the letter to the Hebrews about the priesthood of Christ.

(2) What does the letter to the Hebrews say about faith?

(3) Compare the teaching of the letter of James about faith and works with that of the letters of Paul.

(4) Comment on: Hebrews 1^2, James 2^5, 1 Peter 1^{1-2}, 2^9, 2 Peter 3^{13}.

CHAPTER TWELVE

THE REVELATION

Authorship

THE JOHN by whom this book claims to be written has been traditionally supposed to be John, the son of Zebedee. Even in the third century, however, it was suggested that the author was John the Elder (see p. 123) and not John the Apostle. The book itself does not indicate which John wrote it, and, since John was a common enough name, it is likely that Revelation was written by a John who is otherwise unknown to us.

The style and theology of the book are themselves sufficient proof that it was not written by the author of the gospel or the letters of John. Occasional similarities of thought and style to these writings may be explained by the connection of the author of Revelation with Asia Minor, where the gospel and the letters of John had their origin.

Occasion and Date

The book was probably written about AD 95 during the reign of the emperor Domitian, when emperor-worship was being enforced and the tradition had arisen that Nero would return from the dead. It may well include fragments of earlier writings, and some of the hymns which it contains may have been in use in the early Church. It begins with letters addressed to seven churches in Asia Minor, which had already suffered persecution and were expecting more. The whole book was intended for these churches, and was written to encourage the faithful, to warn the disloyal, and to predict the events which would lead to the end of the world and to the coming of a new heaven and a new earth.

The writer says that he received his revelation on Patmos, a small island in the Aegean sea, and the book itself may have been written there.

The Nature of the Book—Apocalyptic

In the last two centuries before Christ and the first century after Christ many apocalyptic works were written by Jews. These apocalypses (the

Greek word *apokalupsis* means 'revelation') claimed to contain the key to hidden mysteries about the end of the world and about the events which would precede it. The first great apocalyptic book was Daniel, and this was followed by many works which are not included in the Bible. The only apocalypse in the New Testament is Revelation, which is itself often called the Apocalypse; but Mark 13 and part of 2 Thessalonians 2 have the characteristics of this type of literature.

Apocalyptic writings tend to be very colourful and bizarre in their speculations. They speak of great disasters and supernatural struggles which lie in the future, and they predict the dissolution and renewal of the whole universe. Sometimes they have been dismissed by modern readers as too fanciful for serious attention, but now, in an age when the destruction of the earth must be admitted as a real possibility, the message of these works cannot be written off as irrelevant. This does not mean that we should accept uncritically all that is said in a book like Revelation. In common with most apocalyptic writers the author of Revelation believed that the end of the world would take place within a few years. He made detailed predictions about plagues and battles and universal catastrophes. Although the world has not come to an end and the detailed prophecies of Revelation have not been fulfilled, the book has an enduring message which is not invalidated by its prophetic inaccuracies. It proclaims the sovereignty of God, the Lordship of Christ, the salvation of the faithful, and the future transformation and renewal of the universe.

THE CONTENTS OF THE BOOK

Introduction (Ch. 1). John tells of the vision which he received on the island of Patmos (see notes on 1^{1-20}).

The Letters to the Seven Churches (Chs. 2 and 3). These letters, which are written to seven churches in Asia Minor, commend those Christians who have been faithful, and condemn those who have failed to show consistent loyalty to Christ. Warnings are given against false teachers.

The Vision of Heaven (Chs. 4 and 5). John has a vision of God enthroned in heaven with Christ, the heavenly Lamb, receiving the worship of four mysterious creatures, twenty-four elders, and thousands and thousands of angels. Finally, every created thing joined in the hymn of praise. Then the Lamb took from God a scroll which had seven seals.

The Seals (Ch. 6). The Lamb broke six of the seven seals. As the first four were broken, four horsemen appeared, each bringing disaster upon the earth. When the fifth seal was broken, John saw the martyrs waiting for the Last Judgement. When the sixth was broken, the whole earth was shaken, there were strange events in the sky, and all men went into hiding, because the day of vengeance had come.

The 144,000 and the Vast Throng (Ch. 7). John tells how God and the Lamb were worshipped in heaven by 144,000 members of the tribes of Israel, 12,000 from each tribe (verses 1–8). Then he describes the worship offered by 'a vast throng, which no one could count', which was drawn from all nations and had come through 'the great ordeal' of the final conflict with evil (verses 9–17).

The 144,000 and the vast throng are identical. Since 144,000 is not to be taken literally but is a purely symbolic number, it is consistent to call it a 'throng which no one could count'. Here and in Revelation 14^3 it refers to the true and spiritual Israel which consists of all faithful Christians. It represents the completeness of Israel, because 144 is the square of 12, the number of the tribes of Israel, and 1,000 is a conventional expression for a large number of people.

The Trumpets and the Two Witnesses (Chs. 8 to 11). When the Lamb broke the seventh and last seal of the scroll, there was silence in heaven, after which seven angels were given seven trumpets. When the first six trumpets were blown, signs, portents, and disasters followed. An angel told John that the seventh trumpet would mark the coming of the end, and John was instructed to eat a scroll which was in the angel's hand. Two witnesses appeared, who bore witness for three and a half years, after which the beast killed them. When their corpses had been exposed for three and a half days, they were raised and taken to heaven. The seventh trumpet was then blown, and Christ's Kingdom began. But troubles had not ended, and earthquakes and strange signs followed.

It is impossible to be certain of the meaning of the three and a half years and the three and a half days in Chapter 11. In every generation theories have been brought forward to show that these prophecies prove that the Kingdom of Christ will begin in the near future. Sometimes it has been argued that they prove that the Kingdom has begun at a particular time in the past. It is indeed possible that the writer does not intend to predict a date for the coming of Christ's Kingdom and that $3\frac{1}{2}$ has a symbolic meaning. Seven was regarded as the perfect number, and $3\frac{1}{2}$, being half of 7, may have represented the imperfection of the times of tribulation. Another explanation is that $3\frac{1}{2}$ may have been a typical apocalyptic figure for the time of persecution, because the persecution of Jews by Antiochus Epiphanes, which is referred to in Daniel, lasted $3\frac{1}{2}$ years. But human ingenuity has produced so many different conjectures about these statements in the eleventh chapter of Revelation that the wisest course is to acknowledge that we do not know the correct interpretation of them.

The two witnesses mentioned in Chapter 11 seem to have been Moses and Elijah, who represented the witness which the Law and the Prophets gave to the Messiah. Alternative theories, however, have identified the witnesses with other Old Testament heroes, and some scholars have argued that they were Peter and Paul, or other early Christians.

The Woman, the Child, and the Dragon (Ch. 12). A woman gave birth to a boy, who was snatched up to God in order to save him from the dragon which was lying in wait for him. Michael and the angels waged war in heaven against the dragon and threw it down. The dragon pursued the woman, and, when she escaped, attacked the rest of her children.

The dragon was the Devil, the child was Christ, and the other children were the faithful Christians. Although the woman has often been identified with Mary, the mother of Jesus, she stands for either the true Israel or the eternal cause of God rather than for an actual woman.

The Two Beasts (Ch. 13). A beast rose from the sea, and the dragon conferred authority on it. The beast was worshipped by all the human race, except those who were on the Lamb's 'roll of the living'. Another beast which rose from the earth, made all the inhabitants of the earth worship the first beast, and branded them with the beast's mark, the number six hundred and sixty-six.

Throughout the centuries the beast has been interpreted in various ways. It has been identified with the Pope, Luther, Mahomet, Napoleon, Hitler, to mention some of the most conspicuous. Interpreters have displayed a great facility in showing that the number six hundred and sixty-six referred to the person or institution which they specially hated. The most convincing explanation is that the beast stands for the Roman Empire, and especially the emperor Nero, who was expected to return from the dead. The numerical value of the letters of the words Nero Caesar, when they are written in Hebrew, is six hundred and sixty-six. And the Book of Revelation seems to be prophesying that when Nero returns from the dead, he will be the Antichrist, the incarnation of evil.

The second beast stands for the Roman State priesthood, which enforced the worship of the emperor. Those who refused to worship the beast were the loyal followers of Christ.

The Fall of Rome (14^1–19^{10}). In this section further woes are prophesied, including plagues, a great battle at Armageddon, and an unprecedented earthquake. The main theme is the fall of Rome, which is described as Babylon and is likened to a prostitute on a scarlet horse. The fall of Rome is followed by the victory of God and the wedding-day of the Lamb, which implies that the Church is the bride of the Lamb.

The references to kings in Revelation 17^{7-14} have caused great perplexity, and, among the many explanations of them which have been suggested, the most satisfactory is that the eighth king, the beast who 'was alive, and is alive no longer, and has still to appear' (verse 8; see also verse 11) was Nero, who was expected to return from the dead. The other seven kings (verse 10) were Roman emperors, and, since Vespasian seems to have been regarded as the sixth of these emperors,[1] the one who was 'now reigning', these verses may well have been written during his reign, some years before the book took its final form in the reign of Domitian. It is possible, however, that verse 11 was written during the reign of Titus, the successor to Vespasian. The ten kings of verses 12–14 were probably Parthian rulers who were expected to launch an attack on Rome.

The Last Things, the New Heaven and the New Earth (19^{11}–22^{21}). An account follows of a rider on a white horse who fought against the beast and the kings of the earth. The beast and the false prophet were captured and thrown into the lake of fire, and the rest of the rider's opponents were killed. In this account the rider stands for Christ and the false prophet for the supporters of emperor-worship.

After the rider's victory the Devil was thrown into the abyss, and the martyrs rose from the dead (this was the first resurrection) and reigned for a thousand years. When the thousand years were over, Satan

[1] The three emperors, Galba, Otho, and Vitellius, who reigned for only a few months each, are not counted.

was released, and attacked God's people. Satan's army was destroyed, and he himself was flung into the lake of fire.

These events were followed by the final judgement and second resurrection, when all the dead rose and were judged according to their deeds. Death and Hades, together with those whose names were not on the roll of the living, were thrown into the lake of fire.

Finally, a new heaven and earth appeared, and from heaven there came the new Jerusalem, a city of eternal blessedness, ruled over by God and the Lamb. In this city lived all the faithful servants of God, and their life was spent in giving Him worship and sharing in His reign.

The book of Revelation ends with the promise that Jesus will come quickly and that the prophecies contained in John's vision will soon be fulfilled.

The thousand years' reign of the martyrs, otherwise known as the Millennium (see 20$^{4-15}$), has been the subject of much speculation. It has been argued that the Millennium began with the death and resurrection of Christ, but this is hardly consistent with the statement that the beast was captured before the Millennium. It has also been claimed that all the saints rose for the Millennium, but in fact only the martyrs are mentioned in the account given by Revelation. If the beast stands for the Roman Empire and especially for Nero, then the message of Chapters 13 to 20 is that Nero will soon return from the dead, that great disasters will follow, and that, after Nero has been defeated and the Roman Empire has been overthrown, the martyrs will reign for a thousand years.

Christianity does not depend for its validity on the accuracy of these prophecies in Revelation, and the gospel will remain true, even if they are not fulfilled in detail. The permanent message of Revelation is that God will finally rule unchallenged. This message, wonderfully enshrined in the last two chapters of the book, is of more relevance to us than the detailed speculation about the plagues and wars which will herald the end of the world.

COMMENTS ON SELECTED PASSAGES FROM REVELATION

Revelation 1$^{1-3}$—*The Prologue*

The revelation was given by God to Christ, and by Christ, through an angel, to John. Its purpose was to tell men about events which would soon happen, and the written record of it was to be read in public to the churches.

Revelation 1⁴⁻²⁰—*The Preface to the Seven Churches*

The book was addressed to seven churches (1¹¹), all of which were in cities on or near the Aegean coast of Asia Minor, and the letters which John wrote to these churches are contained in Chapters 2 and 3. The churches had been the victims of persecution and were tempted to fall into heresy. Some of John's letters to them are full of praise, others are severe, and others contain a mixture of praise and condemnation. They prophesy the return of Christ, threaten punishment for the disloyal, and promise blessedness for the faithful.

This preface to the letters opens with a greeting (verses 4–5), which in some ways resembles the greetings at the beginning of Paul's letters (see notes on Gal 1¹⁻⁵). The greeting is followed by a doxology to Christ, which may well have been used as an early Church hymn (verses 5–6). Next there is a prophecy of His return as Judge (verse 7) and an assertion that God is the beginning and the end of all things (verse 8). John describes how he received his vision on Patmos, the island where he was imprisoned (verses 9–20). In the vision Christ appears 'like a son of man' (see Dan 7¹³ and notes on Mk 2¹⁻¹²). The description of His appearance resembles Old Testament descriptions of God (verses 14 — 15 : see Ezk 1²⁴, Dan 7⁹), and He speaks of Himself in divine terms as 'the first and the last' (verse 17 : see Isa 44⁶) and 'the living one' (see, for example, Dan 6²⁶).

Revelation 1⁴. *from him who is and who was and who is to come* means 'from God'.

seven spirits. Instead of referring to the Holy Spirit John speaks of seven spirits, because there are seven churches.

Revelation 1⁵. *witness.* The Greek word *martur*, meaning *witness*, soon came to be used of a witness who gave his life; and this is the origin of the English word 'martyr'.

first-born from the dead. This means that the resurrection of Jesus preceded the resurrection of the rest of men. (See also 1 Cor 15²⁰, Col 1¹⁸). For the connection of *first-born* with the *ruler of kings of the earth*, see Psalm 89²⁷.

freed us from our sins with his life's blood. The death of Jesus is regarded as a sacrifice for sin. See notes on Romans 3²¹⁻⁶.

Revelation 1⁶. *royal house ... priests.* See notes on 1 Peter 2⁴⁻¹⁰.

Revelation 1⁸. *the Alpha and the Omega.* These are the first and last letters of the Greek alphabet. Their use here means that God is the beginning and the end of all things. In 22¹³ this title is given to Christ.

Revelation 1¹⁰. *the Lord's Day.* This is the name for Sunday, which was already the special day for Christian worship, because it was the day of Jesus's resurrection (see Acts 20⁷⁻¹², 1 Cor 16²).

Revelation 1[16]. *a sharp two-edged sword*. This is the word of God (see Eph 6[17], Heb 4[12]).

Revelation 1[18]. *I hold the keys of death and Hades*. This means that Jesus has power over both death and Hades, the home of departed spirits. In Revelation *death and Hades* are regarded as supernatural beings (see 20[13-15]; compare 1 Cor 15[26, 55]).

Revelation 1[20]. *angels* are the guardian angels, who had special care for the churches.

*   *   *

Revelation 3[14-22]—*The Letter to Laodicea*

This is the most famous of the letters to the seven churches. Laodicea was an extremely prosperous town, which was so wealthy that in A D 60 it had refused to accept help from Rome after it had been badly damaged in an earthquake. Its complacency affected even the Christians who lived there (verses 15–17). The letter tells them of their spiritual poverty and exhorts them to obtain spiritual riches (verses 17–19).

In spite of its severity this letter is full of hope. Christ might be severe with the Laodicean Christians, but that was because He loved them (verse 19). If they repented, He would come to them and be with them. He was already waiting to enter the heart of every man who repented. To all those who overcame the trials and temptations of human life, as Jesus Himself had overcome them, He would give a place on His heavenly throne (verses 20–2).

Revelation 3[14]. *Amen* is Hebrew for 'So be it'. Here it means that Christ is faithful and true.

prime source of all God's creation. This description of Christ is similar to those found in John 1[3], Colossians 1[16], Hebrews 1[2].

Revelation 3[18] refers to spiritual riches. *white clothes* were symbolic of divine purity (compare also Rev 19[8], where fine linen stands for 'the righteous deeds of God's people'), but this reference has special point because Laodicea was famous for the black clothes which were made there.

ointment was also made in Laodicea. For both *white clothes* and *ointment* see Ecclesiastes 9[8].

for your eyes so that you may see refers to spiritual insight.

*   *   *

Revelation 21[1-8]—*The New Jerusalem*

The previous section of the book has given a graphic description of the conflicts which led to the Millennium, the final overthrow of Satan, and the Last Judgement (19[11]–20[15]). Now follows a description of the new heaven and earth and the new Jerusalem which will come down from heaven and be the home of the redeemed.

The new Jerusalem is like a bride (verse 2) because, as the Church, it is the bride of Christ (see notes on Eph 5$^{25-7}$). The life of the city is one of unclouded joy. Death and sorrow have ended, and God is with His people (verses 3–4). In this new Jerusalem those who have overcome the world will receive living water and be sons of God (verses 5–7), but the unrepentant sinners will be thrown into the lake of fire (verse 8; see 20^{15}).

Revelation 21^1, *a new heaven and a new earth*. This is also prophesied in Isaiah 65^{17}, 66^{22}, and 2 Peter 3^{13}.

The *sea* was regarded as the source of evil and anarchy. The beast, for example, came out of the sea (13^1).

Revelation 21^2. *new Jerusalem*. Compare Galatians 4^{26}, Hebrews 12^{22}.

Revelation 21^3. The Greek word translated *dwelling* can also be translated *tabernacle* or *tent*. It was in the *tabernacle* that the Israelites believed that God was especially present (see Lev 26$^{11-12}$).

Revelation 21^4. Compare Revelation 7^{17} and Isaiah 25^8.

Revelation 21^5. *he who sat on the throne* is God.

Revelation 21^6. *the Alpha and the Omega*. See notes on Revelation 1^8.

water-springs of life. See John 7$^{37-9}$, where the living water is said to be the Spirit. See also John 4^{10}.

Revelation 21^8. *the second death* is eternal death, in contrast with the first death, which takes place at the end of earthly life. It is not envisaged in Revelation as a state of non-existence but as the endurance of punishment.

Revelation 21^{22}–22^5.—*The Life of the New Jerusalem*

Because God and the Lamb are in the new Jerusalem, the whole city is a sacred place, and there is no need for a temple (21^{22}). Since God is its light and the Lamb is its lamp, there is no need for sun or moon, and there is never any night (21$^{23-5}$, 22^5; see Isa 60$^{19-20}$). Its gates are always open (21^{25}), because its citizens are free and without fear. It has a life of ideal prosperity and perfect purity (21$^{26-7}$). Its 'river of the water of life' and its 'tree of life' (22$^{1-2}$) show that it is a second Eden, a new Paradise (see Gen 2$^{9-10}$). Men from all nations will share in its life, and nothing accursed will be there (22$^{2-3}$; see Isa 60^3 and Zech 14^{11}). Its citizens will bear the name of God, in contrast with the mark of the beast which was on the foreheads of the unfaithful (22^3; see 13$^{16-18}$). Their unity with God will be such that they will not only worship Him (22^3) but share in His reign (22^5).

Revelation 21²². *The Lamb* is a title used often of Christ in Revelation. It denotes Him as the sacrificial lamb which liberates men from sin and death (Rev 5¹²; see Jn 1²⁹), and also as the victorious lamb.

Revelation 22³. *every accursed thing shall disappear*. An alternative translation is *there shall be no curse any more*. It probably means that with the new creation the curse imposed on the earth at the Fall (Gen 3¹⁷) has been abolished (compare Zech 14¹¹).

shall worship. This could also be translated *shall serve*. In the new Jerusalem there will in fact be no distinction between the worship of God and the service of God.

Revelation 22⁴. *his name*. In Hebrew thought 'the name of God' was regarded as in a sense the being and qualities of God, an extension of His personality. When the faithful bear God's name, they share in His life.

The account of the new Jerusalem in these concluding chapters of Revelation is a poetical description of future blessedness and should not be taken absolutely literally. John was used to life in cities, and his vision of the future was a vision of life in the perfect city. These chapters describe the final state which is the object of the Christian hope and is a theme of every New Testament writer. Although men can share the life of Christ already, there will be a time in the future when the whole universe will be renewed and God's sovereignty will be undisputed. We do not know what this future blessedness will be like. Our 'knowledge now is partial; then it will be whole' (1 Cor 13¹²). 'What we shall be has not yet been disclosed' (1 Jn 3²). The meaning of the vision of the New Jerusalem is that this future state will be more wonderful than anything that we can imagine. The Bible, which begins with the story of the creation of heaven and earth, ends with the prophecy of a new heaven and a new earth and with the affirmation that in the end all evil will be overcome and God's triumph will be complete.

CHRONOLOGICAL TABLES

I—THE LIFE OF JESUS AND THE HISTORY OF THE EARLY CHURCH

There is wide disagreement about the exact dates and order of these events. Most of the dates given below are only approximate, and alternative schemes of dates will be found in other books. Important events in Jewish history are mentioned in this table.

6 B C	Birth of Jesus
4 B C	Death of Herod the Great
A D 6	Revolt of Judas of Galilee
28	Baptism of Jesus
29	Death of John the Baptist
30	Crucifixion of Jesus
31	Death of Stephen
32	Conversion of Paul
35	Paul's first visit to Jerusalem after his conversion
38	Riots against Jews in Alexandria
40	Caligula's threat to erect his statue in the Temple
43	Death of James, the son of Zebedee
44	Death of Herod Agrippa I
	Revolt of Theudas
46	The Famine
	Paul's second visit to Jerusalem
46–8	Paul's first missionary journey: Cyprus and Asia Minor
49	Expulsion of the Jews from Rome
	Paul's third visit to Jerusalem
	The Council of Jerusalem
49–51	Paul's second missionary journey: Asia Minor, Macedonia, and Greece (Corinth A D 50–1)
53–7	Paul's third missionary journey: Asia Minor (Ephesus A D 54–6), Macedonia, and Greece
58	Paul's arrest in Jerusalem and imprisonment at Caesarea
60	Paul's journey to Rome
62	Death of James, the brother of Jesus

64   Nero's persecution of Christians in Rome
       Death of Peter and Paul
66–70 Jewish revolt against Rome
70   Destruction of Jerusalem
90–5   Persecution of Christians by Domitian
112   Persecution of Christians in Bithynia by Trajan
115   Death of Ignatius
115–17 Jewish revolts in Egypt, Cyrene, Cyprus, and Meso-
       potamia
132–5 Revolt of Bar-Cochba in Palestine

*   *   *

II—THE BOOKS OF THE NEW TESTAMENT

There is even greater disagreement about these dates than about those
in the previous list.

AD 48   Galatians
50   1 and 2 Thessalonians
54–6   1 and 2 Corinthians
57   Romans
61–3   Philippians, Colossians, Philemon, and Ephesians
64   1 Peter
65–70   Mark
75–90   Matthew, Luke, and Acts
90–110 John (the gospel and the three letters)
95   Revelation

Galatians is sometimes dated later than the Thessalonian letters, and
Philippians is sometimes dated to Paul's ministry in Ephesus (AD 54–6).
If Ephesians was not written by Paul, it was probably written between
AD 70 and 90. If 1 Peter was not written by Peter, it was probably
written about AD 112.

It is very difficult to give even an approximate date for the rest of
the books of the New Testament. The range of years within which they
may have been written is very great.

AD 50–95 Hebrews
70–100   James (40–62, if it was written by Jesus's brother)
70–125   1 and 2 Timothy, and Titus (63–4, if they were written
          by Paul)
90–130   Jude
100–150   2 Peter

*   *   *

III—THE REIGNS OF ROMAN EMPERORS

31 BC–AD 14	Augustus
AD 14–37	Tiberius
37–41	Gaius Caligula
41–54	Claudius
54–68	Nero
68–69	Galba
69	Otho
69	Vitellius
69–79	Vespasian
79–81	Titus
81–96	Domitian
96–98	Nerva
98–117	Trajan
117–138	Hadrian
138–161	Antoninus Pius
161–180	Marcus Aurelius

*　　　*　　　*

IV—RULERS OF PALESTINE

This is not a full list. It includes only the rulers mentioned in this book. The reigns or terms of office are given.

37 BC–4 BC	Herod the Great, king of Judaea, Samaria, Idumaea, Galilee, and other territories
4 BC–AD 6	Archelaus (son of Herod the Great), ethnarch of Judaea, Samaria, and Idumaea
4 BC–AD 34	Philip (son of Herod the Great), tetrarch of Ituraea and other territories
4 BC–AD 39	Herod Antipas (son of Herod the Great), tetrarch of Galilee and Peraea
AD 26–36	Pontius Pilate, procurator of Judaea (including Samaria and Idumaea)
AD 41–4	Herod Agrippa I (grandson of Herod the Great), king of Herod the Great's realm (from AD 37 ruler of Philip's territories)

AD 50–100 Herod Agrippa II (son of Herod Agrippa I), king of Chalcis (AD 50–3), and king of Philip's and other territories, including part of Galilee (AD 53–100)

AD 52–60 Antonius Felix, procurator of Palestine (including Judaea, Samaria, Idumaea, and part of Galilee)

AD 60–2 Porcius Festus, procurator of Palestine

*   *   *

BIBLIOGRAPHY

There is a wide range of literature on the New Testament, and only a brief indication can be given here of books that may be read or consulted. Two kinds of book, however, are priorities for a study of the New Testament and indeed of the Bible as a whole. They are a concordance and a one-volume Bible commentary.

(1) *Concordances*

Cruden's Complete Concordance to the Old and New Testaments (This is based on the Authorized Version. An edition is also published which includes a concordance to the Apocrypha.) *New English Bible New Testament Concordance*, compiled by E. Elder

(2) *One-Volume Bible Commentaries*

The Abingdon Bible Commentary, edited by F. C. Eiselen and others
A Concise Bible Commentary, W. K. Lowther Clarke
William Neil's One-Volume Bible Commentary
The New Bible Commentary, edited by F. Davidson and others
Peake's Commentary on the Bible (Revised Edition), edited by M. Black and H. H. Rowley
The Teacher's Commentary, edited by G. H. Davies and A. Richardson

(3) *Bible Dictionaries and Word-Books*

Black's Bible Dictionary, M. S. Miller and J. L. Miller
Hastings' Dictionary of the Bible, revised by F. C. Grant and H. H. Rowley
The New Bible Dictionary, edited by J. D. Douglas and others
New Testament Words, W. Barclay
A Theological Word Book of the Bible, edited by A. Richardson

(4) *Atlases of the Bible*

The Oxford Bible Atlas, H. G. May
Philips' Scripture Atlas, H. Fullard
Shorter Atlas of the Bible, L. H. Grollenberg
The Teach Yourself Bible Atlas, H. H. Rowley

(5) *Series of Commentaries*

(Only cheaper series are mentioned)

The Clarendon Bible
The Daily Study Bible (by W. Barclay)
The Epworth Preacher's Commentaries
The Layman's Bible Commentaries
The New Clarendon Bible
The Pelican Gospel Commentaries
The Torch Bible Commentaries
The Tyndale New Testament Commentaries

(6) *Other Books*

(This list contains books which are available in cheap editions, mainly paper-back. It is not a comprehensive list, and fuller bibliographies can be found in some of the one-volume commentaries, dictionaries, and word-books, mentioned above)

W. Barclay, *The Mind of Jesus*
            Crucified and Crowned
            Jesus as They Saw Him
F. F. Bruce, *The English Bible*
R. Bultmann, *Jesus and the Word*
G. B. Caird, *The Apostolic Age*
C. H. Dodd, *The Meaning of Paul for Today*
            The Authority of the Bible
            The Epistle of Paul to the Romans
            The Apostolic Preaching and its Developments
            The Parables of the Kingdom
R. H. Fuller, *Interpreting the Miracles*
E. C. Hoskyns and F. N. Davey, *The Riddle of the New Testament*
W. F. Howard, *Christianity According to St John*
A. M. Hunter, *Introducing the New Testament*
              Introducing New Testament Theology
              Introducing Paul's Gospel
              The Works and Words of Jesus
              Interpreting the Parables
H. A. A. Kennedy, *The Theology of the Epistles*
F. Kenyon, *The Story of the Bible* (with additional chapter by
            B. M. G. Reardon)

C. S. Lewis, *Miracles*
W. Neil, *The Plain Man Looks at the Bible*
A. M. Ramsey, *The Resurrection of Christ*
A. Richardson, *The Miracle Stories of the Gospels*
D. S. Russell, *Between the Testaments*
J. S. Stewart, *The Life and Teaching of Jesus Christ*
         A Man in Christ
V. Taylor, *The Gospels: A Short Introduction*
W. Temple, *Readings in St John's Gospel*

SYLLABUS OF STUDY

For local preachers 'on trial' who are using this 'guide' to
prepare for the Connexional Examination in New Testament

This course of study is designed to extend over six months, and is divided into twelve fortnightly sections. The chapters of this book for each fortnight, together with the selected passages of the New Testament, are given below. Questions are set on each of the first eleven chapters, but no questions are set on the last chapter in order to give time for revision.

This book cannot be properly read without a careful study of the selected passages from the *New English Bible*. The book is not intended as a substitute for the New Testament but as an aid to its understanding. Students are also recommended to have an English dictionary at hand, and to consult it whenever they do not know the meaning of a word.

It is not necessary for the student to master those parts of the book which are in small print. They will be of assistance, however, to readers who wish to study the selected passages in greater detail.

Students taking correspondence courses should send to their tutors each fortnight answers to at least two questions—but more if possible—on the chapter for study.

Study One. Introduction and Chapter One.
Mark 1^1–8^{26}. (Questions will be set only on Chapter One of the text book and on the selected passages from Mark.)

Study Two. Chapter Two.
Mark 8^{27}–16^8.

Study Three. Chapter Three.
Matt. 1^{18}–2^{23}; 5^1–7^{29}; 10^{29-31}; 11^{25-30}; 12^{38-45}; $13^{24-30, \ 33, \ 36-52}$; 16^{17-19}; 18^{15-35}; 20^{1-16}; 21^{28-32}; 25^{1-46}; 28^{8-20}.

Study Four. Chapter Four.
Luke 1^1–2^{52}; 3^{7-20}; 4^{1-30}; 7^{1-49}; 9^{51}–11^8; 12^{13-21}; 13^{31}–14^{24}; 15^1–16^{12}; 16^{19-31}; 17^7–18^{14}; 19^{1-10}; 22^{24-38}; $23^{6-12, \ 32-48}$; 24^{13-53}.

Study Five.   Chapter Five

There are no selected passages for study. The sayings of Jesus studied in previous weeks should be revised.

Study Six.   Chapter Six.

John 1^1–2^{22}; 3^{1-21}; 4^{1-42}; 6^{22-71}; 9^{1-41}; 10^{1-18}; 11^{1-44}; 12^{20-36}.

Study Seven.   Chapter Seven.

John 13^{1-20}; 13^{31}–17^{26}; 18^{33}–19^{37}; 20^1–21^{25}. 1 John 1^1–2^2; 2^{28}–3^{12}; 4^{1-21}.

Study Eight.   Chapter Eight.

Acts 1^1–28^{31}. (Although questions may expect a general knowledge of the Acts, special comments will be asked for only on Acts 1^1–4^{31}; 6^{1-15}; 7^{44}–12^{25}; 15^{1-35}.)

Study Nine.   Chapter Nine.

Gal. 1^1–3^{14}; 3^{23}–4^7; 5^{13-25}. 1 Thess 4^{13}–5^{14}. 1 Cor. 1^{10}–2^5; 3^{5-17}; 12^1–13^{13}; 15^{1-58}. 2 Cor 4^{16}–6^{10}; 11^{21}–12^{10}.

Study Ten.   Chapter Ten.

Rom 3^{21-31}; 5^1–6^{14}; 7^7–8^{39}. Phil 2^{1-13}; 3^8–4^1. Col 1^{13-20}. Eph 1^{1-14}; 5^{22}–6^{20}. 1 Tim 6^{3-19}. 2 Tim 4^{6-8}.

Study Eleven.   Chapter Eleven

Heb. 1^{1-4}; 4^{14}–5^{10}; 9^{11-15}; 11^1–12^2. Jas 2^{1-26}. 1 Pet 1^1–2^{10}. 2 Pet 3^{8-13}.

Study Twelve.   Chapter Twelve.

Rev 1^{1-20}; 3^{14-22}; 21^{1-8}; 21^{22}–22^5.

INDEX

INDEX